"Roy's groundbreaking book is
indicates that alligators fail m

happy about this! But the real "gator bite," or learning nugget, from Rocky the Alligator is that small businesses must learn from their mistakes and adapt to the challenges of customer sophistication, fierce competition, and, yes, onerous regulation. Remembering that small businesses in the U.S. generally account for 60 to 80 percent of net new jobs growth, this book is a must for small businesses to navigate the swamp and grow with confidence and integrity."

~ **Jeffrey C. Thomson, CMA, CAE**
President and CEO,
Institute of Management Accountants

"The Alligator Business Solution *is a great tool for anyone thinking about starting a business to read thoroughly prior to making the decision to become a small business owner. There is an incredible amount of information compiled from Roy Austin's decades of experience as a very successful business owner and leader. If you are already in business, this book will enable you to structure your company to achieve even greater success. I enthusiastically recommend* The Alligator Business Solution."

~ **Ron Kirby**
President,
Business Consulting & Leadership Development
www.RonKirbyLeadership.com
BNI Global Board
US Executive Regional Business Coach

"When you are truly ready to roll up your sleeves and get to work on starting or revitalizing your business—READ THIS BOOK! Roy Austin shares practical and logical fundamentals to foster your business success, with a passion for helping you succeed."

~ **Bob Nicoll**
Author, *Remember the Ice and Other Paradigm Shifts*

"As managing partner of a regional accounting firm, I see many small businesses' financial results. I believe if more of my clients read this book and paid attention to the details that are discussed, I would have more successful clients. Many of my small business clients are good at certain aspects of their businesses but have many details that are wanting for lack of attention and lack of knowledge on these issues. This book puts into simple readable perspective some of the basic things that businesses can focus upon to achieve greater success. One of the issues I have with the many business books I read is keeping my attention and not lingering on a point too long. This was written well, flowed nicely, and kept my attention. I really believe it will be a help to small businesses that take the time to read it."

~ **Michael T. McCarthy**
Managing Partner,
Hancock Askew & Co., LLP
Offices in Savannah, Atlanta & Miami

"The Alligator Business Solution *is the book I wish I had when I took my first stumbling steps into self-employment two decades ago. I've read hundreds of business books but not one of them was as comprehensive as this one. Roy Austin covers everything from preparing to start your business all the way to really understanding your financials. All of this information, plus the included case studies and encouragement from the author, will save you from the often fatal mistakes made by new business owners. Reading this book is like having your own mentor working with you step-by-step as you navigate the difficult and often lonely road of owning a business."*

~ **Bonnie Jo Davis**
Owner,
Davis Virtual Assistance and Magic Wand Author Services
Amazon Reviewer

"In the last decade, more than 400,000 books have been published about business—how to succeed, how to manage, how not to manage, how to ride the latest wave, etc. The result is a figurative swamp of ideas and advice—some brilliant, most not – that drowns good ideas and thwarts good people.

"If you want to get through the swamp, you need an experienced guide. Not someone who tells you, 'This is the way we used to do it,' but rather someone who says, 'This is what I learned and here's how it applies.'

"Along comes Roy Austin, who has compiled the ultimate guide out of the "management swamp" with an extremely practical, realistic and useful how-to book on starting and running your own business. Sure, the swamp/alligator analogy is a little kitschy, but Austin's examples and no-nonsense advice make it easy to overlook the smilin' gator that leads you through the book. And it fits his down-to-earth sense of humor and humility. If Austin doesn't know something, he tells you who does and where to find it. That makes this an invaluable survival guide. Einstein said genius is the ability to explain the complex in the simplest terms possible—and no simpler. Austin may not be Einstein but he would be my choice for swamp guide."

~ **M. Dan. Suwyn**
Partner, Workplace Dynamics,
Former: Owner of Rapid Change Group,
Managing Editor, Savannah Morning News,
Presentation Editor, Fort Wayne News Sentinel,
Reporter Gannett Newspapers

"Starting and running a small business is, to say the least, a tremendous challenge. We all know that a significant percentage of start-ups and small businesses fail, and that there can be many reasons for this.

"One of the main reasons, without a doubt, is the wide range of skills required of the small business owner/operator. It is extremely rare

that an owner/operators possesses all of the skills required, so it is essential that they both 'know what they need to know' and 'know what they don't know.'

"The Alligator Business Solution *provides an exceptional go-to handbook for the small business owner/operator. It thoroughly covers virtually all of the key elements around small business, from strategy and planning to organization and finance, as well as marketing/sales operations.*

"Most importantly, The Alligator Business Solution *does all this in a manner that is approachable, friendly, and understandable. It educates without intimidating. The author, Coach Roy, does this in a refreshing and innovative framework by using 'The Swamp' and 'The Alligator' as the metaphors. The reader can find everything they need to know under topics such as 'Swamp Fundamentals, 'Finding Food in the Swamp,' and 'Swamp Survival.' Business handbooks work best when they are truly handy, and* The Alligator Business Solution *certainly fits the bill here! I would recommend it heartily to any and all small business owners/operators who are smart enough to know that they don't know it all."*

~ **Professor Mickey Goodman**
Professor of Business & Entrepreneurship,
Savannah College of Art & Design
Co-Founder and Principal with e2Advisors LLC.

"Having completed a number of acquisitions (25+) of early stage companies during 35 years as a business leader, and experiencing varying levels of operating sophistication within them, I appreciate the value of the basic but essential 'words of wisdom' Roy Austin shares in The Alligator Business Solution. He has written a guide, or perhaps better said 'playbook,' for a first-time entrepreneur who is just starting a business and/or a business owner who needs to reset/ pivot a company's direction and priorities. These are lessons one might learn in business school, but for those without this training, it is exactly what a street-savvy, first-time entrepreneur should know and follow in building a sustainable profitable business.

"In The Alligator Business Solution, *Roy provides a thoughtful and practical step-by-step approach essential to establishing a structure, and winning operating culture within a business, by sharing his extensive knowledge and experience. He covers all aspects/functions critical to building a successful business highlighting the importance of planning, processes, controllership, marketing, leadership, and governance within a company. Starting with a vision, statement of values & company culture, and fundamental purpose of a business, he provides the reader an insightful tutorial that should help to put your company on a successful track going forward. I highly recommend Roy's 'Solution' to all entrepreneurs and early stage company owners, whether just starting a business or still in the early stages of development and growth."*

~ **Kenneth Boyda**
Current: Chairman & Director of Razberi Technologies Inc.,
Director of Vidsys, Inc.,
Former: President and CEO of Interlogix/General Electric Security

"This easy-to-read book explains how any business owner can progress from the fundamentals of an excellent product or service to sustainable success. The way to build any business is to develop a product or service with a competitive advantage. Most small business owners know how to make an excellent product or provide an excellent service, but may have limited knowledge about how to achieve a competitive advantage. Mr. Austin stresses that all businesses must constantly make business decisions beyond their product or service and also understand the quickly changing business environment.

"You may have the best product today; but, if you do not adapt, you may find yourself in second place or worse over time. Mr. Austin presents guidelines on how to monitor your business continuously to achieve your goals. In this book the author compares building a business to building a house in the 'business swamp,' which requires a solid foundation upon which to base decisions. In essence this requires knowledge of all aspects of the business, along with the skills and tools to utilize that knowledge. Mr. Austin has done an excellent

job in presenting this blueprint in a humorous and entertaining manner, and I highly recommended his book to every business owner, regardless of the business size."

~ **Allen Yessman, MAcc, CMA, CPA**
Adjunct Professor of Accounting,
Nova Southeastern University

"Fundamental to this book is that businesses are serious and essential to the owners. From the start, Roy Austin's true wish is for every reader's business to thrive. He clearly and thoroughly presents guidelines for success with compassion and wit, liberally supported by enjoyable anecdotes from his extensive network of successful entrepreneurs. What makes the book stand out is Roy's ability to provide workable solutions distilled not only from the experiences of business luminaries (e.g., Jack Welch), great thinkers (e.g., David Kahneman, Mark Twain), and from small businessmen he has met, but also from his own consulting experiences, all distilled into bite-size edibles that small businessmen will relish. You will not put this book down once you start, but you will want to reread with a highlighter to emphasize the prescriptions he offers that parallel your business. His passion for entrepreneurs and small businesses is evident as he asks you the reader to participate in end-of-chapter tasks that will reward you with fresh views of your business that will sustain you for years."

~ **Tim Cairney**
Associate Professor, Georgia Southern University
Chair, Florida Council, Institute of Management Accountants

"Like the alligator, this comprehensive business book has a way of sneaking up on you. There are 76 chapters, but don't let that frighten you. Each one is direct and to the point. If you are looking for a solution to a specific challenge, you can hunt down your issue by chapter topic. At the end of each chapter, the author gives you an assignment so you can implement what you have learned. Roy Austin has shared his years of experience with his readers in an incredibly

organized fashion befitting that of an authentic financial expert. Read from start to finish or bite by bite depending on how hungry you are for these tasty tips on how to succeed in the competitive business world."

~ **Lydia Ramsey**
International Business Etiquette Expert,
Speaker and Author, *Manners That Sell—Adding the Polish That Builds Profits.*

"Roy Austin has a true passion for helping people find ways to be successful in business. His new book, The Alligator Business Solution, *shows not only that passion but reflects his knowledge of what it takes to run a viable business. A joyful read that offers great insight!"*

~ **Shellie West**
CEO & Founder, the Greater Bluffton,
SC Chamber of Commerce

"I found it very informative and think it is an excellent tool for the small business owner. This a fun read that is easy to understand and kept my attention. The short segmented topics are great for the busy entrepreneur, making it easy to pick up and focus on one area."

~ **Terry Peacock**
President, Peacock Cabinetry

"A brilliant reminder that the solution to complex problems can often be discovered by returning to core principles. Warning: This book will make you evaluate the effectiveness of every person and operating procedure in your business."

~ **Ammie Dover**
Principal, Larek Point Consulting

"Roy's messages based on the use of analogies of alligators and swamps to the starting and running of a small business are simple and straightforward. Their value is that they are memorable, logical, actionable, and realistic. A good read!"

~ **Ray Wenig**
President & COO, Salt Marsh Angels

"After retirement from Eastman Chemical Company, I continued in community service, but if I had had Roy Austin's book, I am sure I would have tried my hand at starting a business! It is the best guide for beginning entrepreneurs that I have encountered. It is a pleasant, humorous, easy read and appeared to me to be as complete as such a book can be. It contains real-life examples of the business 'swamp' and greatly emphasizes pertinent points as 'gator bites.'

"I believe it could also be used as a textbook for a class in starting a business. I recommend it to anyone contemplating going into business. It could be your first, and best, investment yet!"

~ **Charles L Seay**
Retired, Director of International Trade Services,
Eastman Chemical Company
District Governor of my Rotary Club,
leading to joint assignments Rotary and
AID (Administration for International Development) in the
Czech Republic and India

THE ALLIGATOR BUSINESS SOLUTION

Tom & Zantha,
You are an inspiration to all of us at Libraries for Kids, Int'l.

All the best
Coach Ray Austin

THE ALLIGATOR BUSINESS SOLUTION

SMALL BUSINESS COMPETITIVE ADVANTAGE

By: H. Roy Austin

NEXT CENTURY
PUBLISHING

The Alligator Business Solution
Small Business Competitive Advantage

Published by Next Century Publishing
Austin, TX
www.NextCenturyPublishing.com

ISBN: 978-1-68102-221-5
Library of Congress Control Number: 2016908614

Printed in the United States of America

DEDICATION

A special thank you to my wife and best friend Sharron for her enormous contribution to this book. After editing the first draft and beautifully condensing my thoughts, she has continued to guide me with constructive comments and suggestions to improve my work. Since meeting in 1994, we have worked as a team, whether on the tennis court, traveling, or on a project. Always supportive, never judgmental, she is my sounding board. Being married to your best friend is a true joy, and I can't thank Sharron enough for helping make this book a reality.

CONTENTS

Section 5

Swamp Team

Section 6

Finding Food In The Swamp

Section 7

Navigating In The Swamp

Section 8

Swamp Survival Skills

THE ALLIGATOR BUSINESS SOLUTION

ACKNOWLEDGMENTS

A special thank you to my wife and best friend, Sharron, for her patience, understanding, and support.

I also deeply appreciate all the clients, successful companies interviewed, employers, employees, friends, and Business Network International (BNI) associates from whom I have learned so much. If I attempted to acknowledge all who have contributed to the content of this book and who provided encouragement and support, I would undoubtedly omit some people. I do want to mention a few individuals who have had a particular impact on my life.

- My father, Rockwell Austin, who taught me that the true measure of a man is to admit and accept responsibility for a mistake.
- My stepmother, Jane Austin, who loved me as if I was her own child (my birth mother, Inga Austin, died a few days after I was born).
- My Aunt Bet, who taught me to laugh.
- Dr. Barrie Richardson, economics professor at Bethany College, who taught me the importance of living up to your responsibilities.
- Individuals I met in Vietnam who taught me that in spite of different cultures and customs, people are the same in their hopes, dreams, fears, etc., all over the world.
- Dr. Charles Walsh, executive director of John R. Hay House, who taught me that people can change no matter what mistakes they've made.
- Charlie Seay, retired Eastman Chemical Company executive, who believed in me when I had lost belief in myself.
- Jerry "J.R." Rutherford, my fraternal big brother, for his friendship, support, and encouragement for over forty years.

- Bob Morine, who took a chance on recruiting me as controller for Savannah Manufacturing, which provided me a second career opportunity.
- Dick Carter and Bill Conaway, owners of D. J. Powers, who taught me patience and how to listen.
- David Harper, who taught me how to teach by asking questions.

FOREWORD

Chances are you know a small business owner. Maybe they're an immediate family member, relative, friend, or neighbor. They likely have a passion for a product or service, and at some point decided to go into business for themselves. And although at times you may respect or even envy them for having the "freedom" of being self-employed, you probably have also seen them struggle at times with the challenges of being an entrepreneur.

The long hours. The lack of a steady paycheck, particularly early on. Having to make all the decisions and figuring out most things alone. Riding the ups and downs of the economic cycle. Keeping a brave face when times are tough.

Notwithstanding the freedom and flexibility that come with being a small business owner, there is also the insecurity of *staying* one. Enduring as a successful small business owner is challenging, and many new and experienced owners could benefit from advice and wisdom rooted in experience and proven practice. Fortunately, this is what you'll find in *The Alligator Business Solution.*

In the twelve years I've known Roy Austin, one thing has stood out: his desire to help and mentor others. In fact, one of the things that first brought Roy and me together was his desire to establish a forum where chief financial officers (CFOs) and controllers could gather and learn from each other. Under his leadership, the Savannah CFO/Controllers Council has grown from an idea to a membership that now exceeds 450 people. Roy brings that same helpful, creative spirit to *The Alligator Business Solution.* For those new to small business, thinking about starting a small business, or wrestling with an established one, this book provides ideas, advice, and guidance to help you succeed.

With Roy's assistance, you'll learn how to avoid the perils of the "Business Swamp" and establish a solid foundation for your business "house," based on rigorous preparation, planning, and self-defining choices. Included are exercises to help you establish your fundamental purpose and values as well as your operating principles and systems.

Along the way, you'll encounter helpful real-world examples drawn from Roy's years of experience assisting other small business owners.

Once the foundation for your business "house" is established, Roy will guide you to then build the "walls" of your enterprise, namely the functions that a business must have. You will examine the importance of operations, employees (including hiring, managing, and retaining them), risk management, marketing, accounting, finance, and performance improvement. You'll be directed throughout by Roy's thoughtful advice as well as his illustrations from small business leaders who have relied on him to help grow and further the success of their businesses.

Although people decide to start a small business for a variety of reasons, they will *stay* in business only if the finances allow it. And for many small business owners, finance is the Achilles heel. Many small business owners, who start off with a passion for business, independence, and serving others, ultimately confront feelings of deep regret and disappointment because they did not manage their finances well. That's understandable, because financial management is not taught in high school or college (unless you're a business major, and many entrepreneurs are not).

So, many small business owners do the best they can, which unfortunately is often not good enough. However, you have ensured against this by choosing to read *The Alligator Business Solution*.

Given the critical importance of finances in any business, and particularly in a small business, Roy goes in-depth into key financial matters such as why you must know your numbers, the purpose and use of your company's financial information, how to find the right accountant, how to read your company's financial statements (profit and loss, balance sheet, cash flow), and setting up internal controls. Using clear everyday English and helpful examples, Roy shows you how to be a better-informed leader of your business and a master of your company's finances. Even if you're number-phobic, Roy will help you understand why financial oversight is so critical and how you can set your company up for success through prudent financial management.

In my work with hundreds of Fortune 500 and Mid-Market leaders, I have had the opportunity to see a broad variety of leaders and managers in action. One of the attributes that distinguishes high-performing leaders from others is their deep desire to develop the talent and potential of those who work with them. What continues to impress me about Roy is his desire to help and mentor others. You will certainly experience that spirit of wisdom and generosity in this book.

With his clear conversational style, Roy will guide you through the "swamp" of leading and managing your company for long-term success. As with all the clients he serves, I know Roy is grateful to be working with you, and is eager for you to achieve the goals, both personal and professional, that you've set for yourself. You're in very good hands.

David Harper

David Harper is managing principal of The Advisory Alliance, which he established after spending more than fifteen years consulting to the Fortune 50, 100, and 500 as well as leading and growing entrepreneurial organizations. He authors the Alliance's monthly *60-Second Read.* His clients include Pepsi, TJX Companies (Marshalls, HomeGoods, T.J. Maxx), Avis Budget Group, PetSmart, Dufry AG, Hudson News Group, eviCore healthcare, Hanover Insurance Group, Georgia Power, D. J. Powers Company, Habitat for Humanity, and Goodwill Industries.

David is an SPHR certified member of the Society for Human Resource Management, a certified consultant and facilitator from the Positive Deviance Initiative of Tufts University, a certified facilitator and administrator of the Hogan Personality Inventory; Development Survey; and Motives, Values, Preferences Inventory; the Myers-Briggs Type Indicator; the Student Leadership Challenge; and the Student Leadership Practices Inventory. He is also a master global certification consultant for the Leadership Versatility Index.

He is a Beta Gamma Sigma Medal recipient and graduate of Columbia University Graduate School of Business (MBA, finance and management), and holds a Bachelors of Business Administration as well as a Bachelors of Arts in psychology from Concordia University, Montreal, Canada.

PROLOGUE

"Whether you think you can or you think you can't, you're right."
– Henry Ford

How do you build a bridge from where your business is today to your long-term vision? How do you gain a competitive edge? Most businesses fail in the first year, and a majority never survive past five years. You can avoid being a statistic by gaining a competitive edge.

Photo by H. Roy Austin, Natural Bridges National Monument, Utah

A competitive edge evolves from making better decisions, which require knowledge, skills, and tools encompassing all functions of your business. You must also have a solid foundation against which to measure those decisions. *The Alligator Business Solution* aligns all your business functions to achieve a competitive advantage and sustainable success.

Generally, small business owners are product, idea, and operations people with excellent skills. They are smart, energetic, and industrious, often possessing a particular skill that leads to starting a business based on this skill, such as cooking, landscaping, construction, or a host of others. The reality is that "doing" this work is merely one aspect of the business.

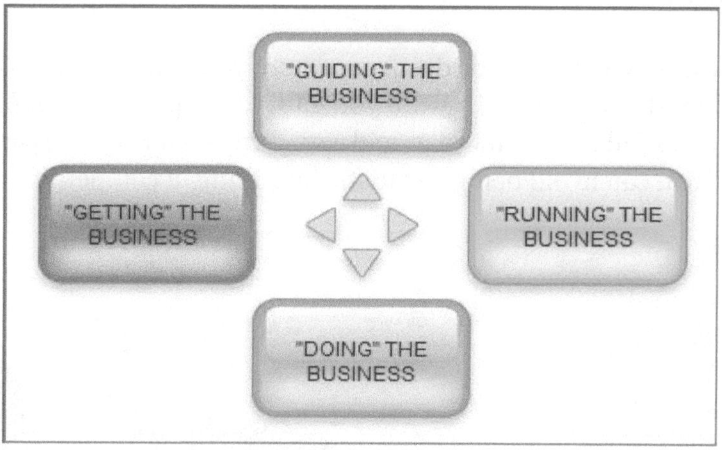

Image provided by Business Design Corp, Touchstone Software

Every business has four interrelated operations. As a small business owner, in addition to "doing" the work, you also have to "run," "guide," and "get" the business—and these are different skill sets. Concentrating on only one aspect, like "doing the business," can have a negative effect on other business functions. For instance, changing something in the "doing" (operations) quadrant can affect the firm's ability to "get the business."

What if operations changes a product formula to reduce cost, but customers don't like the new product? This change ultimately affects "running the business," which includes administration functions like accounting, procurement, human relations, and customer service. "Guiding the business" is the overall management and strategizing, which certainly affects all else. If you negotiate a favorable price on a piece of equipment but that equipment doesn't mesh with the company's overall strategy, is it a good buy?

In order to survive and prosper, you must understand and manage all functions of your business, even the ones with which you are not knowledgeable or comfortable. Wouldn't it be nice to have a user's manual for your small business? This book is intended to be your user's manual, just like a car owner's manual.

This book will teach you how to build your "business house" in the "Business Swamp" and establish a solid foundation. You will gain an understanding of your most important business functions. You will learn how to use various tools to help in decision making and aligning your business functions with your foundation. You will gain the competitive edge needed to realize your long-term vision.

As you progress through the book, continually ask yourself, "How can I apply this concept or tool to gain a competitive advantage over my competition?"

This book is dedicated to helping small businesses enjoy long-term sustainable success. Not only is it *for* small businesses; it is *about* small businesses. Eighteen successful business owners were interviewed, and you will learn from their experiences and journeys in the Business Swamp. Their inspiring true success stories, tragic failures, and humorous tales will help you navigate the swamp.

Assignments are included, as well as references to other books, to help you master various aspects of your business.

Rocky the Alligator will guide you through the swamp by emphasizing key points called "Gator Bites." Why did I name him Rocky? Rocky is my son's name, and "Rocky" is also part of my father's, grandfather's, great-grandfather's, and my name.

Picture created by Roman Larionov, PCSAVED.COM

SECTION 1

SURVEYING THE SWAMP

CHAPTER 1

ALLIGATORS AND BUSINESS

"Success is not defined by heights attained but by obstacles overcome in its attainment." – Booker T. Washington

What could alligators possibly have to do with business success? And ...

Is it good or bad to be a business alligator?

The idea for the title—*The Alligator Business Solution*—came from a newspaper story and a conversation with my granddaughter, Anna Ervin. On Anna's eleventh birthday we were driving back from our "dinner date," and she asked me about the alligators where I live and about my book project. Somehow, her two questions fit together.

When I first moved to the South Carolina coast, a newspaper article reported that a man living in a gated community was suing the community because he was attacked by an alligator in his backyard. He contended that such a large animal should have been removed by the community association. The alligator lunged out of the bushes and grabbed his arm. He poked his fingers in the alligator's eyes to escape. (Remember that if *you* are ever attacked by an alligator!)

A follow-up story several months later announced that the man had withdrawn his lawsuit. Why? His wife had been feeding the alligator for two years, which was why the alligator was lurking in his backyard.

You can't really train an alligator like you can some animals. You can't teach them to sit up or roll over like a dog. However, you can teach them—and they will learn—*where* to find their prey and *what* to look for. And they already know *what* to do with what they find. So what can we learn from this story?

1. Even an alligator can learn some basic things, so you *also* can learn whatever is necessary for your business to succeed.
2. Alligators have been around for 150 million years. They survived the extinction of the dinosaurs, so they have what all of us in business want—long-term sustainable success.

3. Alligators have evolved and adapted to numerous changes in their environment and habitat. You will need to evolve and adapt to a rapidly changing business and technology environment.
4. Alligators have a strategy for success—lurk and lunge. What is the alligator doing when it is lurking? It's preparing to lunge. Preparation and planning are important for the success of your business. By planning, you are preparing yourself to take advantage of opportunities. The alligator doesn't lunge until it is ready and the opportunity is at hand, and neither should you.
5. Alligators fail more than they succeed. You will make mistakes in your business, but just like the alligator, you can learn and improve so the next time an opportunity arises, you will be better prepared. A large part of preparation is learning the skills you need to make better decisions.
6. Alligators have patience and a single focus. Too many new businesses attempt to do too many things at once. Concentrate on your core product, service, and expertise. Do it well, and make some money. Once you are established, you can add other products or services.

Small business owners often say, "I can't do that," or "I can't learn that." If you are going to be successful in business, there are certain basics you simply have to learn whether you enjoy them or not. Small business owners often say things like, "I'm just not good with numbers," or "I can't learn the financial side of business," or "I don't understand marketing." Well, too bad. If you are going to succeed in business, you have to understand all aspects of your business. No excuses.

Image provided by Pixabay

Whether it's accounting, marketing, hiring, or any other aspect of your business, you can learn it. You must learn to manage every part of your business. It does not mean you need to become an expert. You just need to know where to look, what to look for, and how to use the information. That is what an alligator does, and it is what you must do as well.

You just need to know where to look, what to look for, and how to use the information.

Is it good or bad to be a business alligator? Well ... both. Alligators have some admirable traits; however, they also have limited ability to learn. You, on the other hand, have virtually no limits on what you can learn. You are infinitely more intelligent and more adaptable to change than an alligator.

Chapter Assignment

Make a list of the challenges and obstacles that you have overcome in your life. You will be surprised at how far you've come.

CHAPTER 2

THE BUSINESS SWAMP

"You must become interested in every aspect of your business."
– Michael Gerber

The Business Swamp is a beautiful, exciting, and exotic place. It is full of mystery and the opportunity for adventure. New and interesting sights await us as we explore this realm. The swamp is a scenic but also dark and perilous place. There are many hidden

Image by Pixabay

dangers and unforeseen obstacles. What slimy creatures will you encounter in the murky waters? There are predators (competitors) who want to take your business from you, or at least limit your success.

Image by Pixabay

Surviving in the Business Swamp is hard, and *succeeding* is even more difficult. But you can do it if you are properly prepared for your journey. The reality is that it takes more than just a good idea or a single skill to be successful. Although many small businesses fail, numerous small businesses succeed, and so can yours. The biggest difference between the two is that the successful ones:

- **P**lan before starting.
- **L**earn to manage all aspects of the business, including the ones with which they are not familiar or comfortable.
- **U**nderstand their target market.
- **M**anage finances well.
- **B**uild on a solid foundation.

When building a house, you want all of the walls to be plumb, or exactly upright to the foundation. If the walls aren't plumb, then the house will be skewed, which could lead to a host of problems including loss of structural integrity. Likewise, you want your business house to be PLUMB with all functions aligned with the "foundation."

Enterprises that fail often open their doors with little or no planning, lack of proper knowledge of how to run a business, little understanding of their target market, and poor financial management skills. They are not PLUMB.

Business is not astrophysics or microbiology. Recognize that to succeed in the Business Swamp you need a variety of skills and must resolve to work on areas you don't understand or in which you are weak. Everything you need to know can be learned.

Choosing the right path through the swamp is often confusing and difficult. First we will talk about what you need to *survive.* Then we will progress to skills that help you *succeed.* From there we'll get into "Swamp Fundamentals," so your business is built on a solid foundation and does not sink in a bog or quicksand. Once the foundation is established, we'll analyze "Operating in the Swamp."

You will then learn how to "Navigate in the Swamp," so you know where to look, what to look for, and how to use your business information. This section will also explain some best practices. Lastly, we'll cover how to "Interpret the Swamp," so you will recognize danger signs.

No one starts a business thinking they will fail. The sad fact is that most businesses do fail, and you don't want to be part of those statistics. *I* don't want you to be part of those statistics. Do an Internet search on the keywords "business failures." There are many studies by various universities and the Small Business Administration that confirm the high failure rate of small businesses. Depending on the study, the rates range from 25 percent up to 50 and even 75 percent. That rate also varies for different industries, and it appears that restaurants and trucking companies have the highest failure rate.

The studies cite various reasons for why small businesses fail. One by the University of Tennessee cites that "incompetence" accounts for 46 percent of why a business does not make it. What constitutes incompetence? Lack of planning, no experience in record keeping or financing, living beyond means, no knowledge of pricing, and not paying taxes. These are the traits the study defines as incompetent. Incompetence is not stupidity. Incompetence is the lack of necessary knowledge and skills to run the business. *You* can acquire the knowledge and learn those skills.

Lack of managerial experience, which includes hiring and managing employees, poor credit granting practices, too-rapid expansion, and inadequate borrowing practices, accounts for 30 percent of failures. Mismanagement with product or service accounts for 11 percent, and that involves inadequate inventory, no knowledge of suppliers, and wasted advertising.

I am sometimes asked if I know of a business for sale. My reply is, “What industry are you interested in?” Amazingly, the reply is sometimes, “Oh, the industry doesn’t matter. I’m just looking for a business to buy.” But why would anyone buy or start a business in an industry about which they know nothing and for which they have no passion?

Again, do not be discouraged by the statistics, but be aware of reality. It can happen to you if you aren’t PLUMB.

GATOR BITE **Most small businesses fail.**

Business failures can happen to the best of people with the best intentions. Failures occur because too often a skilled and intelligent person has a fantastic business idea but fails or underestimates the need to plan and learn all the aspects of actually *running* a business. You cannot rely solely on “doing” the business.

Failure is heartbreaking. You work hard to bring a dream to life and invest so much of yourself in its existence. The death of a business can be devastating. Watching it falter, then fail, when you don’t know what you’ve been doing wrong or how to save it can leave you feeling helpless and discouraged. This state of mind is hardly going to allow you the energy and creative thinking to find your way back out of the quicksand.

Don’t think for a minute that you can just wing it. A few business owners get lucky and succeed, but most businesses fail because they jumped in with no business plan or strategy for reaching their vision. Have you heard the following old adages? Here they are in in one sentence: “If you keep your eye on the ball, your nose to the grindstone, your shoulder to the wheel, and your ears to the ground, you can succeed.” The problem is that it is difficult to work in this position, which causes you to take your attention away from the skills and strategies you need to succeed.

My experience has been just what the University of Tennessee study reports: Small businesses fail due to lack of planning, underestimating the amount of cash they need, and not having the necessary knowledge in all aspects of their business. Simply put, if you fail to plan, you plan to fail.

If you fail to plan, you plan to fail.

What is a "small business"? The official definition by the U.S. Small Business Administration (SBA, https://www.sba.gov/) is "a business that is independently owned and operated, organized for profit, and is not dominant in its field." The SBA sets the standard for what constitutes a small business based on the average number of employees for the preceding twelve months, or on sales volume averaged over a three-year period. The SBA website contains a table that defines in detail whether a company is a small business. The table organizes businesses according to the North American Industry Classification System for industries, and is forty-six pages long.

In reality, a small business can't really be defined by its size and number of employees. A small business is defined by the nature of the people who pour their blood, sweat, and tears into it. A small business is much more than numbers. It is the realization of a dream, and the careful creation of something solid that came out of a vision. It is the culmination of years of planning, sleepless nights high on possibility, steps taken in the right direction, courage, and hard work. A small business is born and raised in the minds of people who are driven by passion and belief in what they are doing. To a small business owner, their business is a living thing. Owners are devoted to feeding and nurturing it, and obsess about its progress, growth, and development like a new parent does with a child.

Generally, small business owners are motivated by the desire to help people and to solve their problems, and are people who love their work. These owners put in very long hours, and when they are away from the business, their mind is still there. Why? Because inevitably the entrepreneur loves the industry, feels privileged to be a part of it, and wants to make a difference in people's lives.

Small business owners generally thrive on direct, personal relationships with their customers and suppliers. They are idea people who imagine great new products, services, and delivery systems, turning them into reality. They are creative and optimistic, and tend to be risk takers.

As a small business owner, you are incredibly important to our country. Small businesses are the backbone of the U.S. economy and the largest source of new jobs. Look at what the SBA says about trends in small business:

- The 28 million small businesses in America account for 54 percent of all U.S. sales.
- Small businesses have provided 55 percent of all jobs and 66 percent of all new jobs since the 1970s.
- The 600,000 plus franchised small businesses in the United States account for 40 percent of all retail sales and provide jobs for some 8 million people.
- The small business sector in America occupies 30 to 50 percent of all commercial space, an estimated 20 to 34 billion square feet.
- The number of small businesses in the United States has increased 49 percent since 1982.
- Since 1990, as big business *eliminated* 4 million jobs, small businesses added 8 million new jobs.

Source: http://www.sba.gov/content/small-business-trends

The important thing is not the size of a business. Small business success depends on what's going on behind the scenes. You can learn, understand, and manage all the various business functions necessary to succeed. Sometimes it is difficult to know which direction to go, but take heart. You will grow into it one step at a time.

Picture by H. Roy Austin in Northeastern Wisconsin

Eighteen successful companies were interviewed for this book. As we wade through the Business Swamp, you will learn from these companies and their owners, and how they validate the principles in this book. The companies are all profiled in appendix I. All are in different industries and provide different products and services, and each will be mentioned throughout the book to emphasize important lessons.

As you read their profiles, you will note that these companies have a track record of success and perseverance—just like alligators—and that is no accident. The owners have a passion to fulfill their fundamental purpose and make the world a better place. They are amazing business people and an inspiration. As you proceed through the book and read their stories, you will gain a more thorough understanding of why they have enjoyed sustainable success.

Chapter Assignment

As you read this book, create a log of the journey through the swamp so you can quickly go back over key points or update previous assignments. When you finish this book, you will have all the basic components for your business plan. My clients keep their log book in a three-ring binder, which enables them to easily add new pages as their business changes and evolves. Keep your log book in whatever format works best for you. When we have finished our journey through the swamp, you will have developed an "alligator mentality" and will have a journal to help guide your future decisions.

CREATED BY ROMAN LARIONOV, WWW.PCSAVED.COM

SECTION 2

YOU IN THE SWAMP

CHAPTER 3
INTRODUCTION

"Hope Is Not a Strategy." – Book by Rick Page

Surviving in the Business Swamp requires skills, knowledge, and the right attitude. Hope and luck are not reliable strategies for success. Just like the lottery, where the odds are millions-to-one against you, it is possible to pick the right number and come out a winner. But don't count on it.

The right attitude is one where you are positive and realistic but not arrogant. A business owner once told me, "I've never failed at anything I've attempted." That's great, but overconfidence can cause you to ignore warning signs. The most tragic and spectacular failures are due in large part to arrogance. In one case I saw, the loss was in the tens of millions of dollars.

In this section, we will explore the role and responsibilities you have as a business owner in the Business Swamp.

CHAPTER 4
THE ONE THING

"You can only change the outside AFTER you change the inside."
– Bob Nicoll, author, *Remember the Ice*

In a scene in the movie *City Slickers*, Curly (played by Jack Palance) shares his wisdom with Mitch (played by Billy Crystal). Curly is a rough-edged, weather-beaten cowboy who has been riding the range for at least half a century. Mitch is one of the city slickers, and he happens to be in the throes of a mid-life crisis.

In one scene, the two men are out on the range on horseback, herding cattle across the country and talking about life. Curly turns to Mitch and says in his gravelly whiskey voice, "Do you know what the secret of life is?"

"No. What?" Mitch asks.

"This." Curly holds up his finger.

"Your finger?"

Curly nods. "One thing. Just one thing. You stick to that and everything else don't mean sh*t."

"That's great, but what's the one thing?" Mitch asks.

"That's what *you've* got to figure out," Curly answers.

Mitch thinks hard about this advice, and now I'm asking you to do the same. What is your "One Thing"? What is the most important factor affecting your ability to succeed and reach your business goals? Contemplate this for a minute and see if you can identify your One Thing.

The most common answers I hear are along these lines: "My one thing, the most important factor in building a successful life and business, is ..."

- Marketing
- Discipline
- Cost control
- Customer service
- Teamwork
- Passion

Sound familiar? Each of these are definitely important, and you could list many more. But none of them is the real factor on which your business depends. Remember, Curly said it's so important that if you stick to it nothing else matters.

What is the absolute, number-one, most important factor that determines your success? Consider all the possibilities. Before you turn the page to see the answer, write down what *you* think is the most important factor for your success and that of your business.

Ready for the answer? It's ...

DON'T PEEK

Picture created by Roman Larionov, PCSAVED.COM

YOU!

That's right. Who *you* are, how *you* behave, and how *you* make decisions are the center and circumference of your business. *You* are the leader; therefore, all the elements of *you* show up in your business and in your life in one way or another—whether you like it or not. *You* are the One Thing that matters, and *you* matter so much that everything depends on *you*.

Go ahead, take a deep breath. I know it feels overwhelming at first. The truth is that when you understand what it means for you to be that all-important One Thing, you'll realize how powerful that is and you will be excited.

The U.S. Army used to have the recruiting slogan "Be all you can be." Focus on your One Thing and make a commitment to "Be the best *you* that you can be." From there, everything else will fall into place. It's the starting point that changes everything. As you work on yourself, you will begin to notice that everything else in your life will inevitably begin to improve as well.

Be the best you that you can be.

Have you ever heard it said that you will get back *only* what you put into something? The truth is that you will get back *everything* that you put in. The more effort and attention you pay to perfecting something, the bigger and better your results will be. That's all well and good, you say, but what does that even mean in real terms?

It means that you have to take responsibility for all aspects of your business, even if you lean heavily on someone else's support (like an accountant), and you must hold yourself responsible for each success and failure. You must learn how to make business decisions that are based on information as well as intelligence, insight, and instinct.

Michael Gerber puts it perfectly in his book *The E-Myth Revisited.* He says, "You must become interested in every aspect of your business." Note that he did not say you must become interested in the aspects of your business in which you are *already* interested ... or already enjoy ... or already know. He said you must be interested in *every* aspect of your business, including the things that bore you to tears, the things you really don't like to do, and the things you just don't understand—yet (the key word here is "yet.")

GATOR BITE **You have to be interested in every aspect of your business.**

It takes effort to become interested in the things that do not interest you, but that's what it takes to build a business, run the business, and be its leader. And that is what you are—a leader. It is up to you to figure out how to be the best *you* possible. You must figure this out, because your survival depends on *you* and what version of *you* shows up.

When an alligator launches itself toward its prey, it really launches. There's nothing half-hearted or "good enough" about it. He's all-in, being the best alligator he can be in that moment, because he is desperate for his next meal.

You are so much more dynamic and creative than an alligator. If you take the time to work on increasing your knowledge and skills, imagine what you can achieve the next time you launch yourself at a project.

Knowledge is certainly power, but have you noticed that it is also the source of confidence and even enjoyment for so many other things? It turns the complicated, difficult, and uninteresting chores into straightforward, well-run, interesting tasks that you actually enjoy. It's just a matter of paying attention, allowing yourself to believe you can learn whatever is in front of you, and then putting that knowledge, no matter how small, into practice.

Now ... does that mean you may actually end up enjoying paperwork and reading numbers off spreadsheets some day? My friend, numbers are fun when the score is in your favor. It's like being up 21–0 in a football game. But what about when you are behind 21–0 in a football game? Then you know what you and your team must do to get back on top. There is a scorecard in business, and it is called your financial statements. They tell you whether you are winning or losing and give you information on how to better manage your business and compete in the marketplace.

"But Roy, I'm just not good with numbers and I hate paperwork. I only like doing the work." Tough. No excuses, no whining, no complaining. What would you say if one of your employees came to you and said, "I don't like doing this aspect of my job"? Every job includes things you don't like to do, but you do them anyway because they are a requirement.

As the owner, you have to manage every part of your business, which means you have to understand enough about every aspect of your business so that you can tell if something is being done correctly or not. Do you ever follow up and check to see if one of your employees did their work correctly? I certainly hope so. Making sure that the accounting, marketing, and other areas of your business are done properly is part of your job.

There are going to be a lot of different parts to your business that you don't fully understand, or even don't want to know about, which is probably why you don't like or are even bored by them. Financial information is at the top of that list for many business owners. Eyes glaze over when conversation shifts to the importance of financial statements and understanding what is creating their results.

Now here's the good news. You don't have to be an expert in every aspect of your business; you just have to know enough to be able to manage all of them. You just need to know the most basic thing that an alligator knows: where to look, what to look for, and how to use what you find.

GATOR BITE

All you need to know is where to look, what to look for, and how to use what you find.

Does this Gator Bite look familiar? Yes, it was in the first chapter. But it is so important for you to understand that it is repeated here.

Accounting and finance are a part of your business. Some people who are operations oriented (doing the business) would rather do just about anything than sit still and focus on numbers. They want to get on with the business of being in business, which to most people means doing the work.

Alligators are like that too. They want to get on with the business of being alligators. They have no time for crunching numbers; they're all about crunching bones. Like you, when they're out there going about their business—namely finding food and hunting down their next meal—the last thing they want to do is work out where their last catch was and the planning that went behind it. They operate by instinct, ignoring the numbers, and just go after whatever walks by. When I say "numbers," I mean all the numbers in your business, not just the accounting and financial numbers. You also have marketing numbers, operations numbers, employee numbers, vendor numbers, and more.

Many business owners "operate" their business, but don't manage and lead it. These people usually don't last very long as business owners, and if they do, they don't build significant organizations. If you recognize yourself when reading this, it's time to evolve. If you are happy being a small mom-and-pop shop, that's okay; being big is not for everyone. But if you want to be profitable, efficient, effective, and—most importantly—have positive cash flow, then you have to know your numbers. No excuses.

Alligators are in such denial about the need to improve their business model that they don't actually hunt; they lurk. All an alligator has to do is wait for its prey to dip into the water for a drink and—voila!—dinner is served. This strategy has served them well for about 150 million years for two relevant reasons: They lurk where their customers are, and they have evolved to survive on eating only once a week or less.

Do you have 150 million years to develop into something that can survive on a catch-as-catch-can diet? No. But you are human, and therefore you can adapt. You can learn to be proactive. You can learn to interpret your numbers in a way that helps you come up with strategies to encourage customers to go out of their way to visit you. You can work on ideas for keeping those customers. How deadly would alligators be if they had your capability to learn? Using the numbers to your advantage can give you an extremely powerful edge, but you have to know how to work with them first.

As you are becoming a better you, your potential is constantly increasing. If you believe you've reached your potential, then you have. If you believe you can continue to grow, learn, and improve, then your potential continues to increase. If you believe you have yet to reach your potential, then keep growing, learning, and improving. Your biggest breakthroughs are ahead of you.

Your potential is not limited by your high school grades, your SAT scores, your ACT test results, or even your IQ, because learning to be the best *you* has no limits. Yes, there are boundaries to the things you can learn and how much you can learn about different things, but you can choose to keep learning for the rest of your life.

You might not be able to reach the level other people have attained, but you can always be better than you are right now. Avoid comparing yourself to others, thinking, *Oh, I could never be that good or learn to do that.* You're walking down the wrong road with the wrong yardstick. Instead of comparing yourself to others, compare yourself to where you were yesterday. There will always be people who are better than you at one thing or another. The real questions are whether you are making progress toward your goals and whether you are improving your skills and knowledge.

Nothing in nature is stagnant; it is either growing or decaying. When you work on being the best *you* that you can be, you stay in the growing phase. You are becoming, rather than succumbing. You might not be able to achieve what Bill Gates, Warren Buffett, or Steve Jobs have achieved, but you can achieve more than you have in the past.

Nothing in nature is stagnant; it is either growing or decaying.

How do you overcome the inevitable setbacks that occur in life? They will happen. They are a part of life. No one escapes some amount of sadness, tragedy, or failure. You overcome those setbacks by accepting the fact that the past is the past, and there is nothing you can do to change it. No matter how big a mistake you made, it does not determine your future. It might affect your future, but it does not determine it. The critical thing is to learn from those mistakes, figure out why they occurred, and take action to avoid repeating them. Your life is in the present and the future—not the past. Right now, and in the future, you can be the best *you* that you can be.

This is a lifelong process. It does not stop when you graduate from high school or college. It does not stop when you become a manager or vice president, chief executive officer (CEO) or business owner. You will never actually be the best *you,* because your idea of "best" will change throughout your lifetime. However, you can continually get better, and you will achieve greater and more rewarding goals as you focus on personal growth and reaching for that ideal.

You may be wondering why I'm talking about you so much, when the purpose of this book is your business foundation and information systems. My discovery in more than forty years of working for other people, plus the past decade as a business coach working to help small business owners succeed is: as the individual(s) running the show goes, so goes the business. Until you understand how crucial your degree of interest in your business really is, there is no way you will be able to achieve and sustain success.

How do you go about becoming a better you? The first step is to identify your Strengths, Weaknesses, Opportunities, and Threats, or SWOT. You've probably heard of a SWOT in the context of improving a business, which we will touch on later. All of my clients fill out a "Personal SWOT." This can be difficult, because most of us don't see ourselves as other people see us. Find someone you trust who cares about you, warts and all, to help you.

No one, and I mean no one, will ever be as interested, concerned, or emotionally invested—let alone financially invested—in your business as you are. Why should they be? They are interested in their own success, and rightly so. That's why it all comes back to you.

No one will care about your business like you do.

A friend of mine learned this the hard way. Ralph (not his real name) built a profitable business over many years. After careful consideration and assigning specific duties and expectations to his manager, he took time away to pursue humanitarian projects. This was a noble endeavor, and Ralph felt he had indeed brought his business to a point where it could almost run itself. He had faith in the manager to run things in his absence.

All was fine for a while, but eventually the phone calls from disgruntled customers trickled in. "The product quality is terrible," he was told, "and the installation wasn't done properly." Ralph called his manager, who told him not to worry, declaring, "Everything is fine. The customer is an idiot." The calls kept coming from an alarming number of unhappy customers. Each time Ralph would immediately check in with the manager, who duly indicated that it was somehow the customer's fault.

Finally, Ralph decided to see what was going on for himself. What he found appalled him. From poor work habits to slovenly conditions to inexcusable waste, the business was in a horrifying condition. He could not wrap his mind around it. He paid his manager well, so where was the man's pride? Where was his work ethic? How did things get so out of control? To make matters worse, Ralph wound up with a lawsuit against him and then found out that he didn't have liability insurance coverage.

Ralph gave up the humanitarian work that was so important to him and went back to work in his business. He was forced to roll up his sleeves again and work sixteen- to eighteen-hour days in an effort to dig his business out from under the chaos.

What is the lesson here? If you want to walk away from your business to pursue other interests, sell it and don't look back. Whether it's your business or you have a leadership role in someone else's business, no one else will do your work with the same care and attention to detail.

If someone ever tells you that you can set up a business and then walk away and reap the rewards, run from them as fast as you can. Have you walked away from any part of your business, in spirit or in fact? If so, you must come back to it, clean it up, and bring it back to life.

Chapter Assignment

Fill out the Personal SWOT below. Ask a trusted friend to review it to determine if you have missed anything. To complete the SWOT, in the appropriate quadrant of the form, list your personal strengths, weaknesses, opportunities, and threats. Later you will be asked to complete a SWOT for your business, so both business and personal examples are included.

- **Strengths**: What skills, certifications, education, connections, resources, achievements, values, aptitudes, etc., do you have?
- **Weaknesses**: What do you avoid, feel uncomfortable with, or lack confidence in? Do you have negative habits? What do you fear? Do you have financial restrictions? Do personality traits or lack of skills inhibit your success?
- **Opportunities**: Can your strengths translate into opportunities? Will eliminating weaknesses create opportunities?
- **Threats**: What obstacles (such as technology, funding, changes in the economy, competition, alternative products or services) do you face? Do you have safety or health concerns?

Put aside your ego and be completely honest with yourself. Your personal and business success is seriously compromised if you do not confront the facts. Keep the SWOT in your business planning log book and make edits as situations evolve. The first step in becoming a better *you* is a better understanding of who you are and where you need to improve.

Here are some personal and business examples of strengths, weaknesses, opportunities, and threats from clients:

- **Strengths**: Reliable, extensive education, active in BNI, sufficient credit, strive for accuracy and completeness, comfortable with technology, like learning new things, strong value proposition, strong relationships with industry leaders.
- **Weaknesses**: Marketing, hard to motivate myself, more interested in doing what I like than what needs to be done, funding, champagne tastes, lack of brand awareness, accounting and finance knowledge, listening skills, opportunities, hating change.
- **Opportunities**: Better utilize social media and blogging, growing industry, learn accounting and marketing, be a better listener, upgrade equipment and information technology (IT) systems, improve communication skills,

employee events like picnics, new product offerings, improve leadership and management skills, networking.

- **Threats**: Age and fatigue, lack of motivation, cash constraints, aggressive competition, new technology, old equipment, inflation, recession, excess debt (personal and business), misunderstandings between departments, loss of key employees or customers.

NAME ____

STRENGTHS	**WEAKNESSES**
OPPORTUNITIES	**THREATS**

CHAPTER 5
LEADERSHIP

"A leader is one who knows the way, goes the way and shows the way." – John C. Maxwell

My good friend Ron Kirby does leadership training and consulting. The first thing he always says in his seminars is, "No one is born a leader. Leadership is a learned skill."

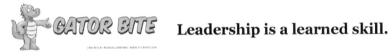

Leadership is a learned skill.

You may argue that it comes easier to some people, but there is no question that leadership is a learned skill. Why? Because it is a skill on which you can improve.

Ron has been training leaders for decades. He was a Sergeant Major in the U.S. Marine Corps. After he retired from the Marines, he was an executive with Best Buy. Now he has his own business and is the senior regional director of the Hilton Head/Savannah Region for BNI (Business Network International).

When he assumed this position in BNI, only one chapter existed in his area. There are now eight chapters, and the region is ranked among the most productive in the world. My chapter alone reported closed business from referrals of over $8 million last year, and was ranked the tenth most productive chapter in the world out of over 5,000 chapters. Worldwide there are over 180,000 members in BNI, and their 6.6 million referrals resulted in closed business of over $8 billion.

Ron built his region by teaching and training people to be leaders. He recently started working with the Savannah area and is training new leaders and building new chapters there. When he says that leadership is a learned skill, he knows what he is talking about—and the people he has trained to be leaders are living proof that you too can become one.

You may or may not identify yourself as a leader, depending on whether you have employees reporting to you or what your idea of leadership is, but the fact is that you *are* a leader. Whether it's your business, your department, your family, your church, or your own career, if any part of its success depends on you, then you are a leader. Everyone is a leader in some facet of life.

As we discussed in the last chapter, the first and most important step as a leader is to work on yourself. Each and every one of us has leadership potential in some form. You must take your own potential and mold yourself into the kind of leader on which everyone, and every part of your business, can depend. Seek out mentors, read books, research online, look for volunteer positions with nonprofit organizations, and practice, practice, practice. Above all, accept responsibility for your mistakes and learn from them. Take note of your growth and improvement, and be proud of it. If you do it right, your business will grow and improve along with you.

Developing and improving your leadership skills is part of being the best *you* that you can be. When you are constantly learning, your potential is constantly increasing. All organizations rise and fall according to their leadership. Today, many companies that we once considered giants in their industry either no longer exist or are a mere shell of what they were at their peak.

Kodak was the largest camera and film company in the world. Today it barely rates a mention. Joseph Schlitz Brewing was once the largest brewery in the United States, even larger than Anheuser-Busch. You may not have even heard of Schlitz. Many successful organizations like these have crashed and burned, while others, due to leadership, have risen from the ashes.

There are many good books on leadership. John Maxwell's books are some I highly recommend. However, there is really no substitute for on-the-field playing experience. You could do extensive reading on how to be a better tennis player, but until you get out on the court and play, you aren't going to improve.

For many people, being the leader is out of their comfort zone. You may be one of those people. Don't be! You have a business to run, customers to satisfy, employees to train, and vendors to work with. If you are serious about building a successful business, then leadership is a responsibility you have to accept and a skill you must develop.

Where do you get the on-the-field playing experience? There are a multitude of nonprofit organizations, churches, and civic clubs that need your help. Leading in a nonprofit is different from leading in a for-profit company because people in a nonprofit are volunteers. Volunteers are there by choice. If they don't like the leadership, they just leave.

Being the boss and ordering employees around is not leadership. Real leadership is all about building a team committed to a common cause. Being a leader in a nonprofit will hone your leadership skills. Start small by chairing a committee. You will make mistakes. That is growth and it is okay, as long as you learn from your mistakes and determine to avoid them in the future.

Chapter Assignment

Make a list of all the situations where you were, or are, the leader. At the top of the page, write the heading *President and CEO of ________________, Inc.* (insert your name in the blank). One position we all have is being the leader of our lives and careers. You will be surprised at how many times in your life you have been a leader in some way. Ask yourself what you learned from each leadership situation.

CHAPTER 6
PREPARATION

"Success happens when opportunity and preparedness meet."
– Zig Ziglar

A key contributor to small business failure is lack of preparation or planning. All too often a business simply opens its doors. With a lawn mower, leaf blower, and a pickup truck, you're now in the landscaping business. If it is just you, or you and another person, this may work out okay. Maybe at this stage it is more of a hobby to you. You work it part time and make some money to supplement your full-time income.

When you decide to make it your full-time occupation and your sole source of income, then you have moved to a whole new swamp. You now need more customers. To support those customers, you need more employees. You will need professionals to ensure the business is compliant with national, state, and local laws: lawyer, insurance agent(s), accountant, payroll processor, banker, and merchant services to process credit card sales. We haven't even touched on marketing services, websites, and computer services. The business may have intellectual property requiring trademarks, patents, or copyrights. And there's more. What about the vendors to supply products and/or services so your business can service and supply its customers?

You may be thinking that all this doesn't apply to you. You are going to set up an incredible website and sell your product or service online—a virtual business with no employees. Sorry, but most of these vendor services are still necessary even in a virtual business. In every type of business, there will be a host of associated legal liability issues. You need professional advice and insurance coverage. As your business grows, new items become necessary. As the number of employees grows, you may need to add benefits such as health insurance and a retirement savings plan.

Whew! There's a lot there to think about. You may feel overwhelmed, but don't be discouraged. A business doesn't go from one employee to one hundred employees overnight. You don't need to know and learn everything immediately. However, you must be aware of the potential needs of your business so you can address them at the proper time. Just keep in mind that success happens when opportunity and preparedness meet.

GATOR BITE **Success happens when opportunity and preparedness meet.**

When I started writing this book, I knew very little about writing, publishing, promoting, legal issues, or trademarks. After the first draft was sent to my editor, I thought I was essentially finished. In reality, I was just getting started. There was so much more to be done.

What's my point? Well, let me ask you a question: How do you eat an elephant? Answer: You eat an elephant one bite at a time. You don't need to know everything about how to run a large business. You will grow into that role and learn along the way. Just take one bite at a time.

Some people say, "I don't bother with planning. I just deal with things as they come along." If you enjoy crisis management, that's fine. But crisis management is very stressful. I live on the coast of South Carolina. The biggest weather danger here is hurricanes. My brother Den lives in the Silicon Valley area of California, an earthquake zone. My cousin Marilyn lives in Kansas City, a part of Tornado Alley. I'll take hurricanes any day because we can see them coming and take action for protection; there are a lot of things you can do to prepare for a hurricane long before it arrives on the horizon. Tornados and earthquakes provide little or no warning, so preparing for them is difficult, if not impossible.

Some people think a business plan is a waste of time. An interesting perspective, but I don't agree. Can you plan and prepare for everything? Of course not. But that doesn't mean you shouldn't prepare for what you can foresee and then make adjustments to your plan as conditions change.

Compare the following true stories. One company did virtually no planning and the other one did. Keep in mind this Gator Bite as you read about what happened.

Proper planning prevents poor performance.

Alpha, Inc. decided to start another company, Omega Inc., in a somewhat related industry. The first company, Alpha, opened Omega with much fanfare but virtually no planning. What little planning it did was related to the potential gross profit on the product Omega was going to sell.

There was no market research, legal setup, financial projections, or consideration of the potential expenses required. Omega would make $40 on what it sold. Sounds good, right? But what about employee salaries, payroll taxes, rent, utilities, legal services, insurance, and numerous other administrative and operational expenses?

In Omega's initial planning, it considered only the cost of buying the product to sell to the customer and none of the other expenses. There was one other issue. Omega had no cash to start with, so Alpha loaned Omega what it needed. What happened to Omega? Initially it was excited as revenues soared, illustrated by this graph.

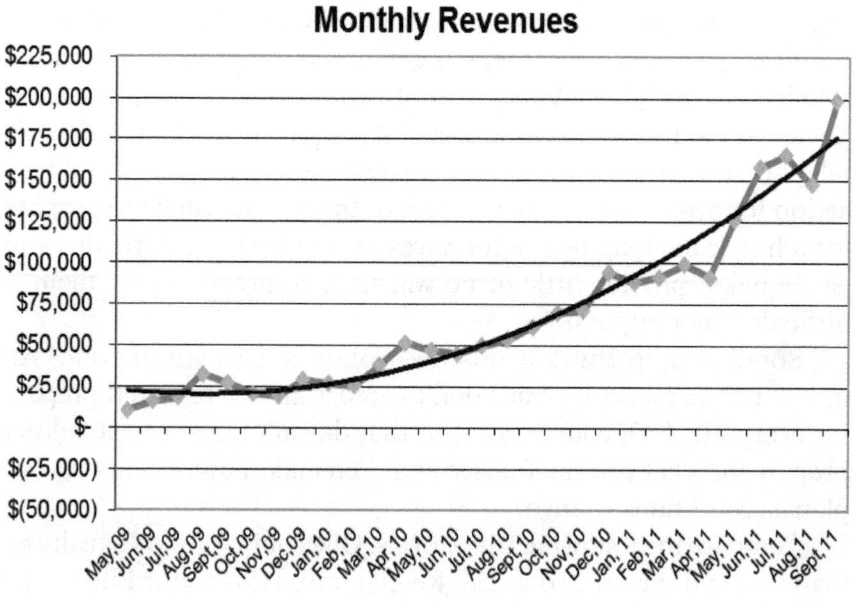

It looks great, doesn't it? Revenues went from $10,000 a month in May 2009 to $200,000 a month in September 2011 (the blue line is revenues, and the black line is a trend line). However, looks can be deceiving—especially when important information is omitted. That's the lesson Alpha learned the hard way. There were a lot of operational expenses directly related to providing the product to the customer that were not considered, plus all the administrative and marketing expenses. As a result, each time sales revenue went up a dollar, expenses also went up by a dollar.

Following is the same chart with pre-tax profit and cash flow added. Pre-tax profit is revenues minus all the expenses of the business, so it is the profit after subtracting operations, sales and marketing, and administrative expenses excluding state and federal income taxes.

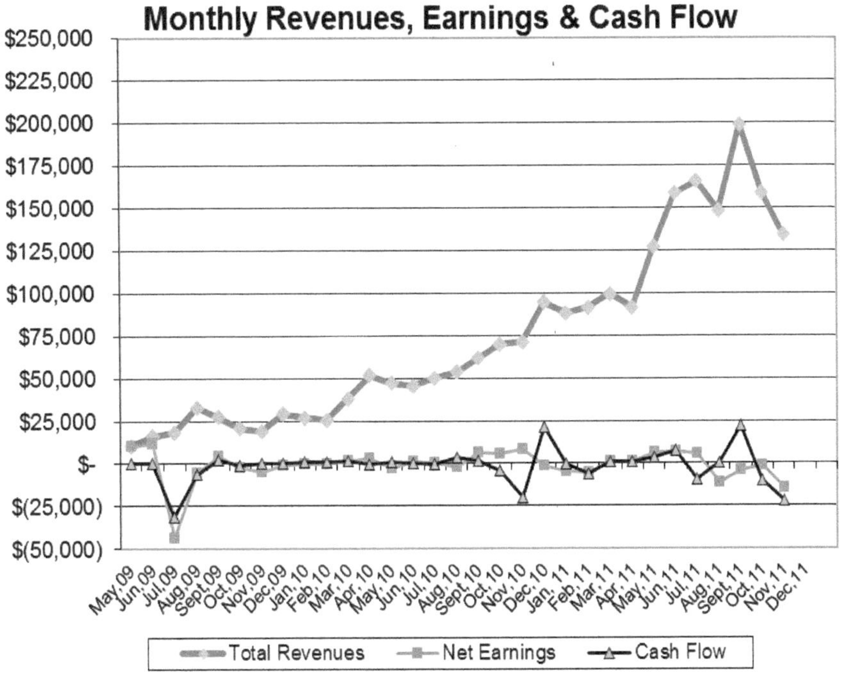

Omega closed its operations a few months after reaching peak revenues. Throughout the existence of Omega, Alpha continued loaning Omega money, thinking that sooner or later these revenues would turn into profits and cash flow. Yet when expenses increase as rapidly as revenues, or even by the same amount, a profit cannot be made by increasing the volume of products sold. Alpha wound up losing about $400,000.

Alpha is not a unique or uncommon situation. Lack of planning and preparation is the most common reason why businesses fail. This example also demonstrates another common reason why small business fail, and that is lack of understanding of basic accounting and financial concepts like gross profit.

On the other hand, what happens when you do the work before opening the doors? Let's look at another small business story to illustrate that.

Foskey Heating and Air was founded by Mike and Christine Foskey. I met Mike at a BNI meeting and over time got to know him. At the weekly BNI meetings, other members kept giving testimonials to the work Mike's company did, and those testimonials had a common theme. Each one told of a situation where the BNI member or someone the member knew had a problem with an HVAC system and contacted a local company. The local company said a new HVAC system costing anywhere from $10,000 to $20,000 was needed. The person subsequently called Mike's company, which came out and made a small repair that fixed the problem—and a new HVAC system wasn't found to be necessary. Numerous BNI members gave testimonials that Foskey did not attempt to sell a whole new system and take advantage of people (Foskey does sell complete systems, but only when they're absolutely required).

In BNI, we do what we call 1-2-1s, where we meet with other members outside the regular weekly meetings to get to know them and learn how to refer business to each other. I learned that Mike had worked in his industry for many years and dreamed of owning his own business. But he knew there was more to running and growing a business than just doing the work. Mike and Christine went to Service Corp of Retired Executives (SCORE) to get help writing a business plan and setting up the new business. They spent over a year planning, and when they finally started, they were prepared.

Certainly there have been challenges along the way, but the company has grown substantially each year. Mike and Christine continue to meet regularly with their SCORE counselor when making changes to their business plan. (As an aside, several years ago I switched my home HVAC maintenance to Foskey even though I was perfectly satisfied with the company servicing my system, and needless to say, I've been extremely satisfied with their work.)

Can your business be successful if you don't do any planning and preparation? Of course it can. I know one that did succeed. The odds, however, are that businesses that plan and prepare are more likely to succeed that those that don't. The successful companies interviewed for this book all had business owners who took at least a year to plan their business (Hilton Head Glass took four years).

Years ago, Fram Air Filters had a TV commercial with the tag line, "Pay me now or pay me later." It meant that if you don't change your vehicle's air filter now, you'll be paying the mechanic to fix your engine later. If you try to wing it, you may succeed eventually, but the odds are against you. You will have to fix things later. If you fall off a cliff, you may survive the landing—but don't bet on it. Alpha lost $400,000, and Omega is out of business. Foskey Heating and Air continues to grow and succeed.

Look at building your business in the context of building a house. When you decide to build a house, first you define your vision. What style of house do you want? How many rooms? What size lot? Building a house begins with a vision of what you want. It might be a Cape Cod, a colonial, an A-frame, or something completely modern. You would picture its size, its color, the landscaping, and a thousand details that feed your dream and keep you focused.

You would spend a lot of time researching and refining your ideal house, looking at magazines, reading articles, searching on the Internet, driving through neighborhoods to see what you like, and organizing the details so you can communicate what you want to an architect. The architect would then translate your vision into blueprints for a plan that fits your needs and wants. Your vision of the house would guide every decision you make regarding its construction.

You can't build a house without a set of blueprints, and you can't create a set of blueprints without a vision of the end product. Would you build a house costing $500,000 and not have an image of what it will look like? I don't think so.

But all too often, people jump into a business and invest a large amount of money without a set of blueprints or a clearly defined vision. If you are going to survive and succeed in the Business Swamp, you need a precise vision and a solid foundation to support your business house.

What should be included in your business plan, and how should you go about the planning? SCORE is certainly an outstanding resource, and it is free. The biggest mistake people make with SCORE is that they don't stick with it; a SCORE counselor can't teach you everything in one or two sessions. Computer programs can also guide you through the business planning process. One is *Business Plan Pro*, which is relatively inexpensive and does a good job. It is interactive, asking questions to guide you through the planning depending on your answers.

No matter how you go about developing your business plan, the important thing about the planning process is that it forces you to think about how you are going to handle all the various functions of your business. Appendix II contains an outline for a business plan and has many of the elements to consider for your plan. Your plan may need elements that are not listed, and some items listed may not apply to your business.

There is a lot to consider. As you work your way through this book and complete the assignments, you will have the basics for your plan in your planning notebook.

Chapter Assignment

On a sheet of paper, create an outline of the elements and sub-elements that need to go into your business plan. As you go through this book, refer back to this outline and make additions and corrections to it. One approach would be to have a separate piece of paper for each major element of the plan. Alternatively, create your outline digitally in whatever format works best for you, such as a spreadsheet or word processing program. I know one author who does all his outlining in Microsoft PowerPoint and uses "Slide Sorter View" to easily move things around. Do it in whatever medium works best for you, but most importantly, *do it*.

CHAPTER 7
CHOICES

"You are where you are because that is where you choose to be."
– Carl Jung

At a seminar I attended years ago, the speaker quoted Carl Jung, saying, "You are where you are because that is where you choose to be." *No!* I thought. *I am definitely not where I want to be. My career isn't where I want it to be. I haven't reached my financial goals. I'm burdened with debt, and my personal life is a mess. I am not where I want to be!*

While driving home, I was stewing about this when I realized that the speaker hadn't said anything about *where* I wanted to be. He was simply saying I was where I am because my choices had led me to my current situation. Although past decisions and choices define where you are today, they do *not* determine your future. Those choices may affect your future, but they do not limit it.

You may be saying, "Wait a minute, Roy. What about people who didn't choose what happened to them, like being in a car wreck or having an illness or being born with a disability?" I understand. Out-of-our-control events do happen, and not just the catastrophic stuff. However, there are people everywhere who blame someone or something else for almost every situation. They fixate on the "if only." "If only I had better parents," "If only I had better teachers," "If only I had been given that promotion," "If only, if only, if only ..."

Conner Stroud (http://www.huffingtonpost.com/2013/08/27/rafael-nadal-conner-stroud-pffd_n_3826713.html) was born with no femurs, hips, ankles, or knees. Specialists told his parents that his feet would never be able to bear weight and recommended amputation of the front part of each foot, leaving only the heels. At age two, Conner had the surgery. He gradually learned to walk on his heels and still does, albeit with a twisting gait because he has no hip joints.

His parents and siblings were tennis players, so he naturally wanted to play as well. He began playing at age five, competing against family. It was either sit there and watch or join in ... and Conner had never been much for sitting around.

"It's hard to remember a time I wasn't playing," Conner said recently. For years, he played strictly able-bodied tennis on his "stubbies" (rubber stoppers attached to the stumps of his legs). Despite being a foot or two shorter than many of his opponents, he won a number of matches. His notoriety spread and enabled him the opportunity to hit with international tennis champions such as Andy Roddick and Jim Courier, and meet Rafael Nadal, his favorite player, at the U.S. Open in 2013. Now Conner is a top-rated wheelchair tennis player.

Do an Internet search for "Conner Stroud." Read the articles. Watch the videos of him playing in his "stubbies." Conner didn't choose to be born the way he was, but he has decided to not let his handicap determine his future.

You may have a legitimate complaint about an unfair disadvantage, but how you choose to react to your circumstances is the critical determination of the result. Your life is shaped by the choices you make and how you choose to react to circumstances both in and out of your control.

Success, however you define it, is a choice.

How do you choose to be successful? Choose actions, attitudes, and behaviors that lead you directly to your goal. If lack of knowledge is standing between you and your dream, learn. Obtain the knowledge and information you need, and learn to apply it.

If you aren't comfortable speaking in front of a group, then do it anyway. If your level of physical fitness is not where you would like it to be, find out how to get in better shape. If you aren't satisfied with your weight, learn about the impact of food choices and adapt your eating habits. If you don't have good people skills, acquire them. If you are shy, tap into your courage and become skilled at meeting and talking to people. If you don't know the right people, get out and find them. Remember, there's a high likelihood that the person you want to get to know, *wants* to be known. Take a deep breath and do it. Generally speaking, people like to meet people. We like to interact with each other. Don't leave opportunities to learn, grow, and improve on the table. Sometimes you just have to step out and make things happen.

Developing relationships with people becomes natural and easy when you begin to focus on how you can help others. Become interested in them, their lives, their goals, who they are, and what they believe in. It won't happen overnight but gradually, little by little, you'll acquire new skills. And that leads to another basic truth ...

Success is not a destination.
It is a lifelong journey.

Success is not defined by financial prosperity, or demonstrated by a big house or expensive car. Success is achieving a goal and then reaching for the next goal. Success is progressive. You never really attain success because you are always in the process of becoming successful. You can always improve your situation, your knowledge, your finances, or your standing in the community. Whatever you seek, once you attain it, you will discover there is more to strive for to make the world a better place.

Success is defined by obstacles overcome rather than heights achieved. You can never honestly call yourself successful because you should always be in the process of becoming successful. Success is reaching your goals one at a time, whatever they may be, and then reaching for the next goal, and the one after.

Guess what? You do not have the right to be successful. However, you do have the right to the opportunity to be successful, and fortunately we live in a country where we have the freedom to pursue our dreams and goals.

Make the choices and decisions to move you toward your goals. Looking in the rear-view mirror as you drive down the road of life will probably land you in a ditch. The road behind you is past. The road ahead is where you will live your life. The next time you get that "Oh, woe is me" feeling, just think of Conner Stroud.

Now let's distinguish between any old decision and a committed decision. At some point in your life, you have made a committed decision, but maybe you didn't recognize it as such. Every year millions of us make New Year's resolutions (decisions) and within a few days forget them. We all decide to do things but then don't follow up on our commitment. In reality, they weren't really decisions; they were wishes. A committed decision is entirely different and really powerful.

Choose to be a DWIT. A DWIT is someone who Does Whatever It Takes to reach their goals. Being a DWIT means staying focused on the objective until it is accomplished, and then moving on to bigger and better goals. When you truly decide to be a DWIT and do whatever it takes to reach your goals, magic happens.

At the 2001 Institute of Management Accountants national convention, one of the speakers was Joel Eisler. He and his partners owned a floor covering company. During his presentation, he mentioned that for the past five years his company had achieved 25-percent-per-year growth in revenues. As controller for Savannah Manufacturing, I was eager to learn how the company had achieved such consistently high growth in revenues.

After his presentation, I introduced myself and asked him how they did it. His answer blew me away, and it is still one of the most powerful statements I've ever heard. I was expecting some revolutionary business or marketing strategy that I could take back and apply. He simply looked me in the eye and said, "We decided to." Wow. Think about that statement. Roll it around in your mind. He and his partners *decided* to commit to the goal of 25-percent-per-year revenue growth and then did whatever it took to accomplish that goal.

Frequently, companies and individuals set goals but never achieve them. Why? Because those decisions weren't committed decisions.

One of my favorite movies is *The Lord of the Rings: The Fellowship of the Ring*. One scene in particular applies to this principle. Frodo is talking with the wizard Gandalf, lamenting about the task he has been given. The dialogue is as follows:

Frodo: "I wish the ring had never come to me. I wish none of this had happened."

Gandalf: "So do all who live to see such times, but that is not for them to decide. All we have to decide is what to do with the time that is given to us."

All we have to decide is what to do with the time that is given to us.

A simple yet powerful statement. Forget the past; you can't change it. Decide what you are going to do with the future.

Chapter Assignment

Make a list of some committed decisions you have made. Think about how satisfied you felt when your committed decision led to accomplishment of your goal.

CHAPTER 8

SECTION 2 SUMMARY

"Control your own destiny or someone else will."
– Jack Welch, CEO, General Electric

To survive in the Business Swamp, you need some basic skills and attitudes. We've already discussed the importance of becoming a better *you* and developing your leadership skills.

To dodge the alligators in the swamp, you must be prepared with a plan for operating in the swamp. Diversions occur in the swamp, so managing your time is critical. Before diving into the swamp, evaluate differing opinions about your ideas and force yourself to consider whether your product or service is really wanted, and whether your strategy is viable. Remember, just because someone needs something doesn't mean they want it. Be a DWIT and make committed decisions to accomplish your goals. Your survival will depend on:

- You
- Leadership
- Preparation
- Time management
- Contrary opinions
- Committed decisions
- Choices
- Learning from mistakes
- Adaptability

These survival skills are all things that you can learn and apply. It all comes back to being the best *you* that you can be.

SECTION 3

SWAMP FUNDAMENTALS

CHAPTER 9
VISION

"Those who can see the invisible can do the impossible."
– Albert Einstein

"If you don't know where you're going, you'll probably end up somewhere else." This quote is attributed to Laurence J. Peter, a twentieth-century American educator and writer, and is the title of a book by David Campbell.

If you don't know where you're going, you'll end up somewhere else.

Some business owners don't have a clear idea of where they are going, let alone how to get there. Others have a vision but lack a plan to achieve it. Your vision, whether personally or in business, is an essential part of success. It defines what success looks like to you and serves as a reference point, like a lighthouse, to double-check that you're headed in the right direction.

What do you want your business to look like in fifteen to twenty years? Common answers to this question are often, "I want to be bigger," or "I want to be more profitable." They're too vague. How do you create a plan to reach "bigger" or "more profitable"?

Most small business owners have a vision but are reluctant to verbalize it. Some don't know how to achieve that lofty vision, so they are afraid to state it. Others are afraid of failure, so they don't want to share their dreams. By the time you finish this book, I hope you will see a clear path to your vision.

If you were going on a long trip and didn't have a map or GPS to guide you, wouldn't you be a little reluctant to start driving?

A client named Pete (not his real name) said his vision was to grow sales revenue to $200,000 from the current $100,000. After some homework assignments, his vision changed to $500,000. At our next meeting, he was grinning like a Cheshire cat. His vision was now $2 million in sales.

What changed? A simple exercise enabled Pete to envision how to accomplish the bigger vision. $2 million in sales was probably always his dream, but he couldn't see a path to its accomplishment. Sometimes the path to your vision isn't clear, and getting there may seem impossible. With a clear concept of how to accomplish his vision, Pete started developing a plan to make it a reality and is well on the road to achieving it.

Image by Pixabay

An excellent example of dreaming big and accomplishing a vision is Robert Asp and the *Hjemkomst*. Robert Asp was a junior high school guidance counselor in Moorhead, Minnesota. He was of Norwegian descent, and he had a big dream: to build a replica of an ancient Viking ship and sail it to Norway. There is little evidence that he had knowledge of sailing, carpentry, or ship building, and Moorhead is 200 miles from the nearest body of water—Lake Superior.

After a year of planning and learning, he started his Viking ship in 1972. He named it *Hjemkomst* (pronounced *Yem-komst*), which is Norwegian for "homecoming." On August 9, 1980, the ship made its maiden voyage on Lake Superior at Duluth, Minnesota. Sadly, Asp died on December 27, 1980. He had been diagnosed with leukemia in 1974 but had continued to work on the ship.

His children adopted his vision and completed the voyage, arriving in Norway on July 19, 1982. Extensive planning and training were necessary to sail this seventy-six-foot ship from Duluth across Lake Superior, then through Lake Huron, Lake Erie, the Erie Canal across New York State, down the Hudson River, through New York Harbor, and across the Atlantic Ocean to Bergen, Norway.

There were monumental problems to solve in building the ship, learning how to sail it, and making the voyage. Robert Asp had a huge vision and made a committed decision to make it come true. He was a DWIT and did whatever it took to make his vision a reality. Importantly, he wasn't afraid to announce his vision to the world despite many doubters.

Those who can see the invisible can do the impossible.

Your vision is a place you'd like to get to in the future, but may have no idea how to do it at present. Your vision is your destination and your inspiration, and once down on paper it guides your thinking, decision making, and attitude as you move toward it.

Your vision begins as an idea that plays in the back of your mind. You aren't sure if it's achievable, but the possibility is exciting. When you bring it forward in your mind, you will find that as you conduct your business, your vision is always out there like a beacon that guides your steps.

Few things are as powerful as an idea or vision, and a person or team committed to that vision. It ensures that you have somewhere to go, which is good, because if you aren't going somewhere, then you are going nowhere. If you feel like you are drowning in a river of alligators, your vision is like a life raft.

To communicate your vision and inspire your team or employees, you need to summarize and encapsulate it in a statement. A vision statement should inspire the entire organization, but that is only possible if it is truly the vision of the owners or leadership team. Often a vision statement is slapped on a brochure or banner but never discussed again. Soon everyone forgets it.

Many businesses create vision statements because it's the chic thing to do, or there's a space for it on the website, or it's a social media expectation. Slapping something up on the wall or online simply because other people look for it or will be impressed by it is wrong. When that happens, you know the people who came up with it probably don't believe in it, let alone believe it is possible.

Often, vision statements use words like "best," "world-class," "largest," "number-one provider," or countless other clichés that are empty unless there's some substance behind them. Substance requires intention and practice. When that vision statement is truly yours, and you believe in it, people will get behind you. People like to be part of a winning team that is going somewhere.

Your vision is not a marketing statement. It is your constant reminder that you are moving in a specific direction to a specific destination. Following are examples of vision statements from the successful companies I interviewed:

- Franchise the business across the Southeast and eventually across the country.
- Be in position to sell the business and retire in ten years.
- Create a golf-themed restaurant.
- Expand from the current two locations to five locations.
- Grow from current $20 million in revenues to $100 million.

Notice that these visions are specific about what the owner wants to accomplish. The owners will know when they have reached their vision. What if they had said something like "We want to be the premier provider of financial advisory services in the Southeastern United States"? How would they know when they had reached that vision? How do you measure which firm is "premier," and what is the definition of "premier" in this context? Your vision needs to be specific so that you can measure your progress and know when you've accomplished it.

After writing down your vision, you need to be a DWIT, commit to the vision, and get started. Accept the fact that in the beginning you don't know everything you need to know. You will learn and grow along the way, and you will acquire all the knowledge and skills you need. You will make mistakes, but so what? As long as you learn from your mistakes and take measures to avoid them in the future, mistakes can be a positive thing. Make a decision and get started.

Remember Joel Eisler and his comment about how his company achieved sustainable revenue growth for years? He said, "We decided to." Decide that you are going to reach for your vision.

Your next step is a concrete plan. Hope, wishful thinking, and wanting something with all your heart is not a strategy. Your plan is your map to guide you through the Business Swamp. Make an outline of the necessary steps, including what you need to learn. Continually fill in the details for each step. There will be changes in the route through the swamp as your plan adapts to changes. While the plan may change, the vision is constant, and that is what keeps you on track.

No doubt, at some point in your life, you have had a goal that you wanted so much that you were determined to accomplish it no matter what the obstacles. Think back to times in your life when you made a committed decision and did not allow anything to get in the way of achieving your goal. Maybe it was athletic or academic in nature, or you wanted a specific career, or wanted to spend the rest of your life with one special person.

On a piece of paper or on your computer, write out the steps you took to get there. Think back on how one thing led to another, and take note of your intentions behind each action. When you're done, look at what you did and realize you have the capability to realize your vision.

Did Robert Asp's vision of building a seventy-six-foot-long Viking ship and sailing it to Norway seem remotely possible? Did Conner Stroud's vision of playing tennis make any sense? What made the realization of their visions possible? They made a committed decision to make it work.

ORGANIZATION CHART

You may have wondered about the exercise Pete completed that opened his mind to a broader vision. His task was to create an organization chart of what his business would look like when he had reached $500,000 in revenues.

An organization chart is a diagram showing the structure of the organization in terms of the position and responsibilities of each employee as well as who reports to whom. There is no "right" way to draw one. Its structure will depend on what best suits your company.

Image by Pixabay

In the diagram above, the top box is probably you, the owner/CEO/president. Reporting to you might be the vice presidents of Marketing, Operations, and Accounting. Use whatever titles you like. Reporting to these three vice presidents could be any number of positions.

Pete's organization chart enabled him to determine how much each position could generate in revenues, and showed eight people in Operations. If each one did $250,000, which he knew to be realistic, that would generate $2 million in revenues (8 times $250,000 = $2 million). Pete's organization chart revealed how he could achieve not just $500,000 in revenues, but $2 million. Your company may not work like Pete's, but that isn't the point.

Picture a beautiful scene in Baudette, Minnesota, with trees and a dock on a river. What do you see? Baudette calls itself the "Walleye Capital of the World." If you've never heard of walleye, it is a delicious

Great Lakes fish. In Baudette there is a forty-foot-long statue of Willie Walleye. Do you have that picture in your mind? Good. Now, when you see the actual picture below, is it what you visualized?

Visualize, Don't Peek

Picture by H. Roy Austin

Picture by H. Roy Austin

Creating an organization chart is similar to these pictures. The actual picture clarifies your visualization. Drawing the organization chart for what your business will look like in ten, fifteen, or twenty years will give you a clearer picture of how to realize your vision. Here are a few more visions of some of the successful companies interviewed:

- Grow to $100 million in annual gross sales revenues and take our stock price to over $150/share.
- Build into a franchise model complete with standard operating policies that anyone could use to run the business, at which point the business could be sold for maximum value.
- Promote tourism in the Sparta, Tennessee, area with a combined inn, restaurant, and brewery on the Calfkiller River, where canoes and kayaks can be launched, picked up, and brought back to the pub. Dave will be cooking brunch on Sunday. Don will be standing in the river serving Calfkiller beer to passing boaters.
- Grow revenues 25 percent per year, and make our company a household name in the communities we serve.

Chapter Assignment

1. Write down where you want your business to be and what it will look like in fifteen to twenty years—just a brief statement of where you want to go. Get the vision out of your head and write it down. Don't just do a mental checklist; write it down. Don't be afraid to discuss your vision with others, even if some people don't think it's possible. Keep your vision statement on hand, and refer to it frequently as you read this book. You may find your vision expanding, as Pete did, as you begin to realize how you can accomplish it.

2. Create an organization chart for where your company will be in fifteen to twenty years.

CHAPTER 10
LAYING THE GROUNDWORK

"Championships are won in the off season." – Pat Summit

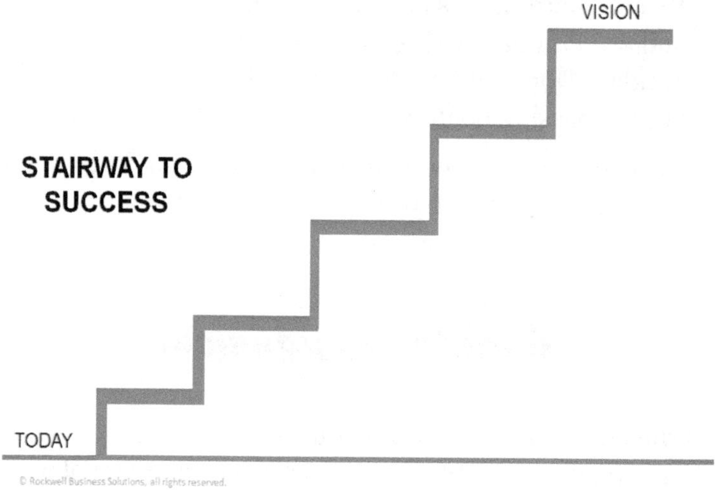

Image by Roman Larionov, PCSaved.com

You now have a vision and are excited to get to work. Before going too deep into the swamp, you need a solid foundation on which to stand. Imagine a staircase beginning from where you are today and leading to where you want to be in the future. Each step brings you closer to your vision, even if in reality there will be some steps up and some steps down. But you are persistent and always headed toward your vision. What is missing from the staircase? The starting point is there, the intervening steps are there, and the ultimate vision is at the top of the staircase.

What is supporting the staircase? In the Business Swamp, the supporting pillars are your "fundamentals."

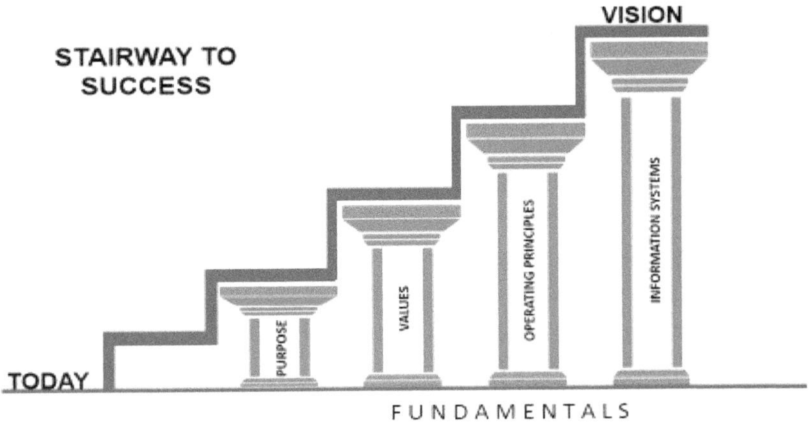

Image by Roman Larionov, PCSaved.com

The foundation of your business (and your life) consists of a set of fundamentals that support and guide your decision making. These fundamentals are critical to your success in business, as well as in life. The four fundamentals are:

- Fundamental Purpose
- Fundamental Values
- Fundamental Operating Principles
- Fundamental Information Systems

The next four chapters will examine each of these fundamentals. Why are they so important? When players are interviewed after their team wins the championship, say the World Series in baseball or the Super Bowl in football, they usually say, "Back in pre-season, the coach emphasized the fundamentals, and we practiced and practiced and practiced them."

Coach John Wooden, the legendary basketball coach for UCLA, won ten NCAA championships in twelve years. Before every practice and every game, Coach Wooden would teach his players how to tie their shoes. He even instructed them on how to put on their socks. Why such attention to detail? Surely the players knew how to tie their shoes? Coach Wooden believed in perfecting the fundamentals of the game. If a shoe wasn't tied properly and the player's foot slipped at a critical moment, it could cost a point, and that point might be the difference in the game.

In section 2, chapter 3, we discussed building your business in the context of building a house. Armed with your vision, you can start on your blueprint—your business plan. Now you are ready to break ground, pour the footers, and lay the foundation. The stability of your foundation will either lend strength to your business or bring the whole thing toppling down. The swamp is a squishy place, so building in the swamp requires a solid foundation.

Your fundamentals support your vision and serve as a place to anchor all the functional parts of your operations. Your foundations define your culture, who you are, what you believe in, and how you will operate.

Your foundation establishes who you are, what you believe in, and how you operate.

Your fundamentals are very much *your* fundamentals. This is why working on yourself and striving to be the best *you* that you can be is so very important. This is your foundation, showing up in your business.

All aspects of your business should be aligned with your foundation, just like aligning the walls of a house with its foundation. If the walls aren't plumb, the house will be unstable. If your business isn't PLUMB, it will be unable to weather storms in the Business Swamp.

CHAPTER 11

FUNDAMENTAL PURPOSE

"The secret of success is constancy to purpose."
– Benjamin Disraeli, British Prime Minister

Other than to make money, why are you in business? The first foundational plank is your purpose for being in business. Your business begins and ends with your customers and satisfying their perceived needs. In reality, all humans need food, water, clothing, shelter, and security, and these can be satisfied at a relatively low income level. Even alligators can get those needs met—except for the clothing—just by following their instincts. Everything else is a perceived need.

Blue Diamond Pool & Spa in Knoxville, Tennessee, cleans swimming pools and spas. Do people really need a pool or spa to survive? No. However, many people have or would like to have a pool, spa, or even both. Why? Because it satisfies a perceived need. The fundamental purpose of your business involves satisfying perceived needs. Your business provides a product or service your customer can't obtain without you. That makes you a problem solver.

The questions to ask yourself are: What problem does my business solve for my customers? How does my business help my customers? How does my business make the world a better place? The answers to those questions are your fundamental purpose. Define it, embrace it, fulfill it passionately, and state it publicly.

Image by David Saba

The next questions to ask yourself are: Why am I in business in the first place? Why do I want to solve this problem for my customer? Is it just for money, or is there a greater purpose?

Why are you in business, other than to make money?

To own your fundamental purpose and live it fully, examine what's in it for you. What motivates you to fulfill this purpose?

Your purpose is not a list of services or products offered at a price. Your purpose is an ideal. Successful organizations own their purpose and have a passion to fulfill it. Many companies create a "mission statement" (fundamental purpose) manufactured from buzz words and marketing slogans. I suggest you create one that is personal and authentic, so that it will motivate you and serve as a touchstone when it's time make a decision. If it doesn't, it is just a blah, blah, blah statement of banalities, and your customers will see right through it.

Your fundamentals, starting with your purpose, will form a set of guidelines for future business decision making. One of the benchmarks for future decision making will be whether the decision furthers your company's stated purpose. If not, it isn't a good decision.

A company must be profitable in order to achieve its objectives, but making money is not the fundamental purpose. Making money enables you to accomplish your purpose.

The interesting thing about your fundamental purpose is that it's not something that can ever be fully reached. Rather, it is always being reached for and always evolving. Every action and business decision you make has to be measured against your fundamental purpose.

Measure every business decision against whether it furthers the company's fundamental purpose.

If a decision is contrary to your fundamental purpose, are you going in the right direction? Small businesses often stray from their purpose and venture into new products or services that are inconsistent with their fundamental purpose, eventually diluting their efforts.

How important is your fundamental purpose to long-term sustainable success? Consider Johnson & Johnson, the size of the business, and the list of products under its brand. In the book *A Company That Cares/Built to Last,* Lawrence G. Foster, Jim Collins, and Jerry Porras wrote, "When Robert W. Johnson founded Johnson & Johnson in 1886, he did so with the idealistic aim to alleviate pain and disease." This fundamental purpose has been in place since the company was founded, and has guided its success for over 130 years. J&J has ventured into new products and services, but they are consistent with their initial purpose.

One business owner sought my advice about a new service he wanted to offer. When questioned why he was considering it, he responded, "To make more money." After some discussion, he concluded that the new service would siphon valuable time that would be better utilized in serving existing clients and gaining new customers. More importantly, the new service didn't fit with his fundamental purpose.

People who love their work and are passionate about it are happy and more fulfilled. They are making a positive contribution to the lives of other people—customers, coworkers, family members, and friends—and they're aware of it. Both a business and an individual will be more successful when a fundamental purpose is bigger than themselves and makes a positive contribution to society.

Here are a few examples of fundamental purpose from the successful businesses interviewed.

- "To build a home with integrity that we can be proud of, the owner can be proud of, and leaves a legacy for future owners." — Pat Strimpfel, owner, Reclamation By Design
- "Help customers turn fear into calm by providing them with customized security solutions, great service, and no excuses." — Bob All, owner, Custom Security Specialists
- "Deliver *value* products to custom home builders so that they can provide them to their customers. Value consists of high-quality products and on-time delivery." — Mike Reeves, president, Espy Lumber Company
- "Ensure our customers drive safe and reliable vehicles so that they and their families have peace of mind." — Berry Edwards, owner, Island Tire

- "Provide high-quality and innovative risk protection for the transportation industry." —Alan Spachman, founder, National Interstate Insurance
- "Provide the best and most reliable warehouse and logistics services to our customers, when they want it, and at a fair price." — Billy Robinson, CEO, Port City Logistics
- "Creatively solve cabinetry problems for clients, particularly ones that people say can't be done, and make it a fun experience for clients and employees." —Terry Peacock, owner, Peacock Cabinetry
- "Make people happy by giving them a beautiful yard to come home to, and by freeing them up to do other things—more enjoyable than mowing, trimming, and planting." —Scott Slawson, CFO, The Greenery
- "Bring people pleasure through culinary delights that promote a healthy lifestyle." – Penny Willimann, owner, Olio Tasting Room
- "Bridge the gap between a client's dream of home ownership and the reality of owning a home." – Bill Fletcher, president, UniSource Mortgage Services

Chapter Assignment

What is your fundamental purpose? Can you identify it and state it in sixty seconds or less?

Write it down. Look at what you have written down. Define it, embrace it, and fulfill it passionately. Your fundamental purpose is the reason you are excited to get up in the morning, because you know you are making a difference. The fundamental purpose of every business is different, and even businesses in the same industry will vary with what they see as their central objective.

Once you have written down the fundamental purpose of your business, write down your *personal* fundamental purpose (in other words, why you personally are in business). Start your sentence something like this: I get to go to work and make the world a better place by

CHAPTER 12

FUNDAMENTAL VALUES

"It's good to stand for something, to believe in something, and base your business on values." – Jerry Greenfield, Ben & Jerry's Ice Cream

The second foundational plank is fundamental values, which are intertwined with your fundamental purpose. Use them to check for stability and to double-check that you are making proper business decisions.

Image by David Saba

Fundamental values lie at the heart of an organization's identity, do not change over time, are not contrived, and are not a matter of convenience. Fundamental values are the glue holding an organization together as it grows. They guide every aspect of the business and may or may not be moral or ethical in nature. Your fundamental values are such that you will never allow them to be compromised.

Never, ever, ever compromise your fundamental values.

Stop reading for a few seconds and think about this Gator Bite. It is critical. In the next chapter, we'll talk about fundamental operating principles and how the line between the two sometimes can get a little blurry. The biggest difference is that fundamental values are *never* compromised.

The Joseph Schlitz Brewing Company was once the largest producer of beer in the United States. Its namesake beer, Schlitz, was known as "the beer that made Milwaukee famous" and was advertised with the slogan, "When you're out of Schlitz, you're out of beer."

Schlitz became the largest beer producer in the United States in 1902, and enjoyed that status at several points up until the 1960s, exchanging the title with Anheuser-Busch/Budweiser multiple times during the 1950s. Schlitz eventually compromised their value of using only the finest ingredients in an attempt to reduce costs, and the product rapidly lost appeal. Schlitz no longer exists, and the original recipe for their beer has been lost.

The fundamental values of your business are intimately tied to your fundamental values as a person. They guide how you conduct your business and your life. Are you polite to customers? Do you meet expectations and stop there, or do you go out of your way to exceed them? Do you give the customer the benefit of the doubt or stand behind your employee in a dispute? Do you choose quality or efficiency when you can't have both? Which is worse to you, blowing a budget or blowing a deadline? Compromising your personal fundamental values or your business fundamental values is a recipe for disaster.

Publicize your fundamental values to your employees. Make sure they understand them, honor them, and live by them. When your employees know what is expected, they will endeavor to live up to that expectation. Do you want employees who don't agree with, or adhere to, your values?

The Landings Club in Savannah, Georgia, has approximately 8,500 residents and 450 employees. Their chief financial officer, Jesse Ruben, shared a copy of the company's values, which are a major factor in their continuing success. The Landings Club's values are:

- Our members: The reason for everything we do.
- Our talented professionals: We choose the best and are committed to growth.
- Team work: We give each other our best.
- Safety: We protect our members, our professionals, and our assets from harm.
- Accountability: We honor commitments and make things happen.
- Initiative: We anticipate and provide service before we are asked.
- Integrity: We do what we say.

- Continuous improvement: We will not stop at good; we aspire to be great.

Each day the staff has a ten-minute huddle and one of these values is discussed. They consider why it is important and what can be done to improve how they live up to it. Think about that. A daily huddle. Their values are ingrained in their culture and have become a way of life for their employees.

Whenever employees need to make a decision or handle a challenging situation, they can go straight to this list and act with confidence; they know what the company leaders expect, and they know they will be supported, as long as they adhere to these values. By being part of the discussion, they know what these values look like and sound like in the real world.

Discussing your fundamental values regularly will not only improve employee performance but will also attract the right employees and repel the wrong ones. In turn, this will attract the right customers.

Discussing your fundamental values should not be confused with meaningless marketing. You're not selling something; you're *being* something. If your fundamental values are just for show and aren't lived by you, then your employees, customers, and vendors will recognize that you aren't who you say you are.

One company posted "The Ten Commandments of Customer Service." You would think if these commandments were posted for all to see, then they must be part of the company's values. As the owner chomped on his cigar and uttered a few profanities, he said of the poster, "It's all a bunch of crap!"

It's no surprise the company went bankrupt twice and now no longer exists. There is no way his customers, let alone his employees, would mistake his words as meaning more than his actions. Authentic adherence to your fundamental values will help build a sustainable business.

Your values are more transparent today than ever before. If a businessperson likes to publicly rip people apart on Facebook, they would be naïve to think that customers won't see it or be affected by it. These defamatory posts say more about the business person's character than that of the victims.

Bob All of Custom Security Specialists makes outstanding customer service one of his fundamental values. He has made it a strength that he can point to as setting his business apart from other security companies. When asked what the real difference between Custom Security Specialists and his competitors is, he replies, "Personal service." Even though great customer service is an expectation today, Bob takes it to the next level. He believes business is personal, and not just about the business. What matters are the relationships he builds among his customers, employees, and vendors.

"Customer service, from the entire staff, starts with a warm hello to answer your call," he says. During office hours, an actual person answers the phone—not a machine or answering service. After hours, the phones are forwarded to an employee's cell phone. "We may be the only alarm company left that actually answers the telephone."

Bob has set up his business so that, if necessary, a customer can speak to someone at any time of the day. This involves a deeper commitment than assigning a person to answer the phone. Late-night calls are rarely a good thing, so he has raised the bar on the quality of work. His entire staff knows that the best way to prevent nuisance false alarms and after-hours calls is by doing the job right the first time.

On his list of fundamental values, he includes the BNI "Givers Gain" philosophy and firmly believes in Zig Ziglar's quote, "You can have everything in life you want, if you will just help other people get what they want." He values the importance of making a difference in the lives of customers, family, employees, friends, and the community, and how asking himself, "What would Jesus do?" guides his decision making in business as well as in daily life.

International Dunnage, LLC manufactures airbags designed to protect cargo in shipping. CEO David Crenshaw says that their number-one fundamental value is to provide a product of the highest quality. To this end, they employ a full range of quality control processes. They use the latest technology and equipment in production, with quality control carried out at every stage under strict ISO 9001 conditions (the ultimate global benchmark for quality management).

The investment of time and money clearly goes hand in hand with their values. A high-quality product meshes with their other fundamental values of excellent service and the promise to provide prompt and creative solutions for customer requirements.

Do you see how your fundamental values can affect everything about how you conduct your business? Test every decision you make against your fundamental values.

Following are more examples of fundamental values from successful companies. Some of them seem simple and obvious, but when choosing a course of action or making a decision, they impact the entire business and everyone in it:

British Open Pub – Damian Hayes

- Use only the best ingredients, not the cheapest.
- Treat employees fairly but expect them to be committed.
- Make sure employees are punctual and on site when scheduled.
- Do what needs to be done—the owner serves tables when needed.

Espy Lumber Company – Mike Reeves

- Honesty.
- Integrity.
- Do what we say, how and when we say we'll do it.
- Employees are our most important asset—in fact, they are our only asset.
- High-quality products.
- On-time delivery.

Island Tire – Berry Edwards

- DIRFT—Do It Right the First Time.
- Safety for customers' vehicles.
- Tell the truth at all times.
- Give back to the community.
- Exceptional customer service.

- Stand behind your work.

Peacock Cabinetry – Terry Peacock

- Fun work environment.
- Teamwork.
- Fairness, kindness, and patience.
- Job must be done right.
- Do the right thing for employees, vendors, and clients.
- Refund the money if the job comes in under bid.

Reclamation By Design – Pat and Ron Strimpfel

- Do it right because it's the right thing to do.
- Never cut corners.
- Don't substitute with inferior materials.
- Continuous learning and education.

The Greenery – Scott Slawson, CFO, and Lee Edwards, President

- Make decisions that are in the best interest of employees, not just profits.
- Respect for every individual.
- Integrity and honesty.
- Community involvement by employees and the company.
- Be all-in.

Port City Logistics – Billy Robinson

- Stand behind our work.
- Maintain the highest level of service.
- Honesty and integrity.

- Work Ethic—Do whatever it takes to get the customer what they want, when they want it.

International Dunnage – David Crenshaw

- Provide a value product to our customers.
- Use latest technology and equipment.
- Extreme attention to quality control.

Covert Aire – Mike Covert

- I believe in old-fashioned "moral" fiber, which includes honesty and integrity.
- Build trust with the customer.
- Give back to the community.
- Have a positive impact on the lives of others.

Olio Tasting Room – Penny Willimann

- Use highest-quality ingredients.
- Know where and who the ingredients come from.

Sweetener Solutions – John Curry

- Use highest-quality ingredients.
- Meticulous accuracy.
- Produce products of the highest quality.

Custom Security Specialists – Bob All

- Givers Gain.
- Measure decisions against the doctrine "What would Jesus do?"

- Make a difference in the lives of customers, family, employees, friends, and the community.

JCB of Georgia – Gayle Humphries

- Always ask: "What is the right thing to do?"
- Honesty and integrity.

Hilton Head Glass/Veronica's Art Glass – Tom and Veronica Zombik

- Accept responsibility for mistakes and make them right.
- Safety first for employees.
- Tell the truth about what we can and cannot do.
- Buy only American made.
- Quality first, not the cheapest.
- Know your capabilities.

Calfkiller Brewing Company – Don and Dave Sergio

- Give our product the time it needs naturally to be awesome.
- Never cut corners on ingredients or the process.
- Treat others the way you want to be treated.

UniSource Mortgage Services – Bill Fletcher

- People before profit.
- Never extend credit just for the sake of making a dollar.
- Refer clients to another trustworthy professional if we can't provide the best product to meet their needs.
- Ensure information supplied by clients is true and accurate.
- Approach *all* of our clients with a steadfast commitment to working as hard as we can on their behalf. We receive absolutely no financial incentive to steer clients to any

particular mortgage product. We approach each and every consultation and transaction with integrity and transparency, which we believe is paramount to building a lifelong relationship with our clients that lasts after the closing documents have been signed.

Chapter Assignment

How does your organization currently act or behave? In what do *you* believe? Write down your fundamental values. Do not shortcut them; spell them out. Do not search for them online; pull them up from inside you. Write down all you can think of, and then narrow the list to no more than five to seven values. Too many will conflict. Fundamental values are not like fruit that you can pick from a tree, keeping the ones you like and throwing the rest away. Remember, fundamental values define who you are, and if you don't know who you are, no list can give it to you.

CHAPTER 13

FUNDAMENTAL OPERATING PRINCIPLES

"Everyone has got the will to win; it's only those with the will to prepare that do win." – Mark Cuban, *How to Win at the Sport of Business*

With your fundamental purpose and fundamental values clearly stated, let's now define your fundamental operating principles.

Image by David Saba

Fundamental operating principles are basic strategies and business philosophies that define how the business operates.

An operating principle is not an operating process or procedure. A principle is a fundamental truth that serves as the foundation for a system of behaviors or a chain of reasoning, whereas a process or procedure concerns the mechanics of how something is done. Principles impose consistency on an individual or organization and are vital to having an enduring framework for long-term success. Processes and procedures can be altered; principles constitute a recipe for success that essentially stays the same and rarely changes.

Your fundamental operating principles need to be rock solid and only change when absolutely necessary, and then only after great thought and analysis. Dramatic changes in the economy, technology, and environment may create a situation where the best—or only—choice is to change the fundamental operating principles of your business. You don't change a recipe unless it improves the food being prepared. Find what works and stick with it.

Fundamental operating principles are not strategies, although they sometimes sound like them. Conserving energy is not a strategy.

How alligators conserve energy—lurk, launch, chomp—is the strategy. Conserving energy is the principle behind the strategy.

Southwest Airlines is an example of adhering to a set of operating principles, and it has been profitable for over forty years while every other airline has gone out of business, gone through bankruptcy, or merged to survive. One of Southwest's principles is to keep its operational costs low while keeping efficiency high. This principle is behind the decision to fly one airplane type, the Boeing 737. Every pilot flies the same plane, every crew member knows the plane's layout, every technician and mechanic can work on the plane, and the spare parts are all the same. Southwest only has to train each employee on one type of plane. Buying parts in volume obtains discounts, and the company can negotiate better contracts when buying the planes.

Another example of Southwest Airlines' operating principles is controlled growth. Southwest chose to limit growth to a specific amount each year to prevent outgrowing its ability to manage the company. Contrast that with WorldCom, which grew at supersonic speed by acquiring company after company (each with its own unique IT and accounting system that did not integrate). WorldCom spectacularly collapsed, eventually resulting in top executives going to prison.

Your principles will depend on your individual philosophy for running your business. They may be opposite or unlike those of other businesses. Below are some common examples:

- Grow no more than ____ percent per year.
- Grow no less than ____ percent per year.
- Consider alternatives before acting.
- Be open to trying new things.
- Be open to trying old things in a new way.
- Always be first to market.
- Never be first to market.
- Put quality first.
- Be willing to take big risks.
- Never take big risks.
- Hire the best, not the cheapest.
- Be prepared for good times.

- Be prepared for bad times.
- Get input from someone who disagrees with you.
- Always be accessible to customers.

As you develop your own principles, pay attention to your industry, niche, solutions to customer problems, and values. Develop your principles accordingly.

The lines between values and operating principles can sometimes blur. "Only use the best ingredients" could be a fundamental value for one business and a fundamental operating principle for another. What is the difference between values and operating principles? Values are the ingredients for your success while your operating principles are the recipe for putting together the ingredients. Values never change; operating principles may need to evolve and adapt.

A fundamental operating principle for David Miller Jr. with Before and After Cleaning Services Inc., a full-service commercial cleaning company, is, "We do not clean timeshare condos. The short turn-around doesn't allow sufficient time to do a good job, and I don't want to jeopardize my company's reputation." Notice that David didn't say he would *never* clean time share condos; he would consider it if there were sufficient time to do the job right. Had he said "never," the statement would be a fundamental value.

Your fundamental values define who you and your business are. Your fundamental operating principles define how you do business.

Fundamental operating principles define how you do business.

Opportunity Cost and Fundamental Operating Principles

Opportunity cost means that if you spend your time or money on one task or item, then that time or money is not available to be spent on something else. Part of sound decision making is ensuring that you are spending your time and money where it's most beneficial and produces the best return. Knowing and defining your fundamental operating principles will ensure that you make decisions to take advantage of the right opportunities.

Damian Hayes, owner of British Open Pub in Bluffton, South Carolina, has a list that begins with doing what it takes to make customers happy. He includes knowing the numbers at all times because margins are thin and costs are always changing. Damian also believes in acquiring ideas from other restaurants. He has defined the type of restaurant he owns. He notes, "This is not an all-night sports bar." There is a big difference between a restaurant where sports play on TVs in the bar and a sports bar that stays open till the wee hours of the morning. These differences influence everything from the menu, to the dress code, to how employees are trained to interact with patrons.

When it comes to competing, growing, and improving yourself and your business, what are the best uses of your time, money, and effort?

Chapter Assignment

Identify your existing fundamental operating principles and examine them for validity and staying power. Whether you are conscious of them or not, you have them. If they are working, give them a place of honor. If not, endeavor to replace them with effective principles.

Following are examples from successful businesses that have weathered the test of time. Note the principles common to many of them. Use these as guides in developing the principles relevant to your own business.

Custom Security Specialists – Bob All

- Stay on top of technology.
- Always be there for our employees and customers.
- Develop a trust relationship with employees.
- Run the company as a family, which includes employees and our customers.
- Continuous education and learning.

- We are here to satisfy needs and to serve.
- Maintain sufficient cash reserves.

Hilton Head Glass/Veronica's Art Glass – Tom and Veronica Zombik

- Only use the highest-quality materials.
- Find and stick with quality vendors. We know the company presidents for the vendors with whom we deal, visited their company, and toured their facilities. If there's an issue, we have a personal relationship with the person we call, and we know the problem will be solved promptly and fairly.
- Take care of repeat customers.
- Train employees so they not only know how to do the work, but why.
- Train employees on how we want them to deal with customers.
- Open communications with employees through regular meetings where all issues and problems are open for discussion.
- Continuous improvement—there is always a better way, and we are cautious about not falling in the "this is the way we've always done it" thinking.

JCB of Georgia – Gayle Humphries

- Define who our customer is and who it is not.
- Know what you do and do it well.
- Maintain adequate cash reserves.
- Same-day shipment of parts to over forty distribution points.
- Online ordering systems allow 24/7 access for parts.
- 24/7 customer service professionals to assist with parts.
- Open Book Management—everyone works together as a team when they know the score as to how well the business is doing.

- Employee surveys.
- Friday morning meetings with managers and key employees.

Espy Lumber Company – Mike Reeves

- Weekly and monthly meetings with management and employees.
- Benchmark with other similar companies who are in other markets and not competitors.
- Provide the highest-quality products, not the cheapest.
- Target customers are custom home builders and new single-family homes and remodels.
- Practice "open book management" (share financial information with employees).
- Know market share in major categories (framing, roofing, doors and windows) versus competitors in our area.
- Rolling twelve-month projections of sales and expenses every month so we can see what is coming. Projection for each store.
- Examine carefully each and every line item of expense each month.

International Dunnage – David Crenshaw

- Minimize bureaucracy and keep overhead low; this means better pricing for the consumer than our competitor can offer.
- Close books and issue financial statements by the third workday of the month.
- Know your numbers on a daily, weekly, and month-to-date basis.
- Track trends in financial metrics over three years, particularly expenses and waste.

- Minimize variances using a small company version of statistical process control.
- Understand that one month doesn't make a trend.

Island Tire – Berry Edwards

- Train, train, train employees.
- Get to debt free so we can provide health insurance for employees.
- Build cash reserves so that the company can weather economic recessions.
- "Bridge the Gap to Maintenance"—a step-by-step process for working with customers from when they step out of their car to when they get in their car to leave.
- Employee performance reviews.

National Interstate Insurance – Alan Spachman

- Avoid doing business in high-risk zip codes; there are areas where losses are frequent and more costly. There is no such thing as a good premium for bad exposure.
- Make sure cash flow is positive.

Covert Aire – Mike Covert

- Timely call back of customer calls.
- Use only original equipment manufacturer. We want our customers to get the best replacement parts, not secondary or refurbished parts.
- Surround ourselves with people who are smarter than we are. These are the people we can learn from.
- Build trust through building strong relationships with the community and customers through community involvement and our fundamental values.

- We want everyone to know our brand, associate it with quality, and have a positive feeling when they see it. We go to great lengths to raise brand awareness and even have a line of condiments with our label, so every time someone uses our condiments, they think of us and say, "I've been meaning to call Covert Aire."
- Hire top-quality people no matter where they come from. If I have to move someone across the country to get the best, I'm willing to do that.
- Know your numbers. I look at financial reports every day. The financial reports are not just for filing taxes. They show the health of the business and how to make it more profitable in the future.
- Structure the business to maintain a 20 percent net profit.
- Share financial information with employees so people know what is going on and how it affects their profit sharing.

Port City Logistics – Billy Robinson

- Teamwork.
- Continuously develop new relationships and nurture existing ones.
- Help our employees earn a good living.
- Help our employees grow as individuals and team members.
- Identify what you are good at.
- Continuous training of employees to help them be the best and most reliable in the industry.
- Track everything so we know what is causing results and can figure out how to improve.

Peacock Cabinetry – Terry Peacock

- Be debt free—started that way and want to stay that way.
- Pay vendors on time.
- Maintain a cash reserve.

- Do without if necessary.
- Build a reputation that will generate referrals.
- Meet weekly with staff.

Sweetener Solutions – John Curry

- Use state-of-the-art equipment.
- Use quality suppliers.
- Continuous training of employees.
- Employee safety.
- Product safety.
- Annual manufacturing audit.
- Invite customers to do a manufacturing audit of our facility.
- Be debt free.
- Meticulous attention to detail.

British Open Pub – Damian Hayes

- Use only the best ingredients.
- Treat employees fairly but expect them to be committed.
- Employees must be punctual and be there when scheduled.
- Do whatever needs to be done, no matter if it is the owner or the dishwasher. If I have to mop floors, then so be it.
- Make sure customers are happy, and do whatever it takes to correct problems.

Reclamation By Design – Pat and Ron Strimpfel

- Adapt to change—the economy, technology, environment, building codes, new materials.
- Only hire people and subcontractors we trust to do it right.
- Minimize waste.

- Clean up the job site when finished. When a house is done, clean it before the new owner moves in.
- Limit the amount of work to what we can control and manage, keeping in mind it is only possible to manage so many projects and still do it right.
- Don't be afraid to re-invent yourself.
- Constantly ask "what if, what if, what if" so you can be prepared for any incident that comes along.
- When at all possible, work out any difference with clients without resorting to legal action—no one wins when the lawyers get involved.

The Greenery – Scott Slawson and Lee Edwards

- Controlled growth—we want to grow, but not faster than we can manage and still provide the quality our customers know us by.
- We want our headquarters to be within a four- to five-hour drive so top management can stay involved and communicate with employees and customers face to face.
- Employee owner mentality—we want all our employees to act like owners.
- Empower and educate employees to make the right decisions.

Olio Tasting Room – Penny Willimann

- Consistent hands-on management.
- Clear standard operating procedures.
- Constantly be on the lookout for new marketing tactics.
- Don't grow too fast.

Calfkiller Brewing Company – Don and Dave Sergio

- Understanding that our business is all about our patrons.

- Always giving 100 percent to make our beer the best that it can be, regardless of cost.
- Educating people about us and our product.
- Making sure the beer is always fresh wherever it is shipped to.

UniSource Mortgage Services – Bill Fletcher

- Ensure clients are educated on products and rates so they can make the best decision possible for themselves.
- Treat people right and they will refer you.
- As a mortgage "wholesaler," we offer better rates to clients than banks will offer. Banks have a "retail" interest rate but extend wholesale rates to us that are not available to their retail customers.
- Pay closing costs for clients out of our compensation from the lender.
- Receive our compensation directly from the lender rather than the borrower. It allows us to advise our clients from an objective stance. Regardless of borrowers' choice of mortgage product, interest rate, loan amount, or assets, our compensation remains a fixed percentage.

CHAPTER 14

FUNDAMENTAL INFORMATION SYSTEMS

"A businessman's judgment is no better than his information."
– R. P. Lamont, Secretary of Commerce, Author

The fourth plank of the foundation is your fundamental information systems.

Image by David Saba

All decisions, business or otherwise, are based on a combination of information (data) and insight or intuition (gut feel). The decisions of engineers and accountants tend to be heavily data driven, while artists are more likely to be intuition driven.

Take buying a car for instance. You could collect volumes of data on various models of cars, engine sizes, gas mileage, and warranties, or you could simply drive a few and buy based on how it looks and feels.

The owner of a small motel in Wyoming drove a beautiful convertible. When asked if he liked it, he said, "The car's a piece of crap, but I look really good in it!" Obviously, engineering specs didn't play a part in his decision making.

No matter how you make your business decisions, here's a simple fact: It is difficult to make a good business decision even if you have perfect information, and it is impossible with bad information.

It's difficult to make a good business decision even with perfect information, and it is impossible with bad information.

"No information" could be added to this statement because many people make business decisions with virtually no information other than their gut feeling. Admittedly, sometimes gut feel works, but it is wiser to have some data to support your instincts. Better information enables better decisions. There are multiple information systems a business owner needs to gather pertinent data. The major systems, which will be discussed in more detail later, are:

- Accounting Information Systems (AIS)
- Customer Information Systems (CIS)
- Operations Information Systems (OIS)
- Employee Information Systems (EIS)

You already have these systems in place to some degree.

Your AIS measures the health of your business, whether you are winning the game in terms of profits and cash flow, and what the future prospects are.

CIS gathers information on who your customers are and their characteristics so you can find new ones and keep the existing.

OIS reports the efficiency and productivity of your operations. You might assume this just applies to manufacturing companies, but think again. Everything you do to process and fulfill a customer's order and provide the product or service is in effect a production process. If you are a freight forwarder and a customer asks you to arrange to move cargo from point A to point B, the steps to accomplish this are a production process.

Last but not least is EIS. When a business is small with only a couple of employees, the EIS is relatively simple. However, there is legally required information to have on file for each employee. As the business grows, you may have benefit packages, performance bonuses, retirement plans, and safety requirements, so your EIS needs will increase.

Most business decisions relate to strategy, employees, operations, finances, vendors, and customers, and are usually more complicated than they appear on the surface. Having all the information at your disposal when you design a strategy does not guarantee success, but it is way ahead of being ignorant.

Take our friendly neighborhood alligator again. He lurks in the shadows waiting for his prey. He has excellent eyesight and an intimate knowledge of the terrain. He watches, studies, and waits, and then launches at his prey with perfect timing. He could not be more prepared, yet he still often misses.

Chapter Assignment

Make a list of the basic elements in your current information systems. As you again look at the list above, determine if some major requirements are missing.

CHAPTER 15

SECTION 3 SUMMARY

"The difference between a successful person and a failure often lies in the fact that the successful person will profit by his mistake and try again in a different way." – Dale Carnegie

You need a solid foundation on which to build a business in the swamp. That foundation is made up of four planks:

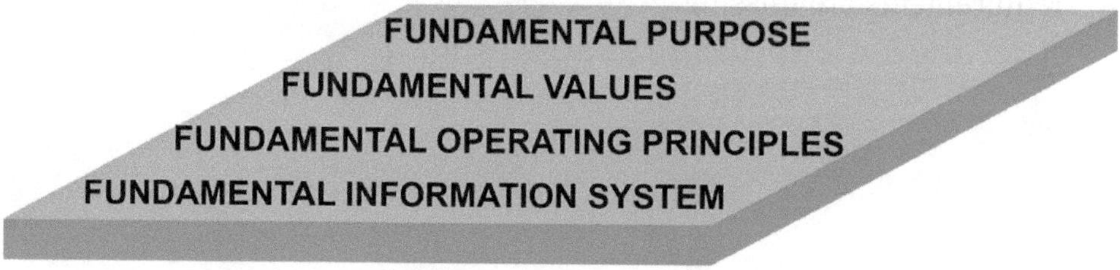

Image by David Saba

Before we continue, make sure you wrote down answers to the chapter assignments. This is the foundation of your business house. Now put on your construction hard hat as you begin putting up the walls. There's a lot more work to do!

SECTION 4

OPERATING IN THE SWAMP

CHAPTER 16
INTRODUCTION

"Management is the accomplishment of results through the efforts of other people." – Lawrence Appley

With the foundation for your business house in the swamp now established, let's add the walls. The walls of a business house are similar to functions that every business must perform. Whether a sole proprietor or a mega corporation, all businesses perform the same functions. The difference is that as a sole proprietor, you must accomplish all of them yourself.

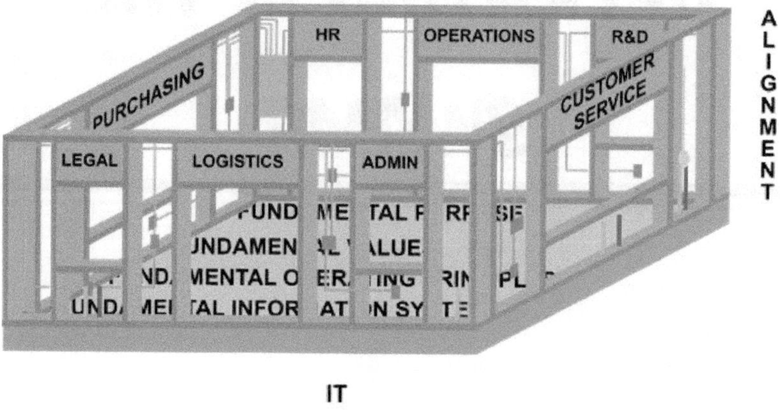

Image by David Saba

The wiring and plumbing are analogous to information technology systems, which connect the business functions and locations. What is the relationship between the walls and foundation? Think about it. If walls are improperly aligned, problems can vary—from cracked walls, uneven floors, and doors and windows that don't open properly, to drainage problems and bulging walls. If the walls are drastically out of alignment, the stability of the house can be compromised.

Despite the walls being placed correctly at first, some settling of the house will occur. Business functions can slip out of alignment with your foundation. Keep the fundamentals of your foundation—purpose, values, operating principles, information systems—in the forefront at all times to ensure PLUMB alignment. When various business functions operate independently with little regard for what is best for the company, expensive problems occur.

Companies with multiple locations are particularly vulnerable to misalignment situations. A remote location often evolves into its own entity by doing business its own way, which may be contrary to the company's purpose, values, and operating principles.

People in one location assume that those in another location are not as competent. They regard themselves as the experts on how to operate the business. In most cases, people in other locations are knowledgeable people who work hard and do the best job they can. Problems often arise, not from incompetence, but because management hasn't encouraged all locations and functional departments to stay focused on the fundamentals and the fact that everyone is on the same team.

Whose responsibility is it to keep the company aligned? Go back and re-read section 2, chapters 1 and 2. *You* are the keystone—the leader.

The first part of this section will talk about the functional walls of your business house. When properly constructed, this house can be a beautiful and profitable structure.

CHAPTER 17
OPERATIONS

"Insanity is doing the same thing over and over again and expecting a different result." – Albert Einstein

The operations side of your business relates to making or buying the products you sell, or delivering on a service you provide. A retail store buys products (inventory) for resale. It may also manufacture by combining parts or raw materials to produce a finished product for sale. Many retailers also have an after-sales service division or may provide some professional service. Your business may be a combination of all these.

Each business is different. Financial planners, warehouse owners, and retail stores selling the same type of merchandise may all operate differently. Regardless of how you do the work, there are two things on which you need to focus:

1. Process: What is the process for doing the work?
2. Information: Is your operations information systems providing vital information?

Every business has a process, or series of processes, for doing the work. Peacock Cabinetry has a process for evaluating customer needs, designing, building, and installing their product. International Dunnage has a process for manufacturing airbags used to protect cargo during shipment and for shipping the product from the factory to the customer. Reclamation By Design has a process for building houses and assuring that the quality is second to none. Ron Strimpfel signs every house just like an artist signs a painting, although the customer will probably never be able to find his signature.

Olio Tasting Room has a process for buying olive oils, vinegars, and a variety of other products, some of which are sold in their original form and others that are combined into new products. Covert Aire has processes for maintaining heating and air conditioning equipment, installing new equipment, procuring parts, and assuring quality control. British Open Pub has a process for procuring food ingredients, preparing food, and serving the customer. Island Tire has an extensive process for evaluating a customer's needs (Berry Edwards calls it the "Bridging to Maintenance," and he is obsessive about quality control). Custom Security Specialists has a process for installing and maintaining security systems.

Every one of the companies interviewed for this book has a process for doing the work. All organizations have such a process or processes—including yours. The point is to recognize that there is a process for doing the work, and every one can be improved. Continually improving your processes is vital to long-term success.

Marketing may succeed in luring customers to your business, but that can be counterproductive if the operations can't support demand. The same is true if the product or service is poor quality, delivery is late, or any of a host of operational problems exist. The marketing will have been a waste, and your company will suffer from Reputation Deficit Syndrome.

Many small businesses don't think about the process for doing the work in the context of process improvement. While they probably recognize there is a process, they are so busy doing the work they don't take time to consider improvements. Manufacturing companies have no trouble recognizing that operations is a series of processes to produce a product. The fact is, regardless of the type of business, if it has a process, then it has inventory.

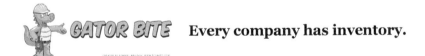

Every company has inventory.

"Now hold on, Roy," I hear you say. "My company provides a service. We have no inventory to sell." Understand that there are three types of inventory: raw materials, work-in-process, and finished goods. Every manufacturing operation has these three, but what about a service business?

Let's go to Bill Fletcher, president of UniSource Mortgage. His company gathers information from prospective clients about their mortgage needs and researches the best mortgage to fit the customer's needs and financial capability. He then prepares the legal documents for the customer to sign. Finally, when all aspects of the mortgage are in place and documents are signed, he closes the file for that customer.

Does Bill have any raw materials, work-in-process, or finished goods? If you answered yes to all three, you get an "A" and go to the head of the class. What are Bill's raw materials? It is the information gathered about the customer, their finances, and the property to be bought or refinanced. What about work-in-process? When the work begins, Bill opens a file, both physically and digitally. That file contains relevant information about the mortgage. From the time he gathers the information until he closes the mortgage, that file is in process. At any given time, Bill will have numerous mortgages in process. Finally, when the mortgage is ready for the customer to sign, Bill has finished goods inventory.

Your business has a series of processes for doing the work, and each process has a degree of inventory. Why is it so important to improve our processes? Processes take time, and the more time consuming they are, the more costly it is to your bottom line. Reducing the amount of time to do the work will get the product or service to the customer sooner.

Streamlining the process and eliminating unnecessary steps frees up employee and machine time to get more done. More work results in more revenue, profit, and, most importantly, cash flow. Improving the process should also improve the quality of the product or service, leading to greater customer satisfaction and fewer returns. Efficient processes can prevent poor quality, potentially minimizing the risk of lawsuits. To recap:

- Every business has a process or series of processes.
- Every business has inventory.
- Every process can be improved.
- Process improvement will lead to higher revenue, profits, and cash flow.

How do you improve your processes?

1. Identify your processes.
2. Systematize all processes.

Identify Your Processes

How do you identify your processes? It isn't difficult, but it does require time and effort. Just approach this with the "you eat an elephant one bite at a time" philosophy.

One method is through the use of a SIPOC, which stands for Source, Input, Process, Output, and Customer.

1. Source: What is the source (suppliers) of the products or raw materials (data or physical items)?
2. Input: What are these products or raw materials (data or physical items)?
3. Process: How are the raw materials combined to make the product or service?
4. Output: What is the product or service being provided to the customer, and how are you going to get it to the customer (fulfillment)?
5. Customer: Who is the customer?

Bill Fletcher has multiple processes operating simultaneously. His "sources" include his customers, banks, lawyers, and credit agencies. "Inputs" include financial information, interest rates, and legal requirements. The "process" is where he combines the respective inputs into a package. Sometimes there are multiple steps in the process where information from one document links to another, which means further calculations must be made. Documents are eventually combined into a mortgage package—the "output." This package is ultimately delivered to the "customer" to approve and sign.

If Bill's business is booming, he has the option to hire additional employees to do the work or he can streamline the process of doing the work—without compromising quality, of course.

As an example, let's assume Bill's mortgage process includes three documents and that each one contains information that applies to the next. Each document has a process for its completion and different inputs. They take different amounts of time to prepare, and a different person prepares each one. Suppose Document 1 takes thirty minutes,

Document 2 takes sixty minutes, and Document 3 takes ten minutes. The entire process takes one hundred minutes.

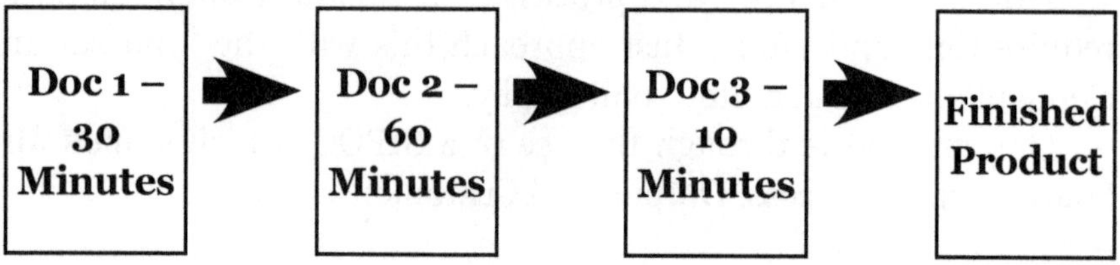

What's going to happen? Document 1's are going to be piling up on the desk of the person preparing Document 2, while the person preparing Document 3 is sitting idle waiting for work. Document 2 is a bottleneck with the entire process getting bogged down at this point. If the goal is to reduce the overall time from one hundred minutes to ninety minutes, what should be changed? The time processing Document 2 needs to be looked at. Perhaps some of it could be prepared by the employee doing Document 3. By clearing the bottleneck at Document 2, we can improve and speed up the whole process.

Don't fall into the "this is the way we've always done it" trap. Take the time to figure out what your processes are and where they could be improved. The world is changing at an extremely rapid pace. If you don't evolve, you will be left behind and find your swamp drying up.

The Goal by Eli Goldratt is a book I highly recommend for business owners. On the surface, the book is about a manufacturing operation, which may not seem applicable to your business if you don't manufacture a product. The real gist of the book is about teaching process improvement and developing strategies to maximize operations. Reading *The Goal* will educate you on how to view your day-to-day operations and the long-term possibilities of your business, no matter what it produces or who it serves. Extract the principles from its pages and apply them to your situation.

Every process can be improved.

The important part of any process is that it is efficient and reduces the possibility of errors. This may mean one or more steps need to be delayed in order to maximize the process as a whole. In our previous UniSource Mortgage example, we can see that speeding up the processing of Document 1 will not help, and will cause more frustration as documents pile up on the desk of the person working on Document 2.

A SIPOC can identify your processes and examine options to improve them. Now let's move on to systemization.

Systemization

One way to think about systemizing the business is "McDonaldizing" it. Ray Kroc was a milkshake machine salesman. When he called on the McDonald brothers' hamburger restaurant, he was impressed by the efficiency of the operation. He noticed a process for each step, including the number of pickles on a burger and where to place each pickle. He immediately recognized that this business was duplicable because every process and procedure was documented and standardized. New employees could easily and quickly get up to speed. Every aspect of the business was done in the most efficient, effective, and profitable manner. Initially, Kroc partnered with the brothers, but eventually he bought them out.

Business Network International (BNI) has a defined process to help members be successful. The process has been refined and perfected for over two decades. Occasionally a person says, "BNI didn't work for me," and admittedly, BNI isn't appropriate for every person or organization. However, in the majority of cases, the people who indicate BNI didn't work for them didn't "work" BNI the way its system teaches. Systemizing your business will improve it, particularly if you have multiple locations.

Small businesses often say they want to systematize their business and standardize operations to easily manage the business. An added benefit to systemization is that if you aren't present, the business can continue to operate effectively.

I searched for years for a better way to help clients systematize their business. Michael Mills with Business Design Corporation has one solution I highly recommend. I was so impressed that I partnered with Michael. His company developed a software product to make establishing and updating processes easy. Check them out at http://go.businessdesigncorp.com/animation/royaustin/whyTsWithRoyAustin.html

Capacity Utilization

Small business owners, particularly service providers, often roll their eyes when I mention capacity utilization. However, every business—not just manufacturers—has a limited capacity for its products or services. How well are you utilizing that capacity?

National Interstate Insurance provides transportation insurance. Their fundamental purpose is to "provide high-quality & innovative risk protection for the transportation industry." They don't have a physical product, and they have an inventory of policies in progress. Since they don't manufacture anything, do they have a limited capacity? If so, can their capacity utilization be measured?

Your employees—your most valuable asset—only have so many hours in a day. If you have ten employees who work eight hours a day, what is your capacity? Obviously, it's eighty hours a day. If one hour is required to perform the service you offer, and your staff processes forty a day, what is your capacity utilization? Full capacity would be eighty a day, so forty a day would be 50 percent. Could you ever achieve eighty policies a day or 100 percent? Possibly, if no one ever uses the bathroom, drinks coffee, or chats on the phone. So, eighty may be possible but unrealistic.

Let's assume that "realistic" is sixty-five policies a day. Now what is your capacity utilization? Forty divided by sixty-five is 61 percent. If you improve production of policies to fifty a day, then capacity utilization is now 77 percent. If you improve your capacity utilization, then you may benefit in ways such as reduced overtime or fewer but more efficient employees.

Chapter Assignment

1. Identify the three most critical processes in your business.
2. Create a SIPOC for those processes.
3. Identify bottlenecks in your process.
4. Brainstorm solutions to minimize the bottlenecks and improve the overall process.
5. Read *The Goal* by Eli Goldratt.
6. Define your capacity and capacity utilization.

CHAPTER 18
RISK MANAGEMENT

"It's the little details that are vital. Little things make big things happen." – John Wooden

Building your business house in the Business Swamp is difficult. You face potential hazards that can sink your business into the bog. Earlier you saw an image of a house with only the foundation laid and the walls erected. Since this leaves the house exposed to the elements, you now need a roof for protection.

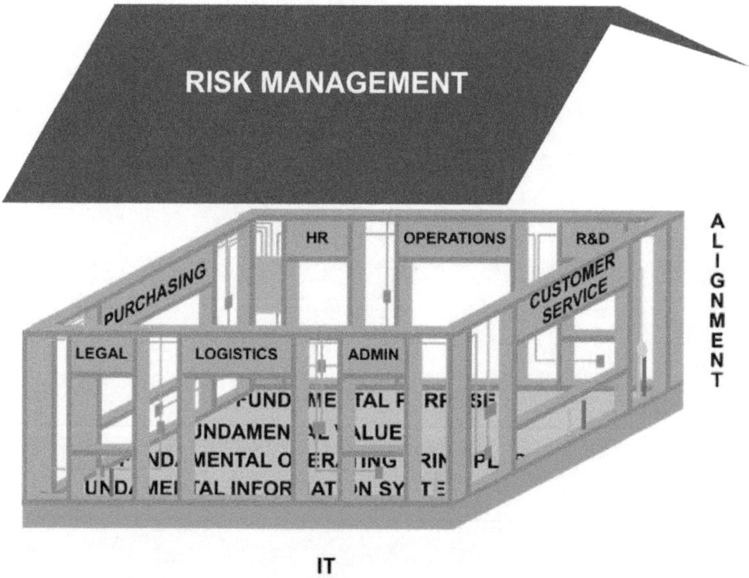

Image by David Saba

Risk management involves identifying factors that may pose a hazard to the success of your company and planning a strategy to deal with those risks before they occur. Every business faces a wide variety of risks and disasters that lurk in the swamp. For each type of risk, you need to identify how it will affect your business and how you would deal with it. The goal is to prevent adverse events from happening; however, if that isn't possible, you need to minimize the damage and be in a position to resume profitable operations as soon as possible. In coastal South Carolina, a big risk is hurricanes. Well-managed businesses have a hurricane disaster recovery plan.

Some risks are inherent just from being in the swamp; others are from external sources. Anticipating every possible risk is probably not possible. However, identifying and planning for many risks is feasible and will increase your chances of surviving and succeeding.

Here are the most common business risks. Every business is different, so some of the risks discussed here may not apply to yours. What plans do you have in place if these took place in your business?

Hazard Risk

Hazard risk relates to the physical assets of an organization such as property, buildings, equipment, and inventory—both external and internal. What are the external risks your products and/or facilities could suffer from damage, destruction, fire, or flooding? Are you properly insured so your facilities can be repaired or replaced? Internal risk management includes preventive maintenance. Are there frayed electrical wires that could lead to a fire? Is there a leaky roof that could lead to damage if not repaired? Does a vehicle need new brakes to prevent a possible accident? Brainstorm with your team to recognize as many potential hazards as possible.

Another option to consider is business interruptions insurance, which covers the loss of income from a disaster.

Financial Risk

Financial risk is the risk that a company's assets could be adversely affected by bad debts, currency exchange rates, interest rates, or inflation. A frequent problem for small businesses is not collecting receivables on a timely basis. If you invoice customers who pay you at some future date, you assume the risk that they will never pay. If your terms of sale state that the invoice is due in thirty days, every day beyond that diminishes the probability you will ever collect. Yet often small businesses carry receivables on their books that are a year to a year and a half old. Why do the work if you aren't going to get paid?

If you do business in foreign countries, fluctuations in currency exchange rates can significantly impact your business. Work with your banker on a strategy to minimize currency exchange rate risk.

Rising or falling interest rates can also affect timing to borrow money.

Inflation in key ingredients or parts you purchase can squeeze your margins. Strategies such as buying in bulk or hedging transactions can minimize the impact of inflation. Your banker, financial advisor, or accountant can help you design a strategy to help your business.

Economic Risk

Economic risk recognizes the reality that the economy goes through cycles. Good times never last and bad times are not permanent, so you must be prepared for both. A common tendency is for small businesses doing well in good times to fail to use that period of prosperity to prepare for inevitable down cycles. They squander precious cash on unnecessary purchases and on their personal lifestyle. When the economy takes a nosedive, their cash reserves are inadequate and they are forced to reduce staff or declare bankruptcy.

Operations Risk

Operations risk considers factors that could adversely affect the company's operations, such as theft, equipment failure, website crashes, telephone outages, or computer meltdowns. What do you do if you can't produce or deliver your products or deliver your service?

Good financial internal control measures can minimize the likelihood of theft of company assets, including theft of cash. Does your IT system have adequate backup, and is it tested to make sure you can retrieve data? How will you communicate with customers, vendors, and employees if your phone system is down? If selling products through your website, what is your plan if the site crashes? If production equipment fails, do you have spare parts for repairs, backup equipment, or alternative production plans? Are people who handle cash covered by an insurance bond for theft?

Strategic Risk

Strategic risk considers risks from competition, product failure, obsolescence, seasonality, and spoilage.

Competition

What are the major threats from other companies selling the same products or services? What are you doing to stay ahead of the competition?

Product Failure

What are the risks of product failure, poor quality, or injury to customers? Do you have adequate insurance for these risks?

Obsolescence

What is the risk that your product or service will become obsolete or be replaced by a new or better product or service? Don't get complacent. Over time, virtually every product or service is superseded. Even if the product or service is essentially the same, delivery methods may change. Technology changes are the most obvious source of obsolescence.

For example, Eastman Kodak had digital technology in 1975, but they were making so much money from film photography that they kept putting off introducing digital. By the time they decided to join the revolution, every competitor had a digital camera on the market.

Seasonality

Are there any seasonal patterns that would affect your sales positively or negatively? In lean months when cash flow drops, how do you cover the essentially fixed ongoing administrative costs of the business? Can you add new services at certain times of the year to make up for lost revenues?

A swimming pool cleaning company located in the Northeast has high revenues in summer and low revenues in the winter. To even out monthly cash flows, it offers customers a monthly payment plan to cover routine pool cleaning maintenance. Parts and chemicals are billed separately as needed. To persuade their customers to adopt this plan, the company offers a discount for those who sign up and opt for the monthly fee to be charged to the customer's credit card or paid by direct debit. This not only helps the company even out cash flows but also helps the customers budget their money.

Many landscaping companies do the same thing. Balanced monthly cash flows also help with employee retention by enabling the company to keep people on the payroll during slow periods.

<u>Spoilage</u>

Is there a risk that the items you sell or have in inventory can go bad? Food can rot, chemicals can deteriorate, and shelf life can be exceeded. What can you do to minimize the risk that your product can no longer be sold in good condition?

Can the products a service company provides go bad? Yes. After extensive preparation of legal documents or a financial plan, if laws and regulations suddenly change, you may have to start again from scratch.

Opportunity Cost

The concept of opportunity cost can also be considered a risk. Choosing one alternative often eliminates choosing another, especially when spending money. If you buy the truck, then maybe you can't buy the forklift. Carefully assess the pros and cons of each alternative. Are you giving up too much in one purchase to allow another? What could the potential cost to your business be? Which opportunity provides the most benefit in terms of increased revenues, decreased costs, or improved productivity—and over what period of time?

Make a list of all the possible capital (large) expenditures and projects you may need in the next few years. How much will each one cost? How much will each one add value in terms of higher revenues, lower operating costs, or increased productivity or efficiency?

Succession Risk

Succession risk recognizes that you aren't immortal. A friend of mine was in seemingly excellent health and at age forty-five had a "widow maker" heart attack. He died immediately. What happens to your heirs and employees if you aren't there? Do you have a succession plan?

A more positive scenario is that you may choose to sell your business or turn it over to a family member. Do you have a written plan in place? Tom and Veronica Zombik of Hilton Head Glass/Veronica's Art Glass have developed a plan so that when they are ready to retire and sell the business, they can obtain maximum value for it.

A business with disorganized financials and accounting records, and sloppy operations procedures, will not attract many buyers. In one situation, two partners had worked together for over forty years but never set up the legal documents spelling out what should occur if one of them died. Sadly, one of them did pass away, and he would be horrified if he could observe the mess that ensued.

Between the partners, they had seven children, and only one was interested in working in the business. The owners may have saved money on legal fees in the short run by not drafting a legal plan of succession, but their heirs have ended up paying dearly in both legal fees and emotional angst.

Contrast that with Bob All of Custom Security Specialists. Bob has put together a ten-year plan to turn the business over to his daughter Robin, who already works there. Bob has a profitable business but wants to make sure that when Robin gets ownership, all runs smoothly, and that the right employees are in place for the next generation.

Size Risk

Many small business owners want to stay small, and that's okay. However, there are risks to being small. For instance, if your business only has a couple of employees, what happens if someone gets hurt, sick, or even dies? If there are three of you and one goes down, you have lost one-third of your staff. What if the person who is injured is the only one qualified to do a particular type of work? If you are a sole practitioner and have health issues that inhibit your ability to perform, your family may face zero income.

A young friend—a sole proprietor—fell off a ladder, broke four ribs, and couldn't work. His income was wiped out. My fraternal big brother, friend, and mentor, J.R. Rutherford, recognized at age seventy the risk that at some point he may not be able to provide tax preparation services for his clients. J.R., who is in perfect health, took the step of merging his operations with a local certified public accountant (CPA) firm in Tennessee to protect his clients.

Employee Risk

The most obvious risk is that your star employees may leave. Strategies for employee retention are discussed in chapter 23. And what about the employees that stay, or the ones you didn't hire?

Discrimination in virtually any form is illegal, and current, prospective, and former employees sue companies frequently for discrimination of various types. These lawsuits can irreparably damage your firm even if you are innocent. Once they become public, at least half of the public will think you are guilty without knowing all the facts. What can you do to prevent these types of lawsuits, and, if they do occur, minimize the impact?

I suggest having a human relations advisor or employment lawyer on your team to advise you. Employment law is complicated, so you want to be sure you have policies and procedures in place that clearly state the company's position. These policies need to be in the employee handbook and supplemented at least annually with follow-up communications reminding employees of company policy.

One business owner proudly asserted, "In seventy-five years this company has never been sued." The words were barely uttered when a former employee filed a racial discrimination lawsuit.

We live in a highly litigious society where people blame others for their own failures. There are those who literally make a living suing other people and companies, pouncing on them if there is even the slightest chance of a payout.

Take steps to prevent a discrimination lawsuit, but if it occurs, you want to minimize the financial impact. One method is with Employment Practices Liability Insurance, or EPLI. These policies cover a range of risks, such as wrongful termination, sexual harassment, contract violations, and wage and hour law violations. In a world where current courts tend to favor the employee, an EPLI policy can be the difference between keeping a business open and being shut down. Fortunately, EPLI insurance is relatively inexpensive.

Another employee risk is theft. Make sure you are properly insured and employees who handle money are bonded. Internal controls for preventing theft are outlined in chapter 50.

Substitution Risk

Is there a less expensive or better performing substitute for your product or service? A common example would be a store brand versus a name brand. Identify potential substitutes for what your business sells and determine how to meet that competition.

Summary

Understanding the risks associated with your business enables you to make smart decisions which could soften the blow if and when the worst happens.

Southwest Airlines certainly did not know there would be a terrorist attack on September 11, 2001. However, they did know that in the future some disaster would affect air travel. Accordingly, they developed a plan to deal with such a scenario. When the Federal Aviation Administration cleared planes to fly again, Southwest was the first airline back in the air, days ahead of every other airline.

Can you be prepared for every possible risk to your business? No. But you can be better prepared than you are now. Identifying the risks, assessing them, and making contingency plans can be difficult and time consuming, but the consequences of failing to do so can be disastrous. Don't delude yourself into thinking, *This will never happen to me.*

Chapter Assignment

1. Make a list of the possible risks that could adversely affect your business. Brainstorm with your team to come up with every possible scenario. Recording every idea, regardless of whether you think the idea is valid, stimulates the thought process, generating more ideas.

2. Complete the SWOT below for your business. Have all of your employees list the strengths, weaknesses, opportunities, and threats to your business. Your employees may see areas and have ideas that you haven't considered.
3. Download and complete the Risk Assessment questionnaire from my website: www.rockwellbusinesssolutions.com/diagrams

BUSINESS ______________________________

STRENGTHS	**WEAKNESSES**
OPPORTUNITIES	**THREATS**

CHAPTER 19
LEGAL

"Pay me now or pay me later." – Fram Oil Filters commercial

This chapter should not be construed in any way as legal advice, since I'm not a lawyer. You need to develop a relationship with a competent lawyer who you can call on if you get in a desperate situation, and, more importantly, help prevent one in the first place. A good lawyer can advise you on the following issues.

Corporate Structure

What legal entity is appropriate for your business? Should you be a limited liability corporation (LLC), subchapter corporation (S Corp), corporation (C Corp), partnership, or some other form of legal entity? There are pros and cons to each. Your lawyer can guide you in selecting the right entity for your business. The right legal structure can protect your personal assets.

Internal Revenue Service

Do you have a FEIN (Federal Employer Identification Number) for your business? Sole proprietors need an FEIN.

Permits and Licenses

Do you need special permits or licenses for your business? Every locality has different requirements and regulations.

Intellectual Property

Do you need a patent for your product or a trademark for your logo?

Litigation

What can you do to minimize the chances of being sued? Even if you win the lawsuit, you still lose. No matter the outcome, your image will be tarnished and you will suffer from Reputation Deficit Syndrome. Half the public will think you are guilty even if the court declares you are innocent.

Law Firms

Larger law firms that have lawyers specializing in different fields may be more expensive, but the cross knowledge can be beneficial. If your business has specialized needs, you may require relationships with more than one lawyer.

Chapter Assignment

Most of the aforementioned items, not counting lawsuits, are often easy to set up and don't cost much. You may be able do some of them yourself and save the cost of a lawyer. However, unless your core expertise is in legal matters, it is better to pay someone to do them correctly. You can be sure of this: failing to establish your business correctly from a legal standpoint can be far more expensive in the long term than paying for a qualified lawyer to do it. Develop a relationship with a lawyer specializing in business law.

SECTION 5

SWAMP TEAM

CHAPTER 20
EMPLOYEES

"Treat employees like they make a difference and they will."
– Jim Goodnight, CEO, SAS

A popular expression in business is "people are our most important asset." Actually, people aren't an organization's most important asset; they are the organization's most *valuable* asset. Unfortunately, this expression is frequently just a platitude and not actually a fundamental value of the company.

Hiring qualified people who are aligned with your fundamental purpose, values, and operating principles demonstrates a true commitment to employees. As Jim Collins writes in *Good to Great,* "Get the right people on the bus, the wrong people off the bus, and the people on the bus in the right seat."

Employees' names don't appear on the balance sheet, but the quality of their work and how they interact with customers, coworkers, and vendors is reflected in your financial statements. It shows up in the form of great or poor performance—and in customers who are happy or leave upset. It shows in going the extra mile to meet a deadline or going home the minute the clock strikes five—and in taking responsibility for honoring the fundamentals of your business or just sliding by on a minimum of effort. Finding, keeping, and growing the best talent is critical to the success of your organization.

A friend and former coworker, Jerry Dahill, told me that after he retired from the Eastman Chemical Company, he took a job as a controller for a small company. I asked how working with a small company compared with working for a large corporation. He said the major lesson he learned was that two Eastman people could do the same amount of work that it took five people to accomplish at the small company.

Jerry said the people at the small company were competent, intelligent people, but they didn't have the training and educational background as those hired by Eastman. (Eastman pays larger salaries and can select from a wider pool of qualified applicants.) Two people accomplishing the job of five was obviously cost effective. In the long run, it is less expensive to pay for the top-tier employees.

In his book *Mastering the Rockefeller Habits,* Verne Harnish reveals, "The Container Store firmly believes that one great person can replace three good people." The Container Store was number one on *Fortune* magazine's list of the best companies to work for in 2000 and 2001. Again, this is a large corporation. Even so, it's an example of the importance of hiring individuals with high levels of potential mixed with education, experience, and alignment with your company's fundamentals.

Typically, a small business doesn't have that luxury. Top-tier employees command higher wages, and the small business selects from a different pool of applicants. There are diamonds (and diamonds in the rough) in just about every talent pool, and finding the person with the intelligence, attitude, willingness to learn, and excitement about the job can be tricky.

There are bright, talented, professional, educated people with solid experience who prefer working for a small local business rather than commuting to a large corporate office. The challenge is finding and keeping great employees, and while difficult, it is not impossible.

Hiring the right people is both an art and a science. No business has a perfect track record in hiring and managing employees, but you can learn to minimize the number of mistakes and misfits. The subject is worth studying, and the more you read up on it, the better you will become at hiring the right people for your business. Books by Jim Collins, Jack Welch, Jack Stack, John Maxwell, and Michael Gerber are excellent resources. Let's take a look at the hiring process first.

CHAPTER 21

WHY ARE YOU HIRING?

"Clients do not come first, employees come first. If you take care of your employees, they will take care of the clients." – Sir Richard Branson

So *why* are you going to hire someone? There are only three reasons. Take a moment and write down your reasons to why you want to add employees. Is your current staff overworked, and would hiring more staff be less expensive than the overtime you are paying? Do you want to provide better customer service? Do you need a salesperson to bring in additional business? Perhaps administrative help will free you up to do other things?

This is the point. Do you have a written procedure to define when and how to add employees?

Companies often add employees for unsound business reasons such as "my cousin is out of work and I want to help her." Naturally you want to help your cousin, but is it in the best interest of your business? Perhaps not. There could be unexpected situations that make hiring a relative a mistake down the road. Think to the future when making hiring decisions.

There are only three business reasons for hiring additional employees. Will the additional employee help ...

- **Increase revenues**
- **Decrease expenses**
- **Increase cash flow**

Initially, adding an employee will increase your expenses. Evaluate whether or not, over time, adding the employee will result in increased revenues or decreased expenses that will make hiring them worth it.

After adequate training and time, if the new person doesn't accomplish at least one of these goals, they are a drag on the business and a threat to its future sustainability. Benevolence is laudatory, but when it comes to your business, your first responsibility is to yourself and your existing staff. Hiring an individual who doesn't eventually increase revenues, decrease expenses, or increase cash flow is risking your future and that of your current employees.

Increase Revenue

The most obvious example of hiring an employee to increase revenue is adding a sales rep. It could be an outside person who calls on customers or someone internal who develops new business through marketing, social media, or via phone. A good salesperson should bring in revenues that are at least three times their salary or compensation.

Several business owners have told me that they didn't want a commission salesperson because they might make more than they are as the owner. Think realistically! So what if you pay a salesperson six figures if they are generating seven figures in revenue. The more productive the salesperson, the more money the owner makes.

Needless to say, there are other ways a new employee can increase revenues. You may have a pipeline of potential new customers you are unable to service given your current employee capacity. Again, evaluate whether another person will increase revenues more than what you pay them.

Decrease Expenses

How can adding an employee decrease expenses? After all, you have to pay the employee a salary. What if that person brings a skill that enables the company to be more efficient and productive, so that going forward you can do more work with the same number of people and maintain a high level of service? A good accountant can find all kinds of savings. They will not only spot waste and overcharges, but can also negotiate better deals with vendors and banks.

Increase Cash Flow

Adding an employee to whom you have to pay a salary will increase expenses, which in turn decreases cash flow. But how can adding an employee increase cash flow? We just noted that a good accountant can find a lot of savings that could translate into stronger cash flow. Here's another example.

One company is terrible at collecting its receivables. It does the work and invoices the customer, but never collects. The partners are constantly loaning the company money to keep it afloat. By not collecting receivables, the company is effectively working for free. It either needs to figure out how to do a better job at collections, or it could hire someone to help them. It could turn the old receivables over to a collection agency, but small businesses are often reluctant to do that for fear the collection agency will damage the company's relationship with the customer.

An alternative would be to hire someone part time to help with collections. There are plenty of retired experienced businesspeople who would be happy to help a small business and would work for less than they were paid when working full time.

Chapter Assignment

1. Make a list of how every position in your company contributes to the three goals of increasing revenues, decreasing expenses, or increasing cash flow.
2. Make a list of possible new positions that could increase revenues, decrease expenses, or increase cash flow by enough to cover their salary and benefits.

CHAPTER 22
HIRING PROCESS

"I'd rather have a lot of talent and a little experience than a lot of experience and a little talent." – John Wooden

Mike Covert, owner of Covert Aire, said the toughest business decision he ever made was hiring his first employee. He wasn't concerned with how to cover the cost of an employee because he had prepared for that; he was concerned about giving up control. Someone else would be out there maintaining and fixing HVAC systems. He knew the quality of his own work, but would the new person deliver the same? If not, the image of Covert Aire could suffer from Reputation Deficit Syndrome.

A fellow BNI member told me he had given up on having employees because the ones he had hired in the past had either stolen from him or done such sloppy work they almost ruined his reputation.

If you have ever hired someone, then you know that sometimes, despite your best efforts, you end up choosing the wrong person. After all, anyone can be deceived by deceitful people; that's what they're experts at. If and when this happens, it is your responsibility to learn from the mistake. Were there any warning signs you missed? Did you have any hesitation about your decision, or did you settle on choosing the best from a bad group just to fill the role? Unless you really can function without help, then you're going to have to try hiring again, and you may as well arm yourself by learning as much from your mistakes as you possibly can.

The first person I hired lasted a week, and it was completely my fault. She was fresh out of college, very smart, and came highly recommended by her professors. I had high hopes for her and talked openly about her assuming a leadership role someday.

At the end of the week, she turned in her notice and said that she had decided to pursue a job in another field. I think the real reason she left was that she wasn't interested in a leadership role at that point in her life. I had assumed that she aspired to work in a managerial capacity. I never asked her about her aspirations. The problem wasn't with the person I hired, it was with me—and in all likelihood, the problem my BNI friend had with hiring employees was at least in part with him.

There are several factors that could have led to the disastrous results my BNI friend experienced. It's easy to say he wasn't paying attention when he interviewed these people, and this is most likely the case. But some people do practice, some people practice deceit to get a job, and he may not have recognized the signs. Why would this be?

If you're a business owner, then you know how difficult it is to get a solid chunk of undisturbed time when you can focus on the person in front of you without constant distractions. It's even harder because your mind never really stops thinking about what's going on in the business while you're doing something else. But you can't split your mind and give total attention to everything trying to occupy it, so you have to fully focus on each interviewee. Put the other things aside for a few minutes. They will be there when you get back. It's worth it to either bring a great person into your business or keep a bad employee out.

In many ways, hiring is like dating. Everyone is on their best behavior and wants to make a good impression, but you really don't know what you've got until six to twelve months into the relationship. That's a lot of time invested in training and development, only to find out you have a lemon. When it comes to hiring, here is a proven rule of thumb from Greg McKeown of *Harvard Business Review*: "Hire slow, fire fast."

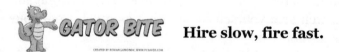

Hire slow, fire fast.

You want to be as sure as possible that you are finding the right person for the job. But as soon as you find out you've made a mistake, correct it. One owner tells people to just send him a warm body and he'll put them to work immediately. Maybe that works for him, but he probably has to kiss a lot of frogs to find a princess. How do you know if you've found the right person?

Hire Experience?

Some companies only hire people with experience in their industry. That's fine, but what if that experienced person doesn't fit the culture of your business? What if they have preferred ways of doing things that are contrary to the way you do them? What if their values are different from yours? What if they don't really buy into your fundamental purpose and are just looking to fill eight hours and collect a paycheck? I don't mean to trivialize the value of experience; it's a great asset. However, experience alone is not sufficient.

What about hiring someone straight out of school and teaching them how to do the job? After all, job skills can be learned, and these people won't come with the baggage of "this is the way we did it where I worked before." But what if they have a poor work ethic, sloppy work habits, and poor attendance? Again, do they share your fundamental values, and will they be committed to your fundamental purpose? Will they be comfortable working within your fundamental operating principles?

You have to decide what the balance is between talent and experience for your business. Here is some sage advice from John Wooden, the legendary UCLA basketball coach: "I'd rather have a lot of talent and a little experience, than a lot of experience and a little talent." You can teach employees just about any skill your business needs.

Look to Your Fundamentals

Fundamental Purpose

Your fundamental purpose narrows the field dramatically, and your fundamental values and fundamental operating principles even further. When you interview prospective employees, find out if their fundamentals are the same as yours.

Would you agree that passion is an important factor for a business to succeed? Steve Adams wrote the book *The Passionate Entrepreneur*. He cites passion as the most critical factor in the success of his business, Pet Supplies Plus. As I read his book, I thought, *Right on, Steve! Passion is really important!* But then the business coach in me took over, and I thought, *How can I teach a client to be passionate*? Think about that for a minute. If passion is important and we want our employees to be passionate about the success of our business, how do we get them to be passionate?

Passion comes from dedication and commitment to a cause that you believe in and want to accomplish. It can't really be taught; it has to be felt. Now, think about your fundamental purpose, about which you are very passionate. Is that prospective employee passionate about your fundamental purpose? How do you find out if your fundamental purpose is aligned with theirs? You ask questions designed to find out not only what their work experience and skills are but also in what causes they believe.

In their LinkedIn profile, what do they list under "Causes you care about," "Volunteer activities," "Organizations you support," and "Opportunities you are looking for"? You want to get to know the person you are interviewing as a person and not just what their education, skills, and experience are. You are probably excited to get up in the morning because you know you are helping people and making a difference in many lives. You want people who share this passion and fundamental purpose.

Fundamental Values

Make sure that their fundamental values are in alignment with yours and your company's. Again, ask questions designed to uncover their values. One of Reclamation By Design's values is "never cut corners." Make up a hypothetical situation and ask them what they would do. One of Covert Aire's values is "Give back to the community." If the prospective employee has never done any volunteer work and has no interest in doing so, are they the right fit for Covert Aire?

Fundamental Operating Principles

Then there are your fundamental operating principles. Does the prospective employee buy into those principles? Would they feel comfortable working in your environment? Do they understand and agree with the way you do business? How long will someone stay with you if they don't agree with your principles? How long will you keep them?

Hiring Process Improvement

Over time you will learn which questions work—and which don't—and you can refine the process. Hiring is a process, and as we discussed in the last chapter, every process can and should be improved.

If the prospective employee doesn't align well with your fundamental purpose, values, and operating principles, then at best, you have an eight-to-five worker who is just putting in time to collect a salary. That may be all you need. But if you are looking for someone who can grow with the company and move into management, then the company and employee fundamentals need to be aligned, and that means getting to know the "real" person. This isn't always easy and will take practice and time.

I was discussing this issue one evening with Bill Dickenson. Bill used to be a psychiatrist but eventually left the profession and founded Wet Willies, a frozen daiquiris bar with over eighteen stores around the country.

Bill said that if you really want to know what the real person is like, take them out and get them drunk. Now, I know Bill didn't mean falling-down drunk (I hope), but it's true that a couple of beers can relax people into being more "themselves." This strategy may not fit with your fundamental values, but it does illustrate the point that getting to know the real person can sometimes be an interesting process.

Chapter Assignment

Make a list of every employee in your company.

1. How does each person align with your company's fundamental purpose, values, and operating principles?
2. If the employee doesn't align with your fundamentals, what do you need to do to achieve alignment? What training does the employee need?

CHAPTER 23
RETENTION

"Letting the wrong people hang around is unfair to all the right people, as they inevitably find themselves compensating for the inadequacies of the wrong people. Worse, it can drive away the best people. Strong performers are intrinsically motivated by performance, and when they see their efforts impeded by carrying extra weight, they eventually become frustrated." – Jim Collins

Here is a fact: Star performers can leave anytime, but mediocre and poor performers will usually stay.

Star performers can leave anytime, but mediocre and poor performers will usually stay.

Star performers have many options and are in constant demand. If they aren't happy, they can find work elsewhere. Mediocre and poor performers don't have as many options. They are happy to work for you because there aren't many other places that want them. So the trick is to keep the stars, nurture the mediocre into stars, and weed out the poor performers. Easier said than done, right?

Generally speaking, exceptional people are scarce, costly, and highly mobile. A nurse practitioner I know is so good at what she does that other medical practices continuously try to poach her. It is in her employer's best interest to keep her happy—and they do, because they value her and understand how difficult it would be to replace what she brings to the practice.

A small business may get an exceptional person like this nurse, but what many business owners fear is the possibility that this impressive employee will use the business as a stepping stone or training ground for bigger opportunities.

Turnover can be a big problem for a small business. You can invest substantial time and money in a person, and then they leave and you have to start over. Add to that the fact that in many cases a small business can't afford to hire that exceptional person nor can they afford *not* to hire them, so they caught between a rock and a hard place.

Keeping Your Stars

How do you retain stars? What would make them want to stay with your company when they get an offer for more money somewhere else? Everyone is different and is motivated by different things. There have been numerous studies showing that money isn't always the highest priority.

If your stars are passionate about your fundamental purpose, they are probably more likely to want to stay. Your cause, and how you help people, is their cause and something they want to share. Stars, if they are ambitious (and most are), want to know that they have a future in the company. Do they have advancement or potential ownership opportunities?

The Greenery is a great example of a company giving its people a stake in the business. The Greenery is 100 percent employee owned. In peak season, it has over 700 employees maintaining and landscaping properties all along the Coastal Carolina and Georgia region. Ownership is through a combination ESOP (employee stock ownership plan) and 401k retirement plan. As the company grows and prospers, employees earn more stock in the company and their retirement plan grows. Every person I've met at The Greenery is committed and passionate about the company's fundamental purpose, values, and operating principles. As a result the company's turnover is relatively low in an industry noted for high turnover.

Give people a reason to stay with your company.

Mediocre and Poor Performers

What about the mediocre and poor performers? This may no longer be true, but for many years the performance evaluation process at General Electric was very strict. The top 10 percent got promoted, the bottom 10 percent got fired, and those in the middle were given opportunities to grow and become part of the upper 10 percent.

This would be tough for a small business to implement. Employees at small businesses become like family. Everyone knows about each other's family, personal issues, and challenges. How do you fire a person you know so well, especially if that person has a sickly child and really needs the job?

Between 2002 and 2007, many companies had employees they really needed to let go. They had people who were the bad apples that spoil the whole barrel. Other employees would be demotivated when they experienced their tardiness, sloppy work, and bad attitude. "If *they* can get away with that kind of work ethic," they reasoned, "then why should I work my tail off?"

You can see the problem. The bad apple is bringing the whole team down, as well as having a negative impact on the company and its customers. They are almost considered family, making it difficult to let the person go. "Pruning the tree" is a decision you will often have to make, and it isn't easy.

At one point I was working for a small company with about $12 million a year in revenues, and it was going down the tubes fast. Top management finally decided that staffing cuts had to be made. I had four people reporting to me, and I had to fire one of them. It was a horrible decision to be burdened with, but I had no choice. I had gotten to know all four and knew some of their personal situations. I know how difficult pruning the tree can be, but sometimes it has to be done or else the tree dies and everyone is out of a job.

Training

Going back to the General Electric example, what would you do with the people in the middle 80 percent? You can't teach people to be passionate, and you can't teach them to be ambitious. They either are or they aren't. But you can give them opportunities to grow and improve.

Let me share a surprising situation I once experienced. I asked a business owner—let's call him George—what kind of training he had for his employees. He immediately responded, "At this company, we don't believe in training."

Wow. That was a new one for me. Obviously, I had to ask why? He said that he wasn't prepared to take the loss. He figured that if the business spent money on training an employee who then left and went to work somewhere else, particularly for a competitor, then his company had paid for training that benefited another business. "That's interesting," I replied, not wanting to damage our relationship.

He was worried that a properly trained employee might leave, but what about the consequences of an untrained employee staying? Essentially, what he is saying by not doing any training is that he wants unqualified, unproductive, inefficient, uneducated employees who can't contribute to the success of the company and probably offer very poor customer service.

George thinks he's saving himself a lot of money and protecting his business, but he's really asking for a lot of headaches and putting his business at risk.

It is amazing that owners see the obvious need for preventive maintenance for their equipment, but even though salaries can be anywhere from 30 percent to 70 percent of their expenses, they spend less than 1 percent of their budget on training.

Employees in most small businesses tend to be good, hard-working people, and prove that business owners take hiring very seriously. A few bad hiring decisions will convince any owner of the importance of hiring good people, but the people that a small business can afford don't necessarily have the qualifications and experience that a huge company can draw. This is why ongoing training is so important for your business, so you can raise the level of your employees' qualifications and skills from within, in just the way you want and need.

How can your employees get better at what they do or how they interact with customers, vendors, and coworkers *without* training? How can they understand how they can help the company reach its goals, and what's in it for them, *without* training? When you provide training, you are saying to that employee, "You are valuable, and I see a future for you at this company." If you have an employee who you wouldn't consider training, do you think you have the right employee?

Now, I understand that not everyone is trainable. When it comes to humans, it's a matter of attitude. If people believe they can learn something, they are right. You can learn virtually anything if it is critical to your success or well-being.

Alligators don't want to be trained, unless it's about coming to dinner. One of my BNI friends, Steve Anderson, is in the business of managing property for gated communities. His company is Advantage Association Management. In our area, alligators abound in ponds and lagoons, and they like to bask in the sun. A lawyer renting a home in one of these communities wanted to get a picture of his ten-year-old daughter standing next to an alligator, so he told the girl to walk up close to it. If you are thinking that this was a bad idea, you're right. The alligator hissed and snapped its jaws, and the terrified girl ran away.

The lawyer then went to Steve and complained bitterly, saying that Steve needed to do a better job of training the alligators. He refused to believe it when Steve told him that alligators can't be trained. As I said earlier, alligators can learn where to look and what to look for, and they already know how to use what they find. Beyond that there isn't much they will learn.

But your employees can learn a great deal. Not only are there important skills that will help them be more productive, but there are also people skills that can help them interact with other employees, vendors, and, of course, your customers.

Performance Evaluation

What else can you do to help retain employees? Employees are people, and people in general want to feel appreciated and know that they are contributing to a winning team.

Performance evaluations sometimes get a bad rap. The purpose of a performance evaluation is to help someone improve and contribute to the success of the organization. It is not a tool to beat people over the head. If you go into a performance evaluation with the objective of helping the person improve, regardless of whether or not that person stays at your company, then it can be a great tool. If used poorly, it can be highly demoralizing.

People want to know how they are doing, and that doesn't mean just once a year. If someone did a particularly good job that day or on that project, say something. If you wait until the annual review and say, "Thanks, Alice, for that nice job you did six months ago," it loses value, and Alice may not even remember what she did.

Recognize accomplishment when it occurs, but make sure it is deserved. A graduation ceremony on Facebook showed kindergartners "graduating" into first grade wearing a cap and gown. Now what did these kids accomplish other than showing up for kindergarten and reaching the age where they are old enough to enter first grade? When these kids grow up, they will learn the hard way that the world doesn't reward or recognize people for just showing up. Recognition for achievement shouldn't be confused with acknowledgement of a person, attention to their needs, and encouragement. Recognition for non-achievement is not encouragement, and it can result in discouragement later in life. Let's look at a couple of examples of how a performance evaluation can motivate or demotivate.

When I was in the army, there was a detailed performance evaluation system. Hopefully it is different today. I don't remember most of what was on the multi-page questionnaire except for two questions, and I vividly remember both.

First, the evaluator was asked to give you a percentile rating relative to all other people in that grade (rank). The lowest percentage I ever got was 95 percent, which meant that I was rated higher than 95 percent of all the first lieutenants. It's a ridiculous process when you think about it. The evaluator couldn't possibly know all the other first lieutenants in the army, so how could he assign a percentage rating to anyone? One captain gave me a 100 percent. Woohoo! I was now the best first lieutenant in the whole U.S. Army, all over the world!

The next question was the real de-motivator: Would you ...

a) promote this person ahead of his contemporaries?
b) promote this person along with his contemporaries?
c) hold this person back from promotion?

Now, I was getting a rating as one of the top in my grade in the whole army. How do you think everyone who evaluated me answered the second question? That's right—promote this person along with his contemporaries.

When I was at Eastman, my boss called me in one day and told me I had been promoted to senior accountant. Naturally, I was pleased and excited. He then proceeded to tell me that at this level more would be expected of me.

"Great!" I said. "I'm ready. What is expected of me?"

"More."

Yes, but "more" of what? He never could tell me. I don't know about you, but I can't hit a target I don't have.

When I was in Vietnam, I was evaluating a young sergeant. He had been wounded in combat, and after he recovered, he had been assigned to my unit. I was managing the officer club system at the 25th Infantry Division at Cu Chi. We had eighteen small clubs and a snack bar for both officers and enlisted men.

This sergeant had a college degree in business, and I wanted to use him to help improve the business so we could better serve the troops, especially the ones who were in from the field. Unfortunately, all I could get him to do was drive a truck. We were trying to offer more and better services at lower prices, and a guy with a business degree couldn't even help.

In his evaluation prior to leaving the country, I gave him a 70 percent, which I thought was generous. My captain called on me, saying that this just wasn't done and that I should change the rating to 90 percent or better. I stuck to my guns and wouldn't change it.

The night before the sergeant left to go home, we sat up late at night and over a few beers discussed the rating I had given him. He didn't like it. We talked about his poor attitude and lack of pride in his work. He argued that he only acted that way because he was in the army but that when he got into a real job back in the States, he would take pride in his work.

I asked him if pride was something he could just turn on or off, or did people take pride in what they did no matter where they are? It was an aha moment for him. He was getting out of the army, so this evaluation would have no effect on his life as a civilian. My goal wasn't to improve his performance there but rather to help him be more successful in the rest of his life. I have no idea what happened to him, or how his life turned out, but I'd like to think that our conversation had a positive effect down the road.

Performance evaluations need to be done, and done regularly. However, doing them is hard for many people. It's hard because all too often people see a performance evaluation as confrontational. In order to be nonconfrontational, business owners often don't communicate the truth with their employees. If you adopt the attitude of "how can I help this person?" it gets a lot easier. Sometimes the conversation can be difficult if there's a serious issue involved, but if you are sincerely interested in helping the other person, you will have conducted a smoother and more productive evaluation.

Having the Conversation

I've mentioned Ron Kirby before. Ron is an amazing leader and trainer, and I've had the privilege of doing several seminars with him. I asked him to share his process for having a conversation with an employee, or what he calls a counseling session. Here is his approach.

Counseling sessions are designed to be productive and an opportunity to get to know your employees' personalities. They are also a great opportunity to discuss weaknesses, strengths, and goals. They should be in private without interruption, allowing you to provide the employee with quality time with you. There should be value taken from the meeting concerning both of you.

1. Initially discuss employee's personal life, hobbies, and interests.
2. Opportunity: Where do you desire them to improve? Give clear guidance. Give them the opportunity to ask questions. Discuss one opportunity at a time.
3. Strengths: Discuss areas you are happy with, and let them know you have recognized their performance.
4. Ask for ideas and suggestions for how the company can improve. You might hear a few gems.
5. Explain your vision on the future of the company and where the employee fits in. In other words, what could their future be with the company?
6. Ask if they have any questions about anything.

What did you notice about Ron's strategy? First, he wants to put them at ease and establish a rapport with the person. He wants to let them know that he cares about them and is interested in them. Then he discusses opportunities for them to improve. He takes a positive approach of "how can I help you?" Then he moves on to recognizing their strengths and contribution to the organization.

A lot of companies' sessions include these elements, but Ron takes it to the next level by asking the person how they think the company could improve or grow. Understand that people won't open up to you until they trust you. Building trust takes time and occurs when people realize that what they say won't be held against them. If they open up and make a suggestion, take it into consideration. Ask them how it might be implemented and how it would benefit the company. You can't implement every suggestion you get, but you can acknowledge and appreciate every suggestion. Also you should be able to give a reason why that suggestion can't be implemented, but don't tell them no at that time. Consider their idea for awhile and when you have a logical reason why their suggestion can or cannot be implemented, go back and talk with them.

The final step in Ron's process is to reiterate to the person what the company's vision is and how that person fits in its future growth. It is also an opportunity to communicate the company's fundamental purpose, values, and operating principles.

Chapter Assignment

Read books and articles on employee retention. Read blogs. LinkedIn Groups offer suggestions. Society for Human Resource Managers is also a good resource. Different approaches will work best for your culture and personality, which means that you have to define what that culture is and your fundamentals. Get an honest assessment of your personality. Take a Meyers-Briggs test. There are free versions online. There are no right or wrong answers for a Meyers-Briggs test, but it will give you an idea of how and why you act and say what you do so that you can better understand yourself and the people with whom you need to communicate.

CHAPTER 24
MANAGING EMPLOYEES

"The best executive is the one who has sense enough to pick good people to do what he wants done and the self–restraint to keep from meddling with them while they do it." – Theodore Roosevelt

Management and leadership skills are learned and can be improved. You can be a better manager if you put in the effort, and your employees will appreciate that effort. No one likes to work for a bad boss. A bad boss not only demotivates people but can also cause them to have poor work habits and a negative attitude.

You may have a great system for hiring, training, and keeping employees, but you still must manage your employees and make sure everything is done right and on time. This chapter is intended to stimulate your thinking with a few proven concepts.

Systemization

New employees can get up to speed much faster if there is a systematized process for their position. In other words, they need a set of standard procedures in place that are easy to learn. Then, if someone is absent or leaves the company, a new employee can step right in and quickly learn how to perform the duties of that position.

Employees will pass through your business. Some will leave because of you. Some will leave in spite of you. They may love working for you, but their spouse gets a job in another city that is too good to pass up. When that great person leaves, there is a gap in the performance of your business. You want that gap filled as fast as possible so that your customers are being properly taken care of and your product or service quality stays top notch.

Affording Additional Employees

Adding new employees costs money. Remember, you only want to add people who can increase revenues, decrease expenses, or increase cash flow. This doesn't happen overnight. It takes time for new employees to get up to speed and reach maximum productivity. Until they do, they are a drain on the company's cash.

Let's say you need a new person, and the salary would be $36,000 a year, or $3,000 a month. People often say, "I don't have an extra $36,000 in the bank, so I can't afford that new employee." Do you really need an extra $36,000 in the bank? Maybe you need less than that. Suppose it takes that new person three months to get up to speed and contribute increased revenues or decreased expenses of $3,000 a month. So we know that it takes $9,000 to cover them for three months until they can cover their $3,000 per month salary. Hopefully, it takes less than $9,000 because they will be gradually contributing over the three months.

If they contribute $1,000 the first month, $2,000 the second month, and $3,000 the third month, then their contribution equals $6,000 in that three month break-in period. What if you have a systemized process for getting them up to speed and it only takes one month for them to cover their salary? Now how much cash reserve do you need? Only $3,000.

We'll talk about accounting and finance later, but this gives you a glimpse of why it is so important for you to have an understanding of the financial side of your business. What if the employee is never productive enough to justify their salary? At that point, do you have the right employee?

Moving Employees

Mike Covert with Covert Aire believes in getting the best employees. One of Mike's fundamental operating principles: "Hire top-quality people no matter where they come from. If I have to move someone across the country to get the best, I'm willing to do that."

Wow. There aren't many small businesses willing to move a person across the country in order to get a great employee. If you have a key position and can't find anyone in your area who can properly fill it, then perhaps moving someone is worth considering. But how can a small business afford to move someone? Think creatively and "focus on the objective, not the obstacle."

GATOR BITE **Focus on the objective, not the obstacle.**

Maybe you offer partial reimbursement for moving costs? Could you pay half initially and the rest over time? Could you offer some special benefits like extra vacation time? If the person leaves within a specified period of time, they could be required to refund the moving costs to the company. Just focus on the objective and not all the potential problems, and you will probably come up with some very creative ways to make it work.

Chapter Assignment

Read books to help you become a manager. I recommend:

- All books by John C. Maxwell
- *The First-Time Manager* by Loren B. Belker

CHAPTER 25
EMPLOYEE LEGAL ISSUES

"A company should limit its growth based on its ability to attract enough of the right people." – Jim Collins

You need a competent employment lawyer and advisor on your team. Every state and municipality has different regulations. Furthermore, employment laws are extremely complex and getting more so every day. There are also regulations related to the Affordable Care Act (national health insurance), Employment Retirement Income Security Act (ERISA), and Fair Labor Standards Act (FLSA), and Occupational Safety and Health Administration (OSHA) and Internal Revenue Service (IRS) regulations, just to name a few.

When your business is really small, some of these don't apply. However, as you grow you will need that competent advisor. You don't make any money when you sit across the desk from a government auditor for days, weeks, or months trying to satisfy their requests. It is much better to have everything in order. Auditors look for red flags; and when they find one, they start digging and digging. Do you really have time for audits?

Documentation

There are certain documents you are legally required to keep for each employee, so you need an employee information system, or EIS. You'll also need to keep file for each employee. What needs to be in that file may vary from state to state, so the following list of items isn't meant to be all inclusive but rather to get you thinking and acting on what is required. Consult with a knowledgeable employment lawyer in your area.

- I-9 Form (employment eligibility verification)
- W-4 Form (employee withholding allowance certificate)
- Employment application
- Consent forms

- Discipline and coaching forms
- Periodic employee evaluations
- Separation forms if the employee leaves or is terminated
- Employment contract
- Employee confidentiality agreements
- Employee non-compete agreement for employees who leave

You also need an employee handbook that is up to date and given to every employee. You may never be audited, but if you are, you will be glad you have everything in order.

Withholding Taxes

This is a high-profile area for the IRS, and where a lot of businesses get in deep trouble. When you pay someone a salary, you are required to withhold their federal and state income taxes, as well as their contribution to Social Security and Medicare. Now let's be really blunt about this. The money you withhold is *not yours*. That is the employee's money. You cannot finance your business with *their* money. That's called theft. The money you withhold *must* be sent to the IRS and/or state Department of Revenue.

All too often, small businesses get in a cash bind and think, *Let's just hold the money until customer ABC Company's check comes in*. But then ABC's check doesn't come in and the money gets spent on something else.

In one situation, the bookkeeper never sent any withholding to the IRS. Three years later, the taxman came calling. The IRS almost never audits last year. They are generally three to five years behind. In this case, the IRS had begun to notice that when the employees filed their income tax returns, there was no receipt of the money by the IRS. Red flag!

When they discovered that the company hadn't sent in any withholding for three years, they not only wanted that money but also a lot of interest and penalties on top. This small business of only a few employees got a tax bill of over $250,000. It put them out of business, and the owner was held personally liable for the money.

If you have a cash shortfall, find another way to finance it and make sure you are forwarding all withholding to the government.

Make no mistake, the IRS is a super predator. Raising red flags for the IRS is foolish.

Independent Contractors

Are you thinking, *I know how to avoid the problem of withholding. I'll just classify everyone as an independent contractor, and that way it's not my problem. The contractor will have to pay their own Social Security, Medicare, and income taxes*? Tread very carefully here. The IRS has a long list of items that attempt to define who is, and is not, an independent contractor, and that list is subject to their interpretation, not yours. You can go to the IRS website if you aren't sure—or better yet, consult your employment lawyer/advisor.

Social Security and Medicare taxes have two components—the employees' portion and the employer's portion. As of this writing, each pay 7.65 percent of salaries for a total of 15.3 percent. You may think you are saving the employer's portion of Social Security taxes by classifying people as contractors, but if the IRS deems otherwise, you could be liable for back taxes, penalties, and interest.

One business owner had a nice business with six people working for him. However, he classified all of them as independent contractors. In reality they were employees because he supervised, scheduled, and managed every aspect of their work. He also supplied them with vehicles, tools, and equipment. He refused to reclassify these people as employees, and I politely refused to work with him. There are three things in life that I don't have time for: illness, jail, and death. I've looked at my calendar very closely and examined all of the possible dates, and I just can't fit these things in my schedule.

Now I don't know if I would have had any legal liability if I worked with him. I would have been an independent contractor. But even if I didn't have any legal liability, I didn't want to suffer from Reputation Deficit Syndrome by being associated with someone who was knowingly violating the law.

Chapter Assignment

Meet with your employee legal advisor and make sure you have all the proper employee documentation located where it can be readily presented.

SECTION 6

FINDING FOOD IN THE SWAMP

CHAPTER 26

INTRODUCTION TO MARKETING

"Man who stand on hill with mouth open wait long time for roast duck to drop in." – Confucius

With the foundation now laid, the walls erected, and the roof over your head, how do you complete your business house? If you were building a house solely for the purpose of selling it, marketing would be akin to the landscaping and interior upgrades such as hardwood floors or premium kitchen cabinets. In other words, what are the things that would attract buyers' attention so they want to look at the house? Before giving your sales pitch, you need to attract potential customers to consider your product or service.

Image by David Saba

Small businesses often just swing open their doors and expect the world to flock to them. Do you wait for customers to find you, or do you find the customers and lead them to your door? Quoting an alleged Chinese proverb:

Man who stand on hill with mouth open wait long time for roast duck to drop in.

You have to learn how to hunt the ducks in the swamp and encourage them to flock to your business.

Sales and marketing have the same goal—to get the prospect to buy—but they are two different concepts. In the business house analogy, marketing gets the potential customers in the door. Then sales demonstrates how your product or service solves their problem or meets their needs.

The marketing message and the sales message also need to be in alignment with the fundamentals of the business. If the salesperson's message promises something different from the marketing message, then the customer will be confused and disillusioned. If the sales or marketing message communicates values the company does not in fact have, the customer will feel it and walk away.

Marketing communicates the value of a product or service to the customer and can include everything from word-of-mouth referrals to expensive campaigns across multiple media. Marketing seeks to increase the value of the product or service in the mind of the consumer. In other words, marketing tries to influence the buying behavior of the target customers so they will consider trying your product or service. Marketing is an umbrella of strategies for communicating your message. It includes, but is not limited to, advertising, branding, public relations, sales, market research, and your customer service.

This section is not intended to be a comprehensive marketing manual. The goal is to introduce you to a few concepts to consider when designing your marketing program and strategy.

CHAPTER 27
WHO IS YOUR CUSTOMER?

"Focus on the customer, not the competitor." – Marsha Lindquist, president, Granite Leadership Strategies

Your success hinges on your employees and your present and future customers. Do you know who your customers are and why they buy? It may sound like a silly question, but it is surprising how many business owners don't know the answer.

Target Market

One of the foundational planks of your business is your fundamental information systems. For marketing, this is your customer information system, or CIS. You must know as precisely as possible who your customers are and how they make purchasing decisions. Your CIS encompasses every possible avenue to learn as much as possible about the demographics and psychographics of your customers and the number of potential buyers.

<u>Demographics</u>

Demographics define who your customers are in terms of their common characteristics and include things like age, gender, race, culture, ethnicity, location, education, religion, household size, income level, occupation, industry, company size, or politics. Understanding who your customers are will help you determine the number of potential customers (in other words, the size of the market for your product). Defining the demographics of your potential customers will help you figure out the best way to market to them and which media to use.

Psychographics

Psychographics is the art of determining why people might buy from you. What are their interests, attitudes, opinions, values, and behaviors? What motivates them to buy? Are your customers looking for prestige or economy? Do your customers have a particular political philosophy? Is there a particular cause in which they believe? Are they physical fitness buffs or couch potatoes?

Market Size

No product or service appeals to everyone. Your product may be fantastic, but if only three people in the world need it, the business isn't likely to succeed. You may only want a small local business. That is fine. Are there enough potential customers to enable you to earn a living year after year?

Geographics

Where are your customers located? Where could your customers be located? What are geographic expansion opportunities?

Customer Tracking

Your CIS also includes tracking your customer conversion rate (the number of prospects converted into customers), customer satisfaction, why customers left, and repeat customers.

Chapter Assignment

1. Create a list of the demographics and psychographics that define your target customer.
2. Define the size of your target market.
3. Define the current, and potential, geographic location of your target market.
4. Create a customer tracking system.

CHAPTER 28
MARKET RESEARCH

"Marketing without data is like driving with your eyes closed."
– Dan Zarella, social media scientist, *HubSpot*

The purpose of market research is to determine who your customers are, why they buy, and how many people or businesses want what you sell. The most critical question of all is: Do people want what you sell? The last thing you do when you build your business house is add the marketing. However, this is one question you must answer before you consider opening a business. It isn't a matter of whether people need your product or service; the question is, do they want it?

Just because people *need* something doesn't mean they *want* it. We all need an estate plan. If you die without an estate plan, the laws of the state you live in determine how your assets and worldly possessions will be distributed, and to whom. What the state determines may be quite contrary to your wishes. If people need an estate plan, why do so many never get around to setting one up? I'm sure you can think up a lot of reasons and excuses, but it all boils down to the simple fact that they don't want it, or they don't want it right now, or they just keep putting it off.

On the TV show *Shark Tank*, entrepreneurs seek an investment from the "Sharks." When the Shark investors ask about their sales, they sometimes get answers like, "We haven't sold any yet," or "Over the past two years sales were $5,000." The Sharks' response to these types of answers is typically, "You haven't proven that anyone wants your product." I'm sure you are familiar with the old adage "find a need and fill it." That's true, but it doesn't go far enough. A more comprehensive mantra would be "find a *want* and fill it."

Find a want and fill it!

Market research is a critical part of the planning process prior to opening any business. It helps you analyze local trends, industry trends, and whether your product has longevity or is just a fad.

The more you know about who your customers are and what motivates their buying decisions, the better you will be positioned to obtain their business. There are numerous software products available to help you track this. Many of these products go by the name customer relationship management, or CRM. When your business is small, you don't need a sophisticated CRM program, but you do need some type of system to help with marketing efforts, even if it is just a spreadsheet or hand-drawn paper forms.

Chapter Assignment

Create a process for defining and tracking what your customers want as well as need. Allow for changing fashions, fads, tastes, and trends.

CHAPTER 29
MARKETING STRATEGY

"To be successful and grow your business and revenues, you must match the way you market your products with the way your prospects learn about and shop for your products."
– Brian Halligan, CEO and Founder, *HubSpot*

Your marketing strategy is the plan for affecting the buying behavior of potential customers so they will consider buying your product. How are you going to get them to visit your store, call you, or go to your website?

In order to develop a plan, you need to know your potential customer. Your marketing plan has to educate potential customers about what you sell (product) and where they can buy your product (place), as well as motivate them to purchase from you (promotion) and establish a price that generates a profit (price). These are the proverbial "four Ps" of marketing.

Target Market/Segmentation (Who is the Customer?)

So we know that the goal of market research is to determine if people want your product or service. These potential customers are your target market, and they comprise a specific segment of the total population.

Tom and Veronica Zombik of Hilton Head Glass/Veronica's Art Glass were part owners in a glass business in New Hampshire before moving to the South Carolina area in the early 1990s. They knew the glass business, but realized they didn't know the market in the Hilton Head area where they had set up. Tom and Veronica spent four years studying the market prior to opening their business, and that research has led to an extremely successful business.

Differentiation (Product)

What makes your product or service different from that of the competition? The most common answer is, "We give great customer service." Sorry, but customer service isn't a differentiator unless all of your competition has horrible customer service. Customer service is an expectation. It is the price of admission. If you don't have a reputation for good customer service, potential customers will not consider your product or service. If they do buy once and have a bad experience, they probably won't return.

Bank websites, promotional material, and advertisements all promote the same thing—customer service, relationships, and competitive rates. So, what differentiates one bank from another? One banker told me, "Roy, you don't understand. We *really* give great customer service." Now I don't doubt that they do, but if all banks say the same thing, how is the customer to choose? What differentiates you from the rest of the competition?

Calfkiller Brewing Company in Sparta, Tennessee, has an interesting differentiator. Being a huge company is not its owners' goal. Dave and Don Sergio want their beer to be a dominant brand in their area, and they believe beer is best drunk when fresh. Therefore, they only sell in kegs to local bars, restaurants, and events. They say that when a patron orders one of their beers, it's often less than twelve hours old.

Differentiation is being unique and doing something different from the competition. But being different is not sufficient. Does your differentiator provide real value to your customers?

Geographics (Place)

Where can your customers buy your product? Do they know where to find you? Most retail businesses need to be in a location that is visible to the public. An obscure location may have lower rent, but is it worth it if no one can find you?

Your product or service may be popular, practical, or legal only in a specific geographic area or climate. Wet Willies, a frozen daiquiris bar, demonstrates this point. One of its fundamental operating principles is finding locations where it is legal to walk around, either inside a venue or in public, carrying an alcoholic beverage. This caveat limits where the company's bars can be located.

Are there any geographic limits to your business? Do customers know where to find your product?

Trends

Fads come and go, often quickly. Your product may be hot now, but does it have long-term sustainability or is it merely a short-term craze? You can profit by capitalizing on a trend, but recognize it as a temporary phenomenon that may soon be gone. Do you remember hula hoops? Assuming your product is not a fad, the next question is to understand the general trends in your market and industry. Nothing lasts forever. Survival often means adapting to a changing business climate.

Price

One of the most difficult aspects of your marketing strategy is pricing your product or service. Your costs include not only the product itself but also any costs associated with the acquisition or production of the product, including any logistic charges to deliver the product or materials to your location or plant, and from there on to your customer.

For example, assume you sell bicycles and each bike you purchase costs you $100. Further, it costs $20 in shipping and handling to get the bike to you, and it costs you $20 to get that bike to the customer. The total product cost of the bike is $140.

Is that all of your costs? What about sales, marketing, and administration? Your price must be sufficient to generate enough revenue to cover all your costs and generate a profit. You need a good accountant to help you determine the price to charge to make a profit. Pricing is part art and part science. Finding the optimal price where you maximize profits and customer satisfaction is difficult. If you have multiple products or services, you may require different strategies for each one. You may be willing to take a loss on one product in order to encourage customers to visit your store and buy more profitable items. More considerations for pricing are:

1. Pricing Too High: If your price is too high, no one will complain if you lower the price.
2. Pricing Too Low: Raising prices is unpopular. Better to start a little higher and come down.
3. Raising Prices: Over time you will have to raise prices to cover increasing costs.

   Damian Hayes of British Open Pub learned the hard way that if he raised the price of a menu item by $1, patrons were upset. However, if he raised the price by 25 cents each quarter, so that by the end of the year it totaled $1, no one complained. Damien is an extremely fair person and has no interest in gouging his customers. Realistically, however, if the cost of the food he purchases increases, he has to raise prices or he will eventually go out of business.
4. Service Creep: Service businesses must guard against "service creep." Service creep occurs when a customer asks for a small favor, and then later another and another. Those favors add up, taking more and more time, and become part of the service provided but at no additional fee. Where do you draw the line? Clearly define exactly what services are covered for a particular fee, and state that additional services will be billed accordingly.

Customer Mix

What percentage of your revenues is each customer? It is a dangerous situation if a large percentage of your business comes from one, or only a few, customers. Although profitable at the time, at some point in the future every one of your customers will be gone. This may occur next week, next month, next year, or even ten years from now, but eventually every one will be gone.

Why? Bankruptcy, merger, retirement of the owner, acquisition by another company, death of an owner, new purchasing personnel at that company, and poor performance of your product or your company. Inevitably you will lose them all. Ideally, any one customer should not account for more than 10 percent of your sales revenues. That way, when a customer leaves, the impact on your business is minimized.

Eventually, all of your customers will be gone.

Remember our discussion on risk management? Having a broad mix of small customers minimizes the risk of losing any one customer. You may think, *This will never happen to me. My customer is solid and will never leave.* Don't kid yourself. The Business Swamp is constantly changing. There are numerous situations where companies either go out of business or are crippled for years because of the loss of one customer.

Part of your marketing strategy should be to broaden the customer mix. If possible, the customer mix should encompass different industries. Recession can occur in a particular industry or geographic region even though the overall economy is strong. Selling in different industries minimizes the risk of overexposure to any one industry.

Promotion

Advertising and promotion seek to educate potential customers about your product or service. There are numerous different media available for communicating your message. Selecting the right media for your business is a challenge and will be discussed in the next chapter.

Merchandising

Merchandising is a form of promotion. It is how products are displayed in your store or on your website. What products or services are most prominent and easiest for potential customers to find? Are they the most profitable products, the biggest sellers, or the loss leaders? Are they on the top or bottom shelf, or at the end of the aisle? Are they an island display in the middle of an aisle?

Many retailers charge fees for the most desirable placement. If your product is heavy, where is it best displayed? If your customers are short in stature, will they find your product on the top shelf? Will visitors spend twenty minutes trying to find what they are looking for on your website?

Chapter Assignment

Marketing and advertising are not synonymous, but many people think they are. Designing an effective marketing strategy requires planning and research, but the rewards for the right strategy are exciting.

Create an outline with all the possible elements for your marketing strategy. Brainstorm with your team to identify specific tactics to include in your marketing strategy.

Determine your differentiator. What do you do best, and how does it add value to the customer that sets you apart from the competition?

CHAPTER 30
PROMOTION AND MEDIA

"The fact is that people never buy what they need. They buy what they want." – Charles Kettering, inventor, engineer, businessman

There are an abundance of people who approach small businesses and say, "I'll handle your marketing." The vast majority of these people are only seeking to handle one aspect of your marketing—the media you use for communicating your message to your target market. What they actually mean is, "I'll handle your print advertising, e-mail, website, billboards, etc." Some (not all) advertising agencies charge a fee to develop an advertising campaign, and additionally receive a commission from the media where they place your ads. This creates the potential for them to place your ads with the media paying the highest commission, which may not be the most appropriate method for your business. How can they be objective in designing a campaign?

How do you determine the best way to promote your business? You, as the small business owner, are the person who can best determine this if you understand the BARE essentials. The BARE essentials consist of the objectives you intend to accomplish with your marketing:

- **B**randing
- **A**cquisition of Customers
- **R**etention of Customers
- **E**ducation of Customers

Sometimes one media will suffice for all these goals, or different media may be necessary depending on your target market and its demographics and psychographics.

Branding

The two aspects to branding are recognition and reputation. Do people recognize your brand? If so, what is their perception when they see it?

Recognition

Do people recognize your name or logo? If not, will they consider your product or service? Are you willing to buy a product you've never heard of from an unknown source? Covert Aire provides HVAC services, equipment, and repairs. Mike Covert believes in brand recognition. He not only has the familiar logo on items like pens and notepads, but he takes the concept further by having packs of Covert Air barbecue sauce. Mike says, "Whenever someone might need HVAC services in the future, I want my brand to be on their mind." While hiking in Utah with my son, my lips got very dry. I reached in my pocket and pulled out—you guessed it—Covert Aire lip balm!

Reputation

When you see a sign for McDonald's or Coca-Cola, it communicates something to you about the company and product. What does *your* brand name and logo communicate? Is it aligned with your fundamentals?

If your fundamental values state you only use the highest-quality ingredients, is that what potential customers associate with your brand? If not, your marketing message is misaligned with your values, resulting in a negative image of your company.

If your fundamental operating procedures state prompt return of customer calls but you don't adhere to that principle, what does that say about your company? If you haven't defined your fundamental purpose, values, and operating principles, then you cannot really design an effective marketing campaign and your brand will suffer from Reputation Deficit Syndrome.

Acquisition of Customers

If your goal is the acquisition of new customers, what is the best media for your business? Billboards and print ads may raise awareness of your brand, but will they cause people to call you or come into your store? Maybe or maybe not, depending on your business and target market. The owner of a home repair and remodeling business said he quit using billboards because they never generated a customer inquiry. Branding may help with customer acquisition, but in addition you need a more direct approach to connect you with the customer. There is no right answer. Facebook or e-mail may work for one business and not another. If you know your target market and the characteristics of your customers, you can figure out the best media for acquiring new customers.

Retention of Customers

Once you have acquired customers, you must work to keep them. Developing strong personal relationships with your customers is a critical aspect of retention. Customers are less likely to leave you if they know you personally. Consider taking them to lunch and getting to know them personally. Learn about their families, hobbies, and work history. Is lunch a marketing media? Of course it is. Anything that connects you with your customers is a marketing media.

If they are geographically separated from you, call them on the phone for a short "just touching base" call. Bill Smith from Litco International in South Carolina calls his customers several times a year just to chat. This isn't a sales call; it's a friend call. His customers love him and are strongly loyal to him.

You can also send customers helpful information to enable their own business to become more successful. I frequently send helpful articles to clients.

Education of Customers

Your customers may be aware of your company and product (brand), but are they aware of all the products and services you provide? One company surveyed its customers to determine whether they were aware of all the services being offered. The results were dramatic. Most of the customers had no idea there was so much more available. If your company offers a number of different products or services, do your customers know what they are? What is the best media for educating current and potential customers about what you offer?

Which Media?

Trying to determine which media to use for each of the BARE essential goals can be a daunting task. Following is a Marketing Media Strategy Grid to assist you. When you download the form, instructions are provided. Here is a small section to give you an idea of how it works. The full grid will be displayed at the end of this chapter. You can download the full form from my website at www.rockwellbusinesssolutions.com/diagrams

Target Market	**News-paper**	
Age		
18 to 24		

In the left column under "Target Market," list all the demographics and psychographics for your target market. To the right are columns for the following media:

- Newspapers
- Networking
- Magazines
- Radio
- TV
- Logo items
- Events/trade shows
- Direct mail
- Website
- Billboards
- Referrals
- Social media
- Texts
- Blogs
- E-mail

This is not meant to be an all-inclusive list. Your business may require other media to accomplish your BARE essential goals.

For each demographic or psychographic, there are four boxes under the media. In each box, fill in the letter designation if that media will accomplish your goal (B, A, R, or E).

In the example below, if newspapers would be an appropriate media to reach eighteen- to twenty-four-year-old customers for branding, acquisition, retention, and education, fill in the appropriate letter in one of the boxes under newspapers.

If you believe newspapers are good for branding and acquisition but not for retention and education, only fill in a B and A. As you go through each demographic/psychographic for each media, you will see patterns emerge. You may discover a particular media would be suitable for branding but not for acquisition, retention, or education. If you find a media that reaches a target market demographic and/or psychographic and accomplishes all four of the BARE essentials, you've hit the jackpot.

Target Market	**News-paper**	
Age		
18 to 24	B	A
	R	E

Chapter Assignment

Complete the Marketing Media Strategy Grid below. You can download a full-size copy from my website at www.rockwellbusinesssolutions.com/diagrams. Look for patterns. Which media works best for a particular demographic or psychographic characteristic of your target market?

MARKETING MEDIA STRATEGY GRID

Target Market	News-paper	Net Working	Maga-zines	Radio	TV	Logo Items	Events/ Trade Shows	Direct Mail	Bill Boards	Face-book	Linked In	Pin-terest	Insta-gram	Blog	Texts	Email

Age (List All Applicable Age Groups):

Gender

Target Market	News-paper	Net Working	Maga-zines	Radio	TV	Logo Items	Events/ Trade Shows	Direct Mail	Bill Boards	Face-book	Linked In	Pin-terest	Insta-gram	Blog	Texts	Email
Cultural / Ethnic Groups																
Location/Climate/Region																

Target Market	News-paper	Net Working	Maga-zines	Radio	TV	Logo Items	Events/ Trade Shows	Direct Mail	Bill Boards	Face-book	Linked In	Pin-terest	Insta-gram	Blog	Texts	Email
Education																
Household Size																

Target Market	News-paper	Net Working	Maga-zines	Radio	TV	Logo Items	Events/ Trade Shows	Direct Mail	Bill Boards	Face-book	Linked In	Pin-terest	Insta-gram	Blog	Bill Boards	Texts	Email

Industries / Occupation

Company Size

Number of Employees																	
Revenues																	
Number of Departments																	
Number of Divisions																	

CHAPTER 32
REFERRAL MARKETING

"First, you have to be visible in the community. You have to get out there and connect with people. It's not called net–sitting or net–eating. It's called networking. You have to work at it."
– Ivan Misner, founder, Business Network International

For small businesses, probably the single most effective marketing strategy is referrals. As an active member of BNI since 2010, I've seen the power of referral marketing in my chapter, May River Business Networkers. In our last fiscal year, our fifty-three members reported closed business from referrals of over $8 million. BNI definitely works if members follow the proven protocols developed over the past twenty-five plus years.

Leads and referrals are two different concepts.

Leads are when you have a name, phone number, or e-mail address but don't know the person, and no one introduces you to them; that person is a lead. Converting leads into customers is a numbers game. If you cold call enough people, you will eventually get a few customers.

Referrals, on the other hand, are introductions to a potential customer by someone who knows you both. Potential customers are more likely to accept your call if their friend introduced you beforehand. By introducing you to the prospect, your friend is in effect recommending and endorsing you.

BNI compiled a study showing that 95 percent of small businesses obtain new customers from referrals. However only 5 percent of small businesses have a referral marketing strategy. Networking and referral marketing, whether through BNI or in any other form, are extremely powerful.

Referral Marketing versus Word of Mouth

Is there a difference between referral marketing and word-of-mouth advertising? Word of mouth is when you find a product or service you like and tell friends and family. Small business owners often say they built their business on word of mouth. Word of mouth is important and is part of your brand image for better or worse. Referral marketing is the act of personally introducing you to the customer. Word of mouth is passive, as no introduction is made. Referral marketing is an active strategy.

Networking is Not Selling

Networking is not selling. Networking is about building relationships. If you approach people with only the mind-set of what you can sell them, you'll likely fail. If you adopt the attitude of "How can I help people?" you will gain friends, referrals, and loyal customers.

When you meet someone, the goal is to develop a relationship with them and learn how you can help them. The BNI "Givers Gain" philosophy is based on helping others. As Zig Ziglar famously said, "You will get all you want in life if you help enough other people get what they want." If you truly listen to what people need, you will find numerous opportunities to help them.

According to a study by the Wharton School of Business, referred customers have a 16 percent higher lifetime value than other customers, and 83 percent of satisfied customers say they are willing to refer products or services.

Chapter Assignment

How do you learn networking and referral marketing? First, join a BNI chapter and take advantage of the training opportunities. Second, the founder of BNI, Dr. Ivan Misner, has written numerous books on the art of networking and referral marketing. Two of my favorites are *Networking Like a Pro* and *The World's Best Known Marketing Secret*. Third, just do it. Meeting and talking with people is a learned skill. The more you do it, the more comfortable and confident you will become.

CHAPTER 32

SUPPLY CHAIN MANAGEMENT

"Logistics is the circulatory system of the economy."
– H. Roy Austin

Supply chain management is the process of analyzing all of the costs associated with moving product from vendors, to you, and on to your customer. No matter what type of business you have, products and services are delivered to customers. Part of your marketing strategy is the delivery or distribution process.

In today's environment, customers expect immediate delivery. If ordering from your website, they want it right now. Whether you're selling to a business or an individual, managing the cost, efficiency, quality, and speed of your product/service delivery system can be a differentiator or a liability for your business. Ideally, you want to minimize the logistics cost both to your company and to your customer, and you also want to minimize the time to deliver the product.

You also need to ensure that the product arrives in good condition. Have you ever ordered something from a website and it arrived damaged? What does that do to the brand image of the supplier, not to mention the additional cost of accepting the return of the merchandise and re-shipping to the customer? In the process, the customer is inconvenienced by spending their time mailing it back. Do you want to inconvenience your customer?

If you are ordering something from China, what is the total cost of getting it from Peking to your location? That total delivery cost includes transportation like ocean freight and trucking, customs entry fees, special permit fees, and import duties. Some companies focus solely on the customs entry fee charged by their broker instead of the total cost of the move, when in fact that entry fee is a small portion of the total cost.

On the flip side, what about the shipping and handling you charge the customer? If it is too high relative to the product cost, your customer may seek another vendor.

Excellence in logistics and supply chain management are an essential part of your company's competitive advantage.

Chapter Assignment

Write down your distribution and delivery process. Put it in the form of a flow chart showing all the intermediate steps in the process. How can the process be improved? Where can costs be cut or delivery times be shortened?

CHAPTER 33
SALES EFFECTIVENESS

"Treat the little customer as if he was a big customer and he will stay with you when he grows up." – Roy L. Smith, American author and clergyman

Through your marketing efforts, potential customers are now aware of your business and are interested in talking with you. Now you want to convert a potential customer into a paying customer.

Customer Conversion

Your CIS provides critical information. One business owner was excited about the number of hits to his new website. I asked how many calls he received as a result of those hits, and of those calls, how many did he get the opportunity on which to bid? And from the bids he submitted, how many of them became customers? His response was, "I don't know."

The old adage that you can't manage what you don't track is true. How could he ascertain the number of calls received from people viewing his website? Simple. Ask the people calling or coming into your store how they heard about you. You don't need a sophisticated CRM program for this. Keep a simple log on a piece of paper or in a spreadsheet to track the following:

- "How did you find out about us?" This will tell you which media is producing the best results. If they came from a referral or word of mouth, thank the person who provided the referral.
- Of the calls received, how many did you get to bid or quote?
- Of the bids or quotes, how many were accepted?

If you don't know your track record in converting potential customers into actual customers, how can you improve the process?

How will you know if your sales efforts and salespeople are being effective?

Customer Acquisition Cost

This is the cost incurred to acquire a new customer. Add up all costs associated with acquiring a new customer and divide by the number of new customers for a specific time period. Potential investors are particularly interested in this metric. Here again, a good accountant can help you, because there are probably costs associated with customer acquisition of which you aren't aware.

Chapter Assignment

1. Create a process to track your customer conversion rate.
2. Calculate your customer acquisition cost and track it over time. Is it getting more or less expensive to acquire new customers?

CHAPTER 34
CUSTOMER SERVICE

"If you do build a great experience, customers tell each other about that. Word of mouth is very powerful." – Jeff Bezos, founder, Amazon

Even though customer service is an expectation and not a differentiator, your business cannot overlook the importance of providing excellent customer service. Customers won't stay if they feel unappreciated or poorly served.

If your product or service is the perfect brand, you don't have to worry about customer service. I define the perfect brand as a product or service everyone wants, where there is no competition and customer service is horrible, but customers still purchase. Would you like to have the perfect brand? Impossible, you say. I found such a product that fit this description of a perfect brand.

A few years ago, my wife, Sharron, and I took a bus tour of Alaska and the Yukon Territory in Canada. Every two hours, the bus stopped at interesting places with unforgettable scenic beauty or at fascinating and unique shops. One place at which we stopped was famous for its cinnamon buns. I had just had a nice breakfast and I wasn't hungry, but I love cinnamon buns so I couldn't pass up the opportunity.

As we made our way toward the store, our tour director cautioned us that the owner of the establishment was not a particularly pleasant person and he had strict rules about how you conducted yourself in his establishment. She compared him to the "Soup Nazi" character featured in an episode of *Seinfeld*.

The minute we entered the door, we were ordered to line up on the left. When we reached the counter, he barked at us in a most unfriendly voice, "Whaddaya want?" We purchased a cinnamon bun and here is what we got ...

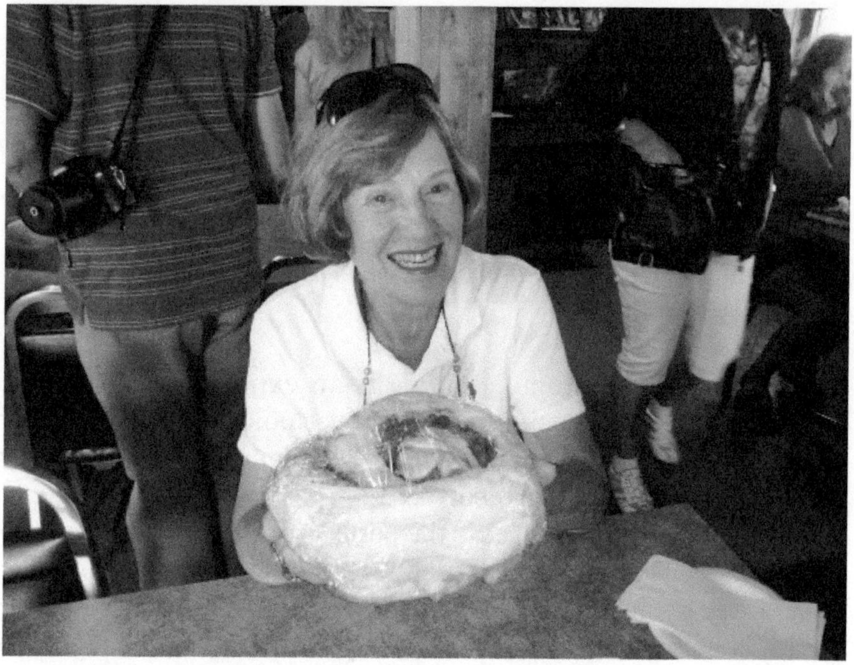

This was hands-down the best and largest cinnamon bun I'd ever eaten—and we feasted on it for three days.

The tour director said that during one visit, a helicopter landed, two men got out, bought two buns each, and flew off. These cinnamon buns are a product that everyone wants, the business has no competition, and customer service isn't a factor. If the owner had nearby competition, he'd be forced to make outstanding customer service a fundamental operating principle. The owner can ignore customer service because he knows a very high percentage of his customers, perhaps 90 percent, will not return to his area. He also knows that his few repeat customers will return because they live nearby (or they have access to a helicopter) and the exceptional quality of the cinnamon buns lures them back.

His underwhelming customer service has zero influence on his customer numbers; it's all about quality cinnamon buns. He has a captive audience on the route between Whitehorse and Dawson City, putting him exactly where the tour buses and ice road truckers need a break.

Making sure your customer service is at an exemplary level may seem like a waste of time, money, and effort, but reconsider. Unless you are located in some equally remote place, you have competition. To survive, you must be better and different from the competition. What is it that you have to compete for first and foremost to survive? Customers. Customer service helps keep customers returning.

How do you improve customer service? Customer service is a process containing multiple elements depending on the type of business or industry you're in. Analyze and document all the elements of your customer service. How can you make the customer feel appreciated? How can you process orders faster? One of Port City Logistics' fundamental values is, "Do whatever it takes to get the customer what they want, when they want it."

Study the competition. Damian Hayes of British Open Pub says, "I learn from others, particularly other restaurants."

Chapter Assignment

Identify all the touchpoints where you or your employees interact with customers, including indirect contact through marketing media. Brainstorm with your team to determine how to improve every aspect of customer service.

Continuous learning is a key element to improve customer service. Attend seminars, and read books and articles on customer service. An excellent book is *Customers for Life* by Carl Sewell.

CHAPTER 35
MARKETING SUMMARY

"Marketing is too important to be left to the marketing department." – David Packard, American businessman

How many of your employees are involved in your marketing? The answer is ... all of them! Every employee in your organization represents your business in every facet of their lives.

This section has helped stimulate your thinking about the various aspects of marketing and selling your product or service. Marketing is critical to the success of every business, regardless of size. For small businesses, because of limited time and resources, marketing is a challenge.

Ideally, you will design your marketing before opening your doors. Planning the marketing prior to commencement of the business will help ensure that you have a good strategy that is aligned with your fundamentals. Once open for business, you will be so busy working *in* the business that it will be hard to find time to work *on* the business.

If you are already open, don't stress. You can still design an effective marketing plan. If you've built your business house correctly and put together a strong marketing program that is in line with your fundamentals, then you can build a spectacular business house.

Chapter Assignment

Adopt the Ten Commandments of Good Business:

1. Customers and employees are the most important people in any business.
2. Customers are not dependent on us; we are dependent on them.
3. Customers are not an interruption of our work; they are the purpose of it.
4. Customers do us a favor when they call; we don't do them a favor by serving them.
5. Customers are a part of our business, not outsiders.
6. Customers are not a cold statistic; they are flesh-and-blood human beings with feelings and emotions like ours.
7. Customers are not people with whom to argue or match wits.
8. Customers bring us their wants; it is our job to fill those wants.

9. Customers are deserving of the most courteous and attentive treatment.
10. Customers are the life-blood of this and every other business.

SECTION 7

NAVIGATING IN THE SWAMP

CHAPTER 36

SECTION INTRODUCTION

"Any difficult task seems easier if you break it down into manageable steps." – Claire B. May and Gordon S. May, authors

Navigating the Business Swamp requires a map. A map tells us where we've been, where we are, and which route to choose to achieve our vision. That map is your financial information. Your financial information will help you find the best route through the swamp. If things are really bad, you will of course know it. When alligators start chomping on your boat, you know you're in a desperate situation. This situation could be the bank showing up to foreclose on your mortgage, having no cash to pay the bills, or a having a major customer leave, just to name a few.

Waiting until alligators start chomping on your boat is not a good strategy for long-term success. Wouldn't it be better to change course to avoid the alligators before they become a problem? Your financial statements and the information contained in them can help you spot potential problems and chart a course through the swamp.

CHAPTER 37

WHY ACCOUNTING?

"You gotta know your numbers." – Robert Herjavec, *Shark Tank*

One of the biggest mistakes small business owners make is not paying enough attention to the numbers. Here is a quote from the book *Shark Tank: Jump Start Your Business* by Michael Parrish DuDell: "You don't need to be an accountant, but if you don't know your numbers, you can't run a business. It's that simple."

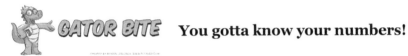

You gotta know your numbers!

In this chapter we will discuss the Accounting Information System (AIS), which is a part of the fundamental information systems foundational plank. Relax. There are no numbers, financial statements, and metrics—yet. That comes later.

Whether you enjoy working with numbers or not, it is absolutely imperative that you understand and manage your AIS. Failure to manage the financial side of the business is a major cause of business failure.

Here is a true story to dramatize my point. A man—let's call him Bubba—received a substantial inheritance. He had minimal business experience but assumed he was knowledgeable.

He bought several small businesses, the largest of which was a manufacturing plant purchased from a major Fortune 500 company. Sadly, Bubba knew nothing about manufacturing and didn't do proper due diligence before purchasing the plant. Due diligence, as it relates to buying a business, is the process of taking all reasonable steps to investigate and evaluate the company to be acquired so the purchaser can make an informed decision. One of these steps should be a full and complete audit of the financial records as well as investigation into the company's employees, target market, and operations, so you can determine if purchasing the company is a sound business decision.

Bubba didn't like accountants, so there was no financial audit. Had an audit been done, it would have revealed a number of provisions in the purchase agreement that made it almost impossible for Bubba's new plant to succeed.

Upon purchasing the plant, Bubba proceeded to contact potential customers, many of whom suggested that next year they would buy 1 or 2 million cases of product. No purchase orders or contracts were signed; he just had a hint that business might be heading his way.

Being the eternal optimist, Bubba started making extensive upgrades to the plant and hired additional employees in anticipation of the business that would come "next year." What Bubba didn't understand was that the potential customers were just lining up sources to supply them *if* they needed an additional supplier.

Bubba boasted to all that in the next year, production and sales would quadruple. In manufacturing, a four-fold increase in production is unrealistic in most situations. Additionally, the raw materials and finished product at Bubba's plant required an air conditioned environment. To further compound the situation, the warehouse was full at current production levels, and no climate controlled warehouse was within one hundred miles of Bubba's plant.

Bubba enticed his banker to join him as the "business manager" for all of the companies he had bought. As things spiraled down at Bubba's plant, he hired three different consultants for advice. All of these consultants, as well as his controller (chief accountant) and business manager, told him the same thing: "If you could quadruple production, you would just be at break-even." That wasn't what our man wanted to hear.

Eventually Bubba's business manager resigned because he was being asked to perform duties he considered unethical. His controller resigned when illegal activities were requested. The company went bankrupt, and excellent employees lost their jobs because Bubba ignored the financial information.

How much money had Bubba inherited? Astoundingly, he'd inherited $30 million, and in just six years it was all gone. Having adequate capital to finance the business was not the problem.

The moral of the story of Bubba is that an arrogant attitude of "I know everything I need to know" and ignoring the financial information is a huge roadblock to success. Successful companies all have positive and realistic attitudes, and a good dose of humility.

You can learn what is necessary to start and succeed in your business, including accounting—and humbleness.

Chapter Assignment

Whether or not you are a numbers person, make a pact with yourself to learn the financial side of your business and adopt the Business Owners' Commandment: "Know thy numbers."

If you are new to accounting it may seem a little overwhelming at first. I've tried to keep the discussion simple and easy to understand. However, sometimes, another author can say the same thing using different words and it all makes sense. Two books on accounting that may help you are:

Simple Numbers-Straight Talk, Big Profits by Greg Crabtree

Accounting for the Numberphobic, A Survival Guide for Small Business Owners by Dawn Fotopulos

Both of these books have interesting stories and easy to understand examples. Making accounting entertaining and exciting is a daunting task. Hopefully, the chapters in this section will enable you to understand accounting and these two books will further your knowledge and comprehension. To navigate the business swamp, you absolutely have to know your numbers, NO EXCUSES. Imagine being suddenly transported to a foreign country with no money, no identification, no map, and no cell phone. You would be lost with no way to figure out where to go or anyone with whom to communicate.

CHAPTER 38

MY ACCOUNTANT HANDLES THIS!

"The buck stops here." – Harry S. Truman

"Roy, can't I just let my accountant take care of all this numbers stuff?"

Sorry, but the buck stops on the owner's desk for managing the financial aspects of the business. As Dawn Fotopulos points out in *Accounting for the Numberphobic*, "You can hire someone to do your accounting but you can't hire someone to understand your numbers."

Many businesses fail because they run out of money. Conventional wisdom says that they were under-capitalized, which is a fancy way of saying that they didn't start with enough money. While under-capitalization may be the problem, more often the bigger problem is how the cash is managed. Remember Bubba? He had plenty of money at the outset.

Of the successful companies interviewed for this book, all indicated the importance of properly managing their cash. Each understood that cash management required understanding enough about their financials to know where to look, what to look for, and how to use the information. John Curry, CEO of Sweetener Solutions, put it this way, "We were engineers by background, not financial people. But we had to learn the finance and accounting side of the business in order to survive, grow, and prosper."

A prime illustration is a business owner who didn't suitably manage her accountant. She needed to put together financial statements to obtain a bank loan for new equipment. Her financial records contained only revenues and receivables. She was using her *QuickBooks* to invoice customers and nothing else. There were virtually no expenses, no assets, and no loan liabilities being recorded. Needless to say, there *were* expenses, assets, and loan liabilities; they just weren't on the books.

The financial transactions were reconstructed and recorded except for one thing—how much cash did the company have? Determining the cash balance required reconciliation of the bank statements to the check register. The owner said her CPA reconciled the bank statement. The CPA was asked for the most recent bank reconciliation. He replied, "I've been really busy, and I haven't reconciled the bank statement in three years." Who is at fault here? If you answered, "The business owner," you nailed it. You can delegate the responsibility for any business task, but you—the owner—are responsible for assuring tasks are completed properly and on time.

You—the owner—must manage your accountant.

Chapter Assignment

Create a checklist of things you need to monitor and review to manage your accounting and your finances. As you go through the chapters in this section, add items to the checklist.

If your checkbook register isn't up to date, get it done. If you don't know how much money you have, you are rowing blindly through the swamp.

CHAPTER 39

THE PURPOSE OF FINANCIAL INFORMATION

"Being great at numbers isn't a requirement for being an entrepreneur. You must, however, have a decent understanding of certain numbers that affect the daily life of your business. Although it is tempting to outsource all of your financial tasks, there are certain fundamentals that every small business owner must understand to run a successful business." – Michael Parrish DuDell, author, *Shark Tank: Jump Start Your Business*

The goal of every business is first and foremost to improve cash flow and reach the point where cash is available for you, the owner. What about profits, shareholder value, and return on assets? If a business doesn't have cash, it dies. A business can earn profits and still run out of cash, which we will talk about later.

There are two ways for you to get a return on your investment. You can take a distribution, which means you withdraw money from the business. Distributions are not salary, but are similar to a major corporation declaring a dividend. The other way for owners to realize a return on their investment is to sell the business.

However, all too often business owners siphon money out of their business to enhance their personal lifestyle. They take distributions even though important business needs aren't addressed, which handicaps future success and salability of the business.

Mike McCarthy, managing principal for Hancock Askew, the largest public accounting firm in Savannah, Georgia, comments, "It is interesting that most business owners who buy planes end up doing very poorly. I think it indicates a spending pattern of excess distributions from the business."

Berry Edwards, president and owner of Island Tire, has the philosophy, "We decided that we would not take any dividends until we were debt free and had sufficient cash reserves in order to be prepared for significant challenges to the business."

Understanding the financial side of your business enables you to determine when to take distributions (get a return on your investment) and the appropriate amount. If the business doesn't survive, there are no future returns, so take care of your business first and you will be able to afford almost any lifestyle you want.

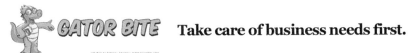

Take care of business needs first.

In section 10, there is a tool for determining when to take your return. Here's a clue: You—the owner—get your return after you have taken care of all the essential business needs.

Chapter Assignment

Make a list of all the current and future needs of your business. As you progress through this section, add to the list.

CHAPTER 40

FINANCIAL INFORMATION'S USEFULNESS

"Financial decisions are too important to be left up to financial people." – Jack Stack, author, *The Great Game of Business*

The reality is that you don't manage a company based solely on what is reflected in the financial statements. However, you do need concise statements in order to make informed decisions.

Even with perfect information, you can still make the wrong decision. The variables and unknowns can make finding the right path difficult. However, can you make a good business decision with flawed—or no—financial information? You can if you're very lucky, but luck is not a reliable business strategy.

It is impossible to make a good decision with bad information.

Why do sports teams keep score? They want to know if they are winning or losing. Also, they want to know *why* they are winning, so they can keep winning or prevent losing. Your financial statements are your scoreboard and contain the details to improve your score.

The hit movie *Moneyball* chronicles the Oakland Athletics baseball team under general manager Billy Beane. He studied computer analyses of his players' statistics. By using those numbers, he developed a strategy that allowed the 2002 team to compete with the New York Yankees (who had a virtually unlimited payroll) despite a meager A's budget. His method took the team to the playoffs, and at one point late in the season they won twenty consecutive games, an American League record. This principle of understanding and analyzing the numbers also applies to business.

To take advantage of your strengths and improve upon your weaknesses, you must know where you are strong and where you are weak. Extract data from your AIS to create performance metrics with target goals. What kind of goals? A performance metric measures a particular business activity to help you determine why you are winning or losing. It could be a purely financial metric, or it could be a cross of financial and non-financial data such as revenue per square foot in a retail store.

Billy Robinson, president of Port City Logistics, says, "We track everything so we know what is causing results and we can figure out how to improve." When Billy says *everything*, he means *everything*, and not just financial data. If his warehouses can decrease the amount of time it takes to unload and load cargo, then he can increase his capacity to handle more business (increased revenues) and decrease costs (accomplishing more with the same people and equipment).

Mike Reeves of Espy Lumber is also fanatical on tracking. Espy has weekly meetings to go over the numbers. In Mike's own words, "We go over each and every line item of expense every month." It isn't enough for Mike to know whether the business has profits; he wants to know why they have profits and what can be done to improve them. The building industry is cyclical, so it is important to detect trends before they become problems.

In his book *The Great Game of Business*, Jack Stack, founder of Springfield Remanufacturing Company, encourages his readers to look at their business as a game. As in any game, there are winners and losers, and he includes some heartwarming stories about people and companies that have overcome great odds or come from way behind to win.

Every employee at Springfield Remanufacturing has a responsibility for a particular line item on the profit and loss statement (P&L). The company is so successful that people come from all over the world to study it.

If successful people and businesses emphasize the importance of knowing the score—and what is causing the score—then shouldn't you be doing the same? If you don't know the score, how can you develop a winning strategy?

Your financial statements are largely historical documents reporting past activity and results. Even so, they hold a treasure trove of information that can make or break your future. Put it in the archives and it becomes useless. Understand the information and use it intelligently, which will increase the probability that your future financial performance will be improved.

If you think of your AIS as the scoreboard for your business, accounting information can become pretty interesting (and maybe even exciting).

Don't be intimidated by the idea of learning a perhaps unfamiliar subject like accounting. Remember, change is constant and in today's modern world the pace of change continues to increase. Realize that you're actually learning new things constantly. No one can assimilate all the changes, but you can improve your knowledge base and learn to use information and tools crucial to your success. Be open to learning, even if you have significant accounting knowledge. New information, ideas, or ways of looking at things can benefit your business. Remember, each of your foundational fundamental planks are of equal importance.

Chapter Assignment

Ask yourself, "Does my current AIS give me all the information I need to make sound business decisions?" Make a list of gaps in your AIS and in your knowledge of accounting. Remember, you don't need to be an accountant; you just need to know where to look, what to look for, and how to use the information.

CHAPTER 41
TYPES OF ACCOUNTANTS

"An accountant is someone who tells you about a problem that you didn't know you had and explains it in a way you don't understand." – Popular accounting joke

When hiring an accountant, it is imperative to find the appropriate person for your business needs. Due to limited resources, small businesses need to be shrewd in selecting an accountant who is qualified, affordable, and reliable. The following will help you differentiate among bookkeepers, management accountants, public accountants, and CPAs.

You can either hire an employee or contract with a firm to help with your accounting. You may not need a full-time person, in which case contracting with an accountant can be a cost-effective solution. You may be able to do the customer invoicing and vendor payments yourself, and then contract with someone to be an outsourced CFO. A good option for an outsourced CFO is a retired accounting executive who wants to work part time, as these retirees have vast experience and are relatively inexpensive.

BOOKKEEPERS

A bookkeeper records the day-to-day financial transactions of the business, including invoicing customers, recording bills from vendors, paying vendors, preparing payroll, receiving payments from customers, and depositing funds. Some bookkeepers simply record transactions, while others offer more comprehensive services such as payroll and preparation of financial statements and reports.

The level of knowledge and experience with bookkeepers varies dramatically. The American Institute of Professional Bookkeepers offers Certified Bookkeeper designation to candidates who pass a four-part examination and have two years' full-time experience.

PUBLIC ACCOUNTANTS

Public accountant is a globally recognized term for all accountants serving the public, whether in practice, commerce, industry, government, or the education sector. Many public accountants are members of the Institute of Public Accountants. Dun & Bradstreet's international definition of public accountant is: "Independent Public Accountants perform many functions, including auditing financial statements, designing financial accounting systems, assisting in managerial accounting function, providing managerial advisory services, and tax preparation. The Public Accountant may perform services for corporations, partnerships, individuals, and other organizations."(Http://cmaindia.informe.com/forum/management-tips-articles-education-humor-f21/what-is-a-public-accountant-t6773.html)

CERTIFIED PUBLIC ACCOUNTANTS

Certified public accountant (CPA) is a designation given by the American Institute of Certified Public Accountants to those who pass an exam and meet work experience requirements.

If your company is growing and the tax returns are becoming more complicated, my recommendation is to hire a firm employing several CPAs to do your taxes. A larger firm will usually be more expensive but will have people with a diversity of experience that a small firm doesn't have. Some CPA firms also offer other services such as payroll, bookkeeping, and business valuation, but their primary focus is taxes and audits.

MANAGEMENT ACCOUNTANTS

The Institute of Management Accounting (IMA) defines management accounting as "a profession that involves partnering in management decision-making, devising planning and performance management systems, and providing expertise in financial reporting and control to assist management in the formulation and implementation of an organization's strategy." (http://www.imanet.org/docs/default-source/thought_leadership/transforming_the_finance_function/definition_of_management_accounting.

pdf?sfvrsn=2) My definition is that the management accountant's job is to determine why the financial results are what they are and work with the owner or management team to develop a strategy for improving results.

Most management accountants are employees of a business and are involved in all aspects of accounting, including everything from posting transactions to preparing financial information reports to help the company make better decisions. They fit into the broad category of "staff accountants," and most have a college degree in accounting and are highly competent.

IMA has certification programs where an accountant can earn the Certified Management Accountant (CMA) designation. Regardless of what level of accountant you hire, they all must be supervised.

If your company can't afford a full-time management accountant, an alternative solution would be to contract with a retired management accountant for a few hours a month.

Payroll Accounting

Small businesses frequently ask who should be doing their payroll. Should they hire employees or contract with a company that provides payroll services?

Doing payroll involves more than writing checks to employees. Social security and income taxes must be withheld from employees' pay and remitted to the IRS. There may be additional withholdings like wage garnishments, insurance premiums, and 401k contributions. Quarterly and annual reports also need to be filed with the state and the Federal Government.

My recommendation is to hire a competent payroll provider. I emphasize *competent* because there are some incompetent providers. You want to be sure that your payroll is done correctly and all legal requirements are met. In one case, every single payroll for two years had an error and the provider was finally replaced.

Doing it "in-house" is usually not a good idea. Most small businesses don't have time to stay abreast of all the legal requirements or invest in the IT systems necessary to track everything related to payroll. Also, where is your time best spent? Do you have the time and money to spend resolving discrepancies with government entities?

When I joined D. J. Powers, we did payroll in-house. The accounting manager was Maria Fernandez, and she was efficient and mistakes were extremely rare. However, one year the State of Georgia determined there was a discrepancy when comparing our quarterly reports to the annual report to the IRS. We endured two and a half years of constant phone calls, letters, and transmission of records before the state finally agreed there was no discrepancy. What a waste of our time! This experience convinced us to outsource our payroll, and Maria was then able to devote her valuable time to other duties.

Which Type of Accountant Should You Use?

A good approach is having a bookkeeper to enter transactions, a management accountant (either full or part time) to prepare financial statements and reports and develop key performance indicators (KPIs), and a CPA to do your taxes.

For a CPA firm, I recommend finding one that has at least five employees. Many sole practitioners can do the job, but if they are sick or injured, their clients are left with no one to perform the services.

The distinction between a public accountant and a management accountant is important. Your public accountant's job is to ensure your taxes are correct and (if they are doing an audit) to determine if the transactions are properly recorded and accurately reflect the financial position of the company. In other words, are your bottom-line profits correct and are your assets and liabilities accurate? A management accountant's job is to ascertain why your profits or losses are what they are, how to improve profits, and how to improve cash flow. All too often, public accountants focus on tax minimization, which is important, but tax strategy should never trump business strategy.

Chapter Assignment

Do you have an accountant? If you are doing the accounting yourself, is that the best use of your time and qualifications?

Do you have the correct accounting personnel in place to meet the needs of your business? If not, start researching options for obtaining qualified and competent help.

CHAPTER 42

FINDING THE RIGHT ACCOUNTANT

"Risk comes from not knowing what you're doing." – Warren Buffett

Skimping on an accountant, or hiring the least expensive bookkeeper, is a bad business decision. You will inevitably get what you pay for. Invest in hiring a qualified account for your team. The cost may be higher initially, but in the long run a good accountant will save you more money than you pay them.

Another cost saving technique is to do it yourself (DIY). Perhaps you have the capability to do your own accounting, but is that a good idea? Could I do my own electrical, plumbing, car repair, website design, signage, home inspection, legal work, landscaping, human resources, information technology, and still find time to edit my own book? Possibly, at some basic level. But should I? The results will be less than optimal, and what if I do it poorly?

The cost of short-term savings is in the long-term consequences. "Do it right or do it over" applies to your business accounting just as it does with other aspects of life.

Does DIY accounting, or the cheapest bookkeeper, really save you money? As the old Fram Oil Filter ads used to say, "Pay me now or pay me later." Can you do your own accounting? Yes, but *should* you do your own accounting? If you have an accounting background or you're a small company with only a couple of employees, it may be feasible in the short term, but is it the best use of your time? Doing your own accounting robs time from marketing, networking, finding customers, production work, managing employees, and selling your services or product.

Let me guess—you are doing the accounting at night or on weekends. Is that really how you want to spend your free time? Is it fair to your family and friends? Isn't it more productive to devote your time to making improvements, working *on* your business?

Accounting tracks your financial status and becomes history. Working on your business in other areas will pay dividends in the future. If you are audited by the IRS, which can and does occur, you may spend days, weeks, and possibly months trying to resolve issues with the auditor. Can you afford to? Bottom line, accounting is necessary and important, but you don't make money doing accounting. You make money providing products and services to your customers. What is the best allocation of your time?

The right accountant knows there is more to accounting than just posting financial transactions. Accountants can prepare financial statements for various uses like bank loan applications or investor presentations. The right accountant can create financial reports that are more useful for internal management.

The important questions are:

1. Why did we have the financial performance we did?
2. What can we do to improve financial performance?

To answer these questions, your accountant can "get underneath the numbers." A popular buzz word today for this is "analytics," which means determining what is causing financial results. Only then can you do something to improve performance. Your accountant should be a member of your executive team and a partner in helping set strategy.

The right accountant will save you money. They can scrutinize your vendor invoices to find out if and where you may have been overcharged. They can negotiate better prices with vendors, better interest rates with banks, or better deals with insurance carriers. They frequently discover unnecessary expenditures, spot trends in both revenues and expenses (especially if they're going in the wrong direction), and help determine the cause as well as how to turn things around. The right accountant makes sure everything billable actually gets billed. Customers are not going to call you to say, "You forgot to bill me for the widgets."

A common problem for many small businesses is failure to invoice for services rendered, especially if customers are invoiced once a week or once a month. Documents for invoicing can and do get lost or misplaced.

How do you know if you have a competent accountant? Your accountant should have certain skills and be able to provide some basic services. Interview several accountants and determine whether they can perform the following tasks. These questions are based on personal experience. As with every occupation, all accountants are not equally competent.

- If she can't reconcile your bank statement, you probably have the wrong accountant.
- If he doesn't know what generally accepted accounting principles (GAAP) are, you probably have the wrong accountant.
- If she can't prepare a cash flow statement, you probably have the wrong accountant.
- If he can't prepare a P&L or balance sheet comparing one time period to another, you probably have the wrong accountant.
- If she doesn't know how to capitalize and depreciate fixed assets, you probably have the wrong accountant.
- If he doesn't know that a loan payment has two components (principal and interest), you probably have the wrong accountant.
- If she doesn't understand depreciation and amortization, you probably have the wrong accountant.
- If he doesn't know why pre-tax profit and cash flow are not the same thing, you probably have the wrong accountant.
- If she can't help you devise KPIs (Key Performance Indicators) for your business, you probably have the wrong accountant.
- If he can't prepare financial statements to submit to banks when applying for a loan, you probably have the wrong accountant.
- If she can't prepare charts that show trends for KPIs, or various line item accounts on your P&L or balance sheet, you probably have the wrong accountant.
- If he can't help you prepare a forecast, you probably have the wrong accountant.

Chapter Assignment

Do you currently have a competent accountant in place? If not, begin a search to find the accountant who will best serve your business.

CHAPTER 43

DON'T SHOOT THE MESSENGER!

"Truth is like the sun. You can shut it out for a time, but it ain't goin' away." – Elvis Presley

Accountants dislike reporting bad financial results. It's no fun to be the bearer of bad news. However, the accountant's job is to report the facts, positive or negative, and to work with the executive team to develop a plan to improve the financial performance of the company.

When the numbers tell a negative story, it's a golden opportunity to make things better. A wise leader seizes this opportunity to turn the ship around and knows that when you assess AIS data, in combination with other information, it can exponentially increase the likelihood of determining successful solutions.

Fixing the problem does not mean reworking the numbers; it means reworking the behaviors and decisions that created the numbers. Remember, the numbers are just a reflection of what is going on *in* the business.

Never be afraid of your financial information. Business owners who ignore financial information they don't like and deny it or get angry about it, are only making things worse by not addressing it. The so-called leader who exhibits anger and frustration toward the accountant reporting undesirable numbers isn't likely to succeed.

One owner didn't like what the financial statements reported, so he fired the CFO. The CFO had to be the problem, so the obvious solution was to replace the "wrong" CFO with one who would report better numbers. Over the course of an eight-year period, this business went through seven CFOs. Did the owner ever solve the problem and "fix" the numbers? No. The business ended up declaring bankruptcy.

Decision makers need to know the truth and need to have the strength, courage, and intelligence to accept it. It's the only way to solve difficult problems. Your accountant or CFO should be part of your executive team to provide a unique perspective anchored in a reality not everyone can see.

Your accountant can provide a strong counterbalance to purely creative suggestions. You need both the pragmatic and creative on your leadership team. Your CFO will be motivated by the enjoyment of working with numbers and projections, and the excitement of developing a plan for your business success.

The moral of the story is that your CFO/accountant is an excellent asset with the invaluable ability to understand the language and relevance of those numbers. Whether you employ a bookkeeper, accountant, or CFO, utilize this resource. Embrace positive and negative financial results as opportunities.

Chapter Assignment

Whether it is good or bad news, seek the financial truth. Review all of your financial information on a regular basis. I asked Mike Reeves, president of Espy Lumber, "How do you have time to track all this stuff?" He replied, "How can you *not* take time? How do you know where you stand if you don't track your financial information? You have to *make* the time."

Make time to understand and review your financial information.

CHAPTER 44

INTRODUCTION TO FINANCIAL STATEMENTS

"If you don't have time to do it right, when will you have time to do it over?" – John Wooden

David Williams is a CPA on Hilton Head Island and a member of my BNI chapter. A new client of his said he hadn't filed an income tax return in years and was concerned the IRS would show up eventually. He asked David, "How much do I owe the IRS?" David replied, "Let's take a look at your financial statement and figure out your tax liability." The man replied, "What are financial statements?"

To better understand your business accounting, think about your own personal finances. In many ways, your personal accounting and financial statements are similar to your business accounting and financial statements.

If you organize your personal finances the same way as a business, it may help you better understand your business financials. There are three basic financial statements:

1. Profit and loss statement or P&L (sometimes called an income statement)
2. Balance sheet or BS (sometimes called a statement of assets and liabilities)
3. Cash flow statement

How would you organize your personal finances into these three statements?

Profit and Loss Statement

Your P&L statement is simply revenues minus expenses for a specific period of time (month, quarter, or year). If revenues exceed expenses, there is profit; if not, a loss. For you personally, what would fit into the categories of revenues and expenses?

Revenues

What revenues do you personally have? Revenues for a business would come from sales of a product or service. On a personal level, revenues could include salaries and wages, interest from a certificate of deposit (CD), or dividends from a stock.

Expenses

What expenses do you have? Expenses are the products and services you buy. Look at your checkbook, bank statement, or credit card statement to see who you pay. If you pay cash for everything, hopefully you keep receipts. In the interest of simplicity, let's assume your only expenses are rent, utilities, food, and car.

Personal P&L Statement

Using just the elements of revenue/income and expenses listed above, your personal P&L might be as follows:

Fred's P&L for Month of July 2016

Revenues:	
Wages	$2,000
Interest Income	10
Dividend Income	20
Total Revenue	$2,030
Expenses:	
Rent	$800
Utilities	250
Food	500
Car	400
Total Expenses	$1,950
Pre-Tax Net Profit or (Loss)	$80

Yes, Fred had a profit. Does this mean that he has $80 more in the bank at the end of the month than he started with at the beginning of the month? Not necessarily, but we'll address that later. Your personal P&L is fairly simple, isn't it?

Revenues/Income minus Expense = Pre-Tax Net Profit/(Loss)

Profits will be referred to as "pre-tax net profit," which are the profits before federal or state income taxes are considered. The word "loss" is in parenthesis, or what you may call "brackets." Accountants often put negative numbers in parenthesis, so if Fred had a loss, it would appear as $(80).

Your personal P&L details financial transactions during a specific time period (in this example, one month). The P&L organizes financial transactions that occurred during the month into categories of revenue and expense.

Your personal or business P&L can be as detailed or as simple as you like. Some people prefer more detail so they know where they are spending their money. In the example we just used, you could break down "Utilities" into gas, electric, and water, and "Car" into fuel and maintenance. More detail makes it easier to spot anomalies. For instance, what if one month the water bill spiked up dramatically? An investigation might reveal a leak. If the water bill had been combined together with electricity and gas, the jump would have been less noticeable.

Balance Sheet

Your balance sheet reports your financial position at a point in time. In other words, what are you worth as of July 31 this year? The BS consists of three major categories: assets, liabilities, and equity. Equity is sometimes referred to as net worth.

The message of the balance sheet is that if you converted all of your assets into cash and then used the cash to pay off all your liabilities (debts), how much money would you have left. In other words, what are you worth in a financial sense? The answer to that question is constantly changing because financial transactions are constantly occurring. The value of your CD changes every day, and the value of what you may own in shares of a stock or bond changes every minute. Since creating a balance sheet minute by minute would be impractical, pick a specific time, such as midnight on the last day of the month, and create a BS as of that moment in time.

What are your personal assets and liabilities today? If your assets are greater than liabilities, you have positive equity or net worth.

<u>Assets</u>

Assets are things you *own*. Ask yourself, "What do I own?" Personal assets would include items like cash (either in your wallet or in the bank), investments like a CD or savings account, money owed to you (maybe you loaned your brother some money—accountants call these receivables), and physical belongings like furniture, appliances, a car, or a house. Shares in a business would also be an asset. The example of Fred's P&L above showed a rent expense, so we'll assume he doesn't own a house.

Liabilities

Liabilities are what you *owe*, or in other words, debts. Liabilities can be short term or long term in nature. Short-term liabilities might include the balance due each month on your credit card. Long-term liabilities include the balance you owe on a car loan, home equity loan, or mortgage (debts you are repaying over a period of years).

Balance Sheet Statement

Fred's Balance Sheet as of July 31, 2016

ASSETS:	
Cash	$1,500
Certificate of Deposit	5,000
Shares in Home Depot	5,000
Receivable from brother	1,000
Car	15,000
TOTAL ASSETS	$27,500
LIABILTIES:	
Credit card debt	$1,000
Loan balance on car	7,500
TOTAL LIABILITIES	$8,500
EQUITY OR NET WORTH	$19,000

If Fred converts all of his assets into cash (collected from his brother, cashed in the CD, and sold his Home Depot stock) and then paid off his credit card and car loan, he would have $19,000 left over. Fred's financial net worth in this example is $19,000.

Organizing your personal finances into a P&L and balance sheet is fairly simple. Your business P&L and BS are conceptually the same.

The only difference is that your business has to adhere to the rules and guidelines of GAAP (Generally Accepted Accounting Principles).

Comparability

What is missing in the example? Wouldn't you want to know if your personal financial situation is improving? Financial statements have minimal value unless you make comparisons. For your personal P&L, what are the previous months' (or years') revenues and expenses? Remember the water bill? Knowing what it is normally will indicate if the current month makes sense. Are you consistently having a pre-tax net profit or loss? On the balance sheet, is your personal net worth increasing or decreasing? This information prompts you to ask why things are changing. Knowing why changes are occurring enables you to make corrections. To manage the financial side of your business, you don't need to be an accountant; you just need to know where to look, what to look for, and how to use the information.

Know where to look, what to look for, and how to use the information.

Cash Flow Statement

Recall that Fred had a pre-tax net profit of $80. However, this doesn't necessarily mean that his cash balance went up by $80. Fred's P&L showed food purchases of $500 for the month. What if Fred charged some of that to his credit card? The purchase/expense occurred in July, but Fred didn't pay the credit card until August. We'll elaborate on that in the chapter on cash flow statements. For now, keep this rule in mind:

The date when money comes in, or goes out, is not always the same as the date recorded on the books.

A critical concept to understand about your business financial statements is that pre-tax net profits, or losses, do not equate to changes in your cash balance.

Pre-tax net profits do not equal cash.

The cash flow statement ties together the P&L and BS because cash is the common denominator in both statements. The cash flow statement is the most important financial statement, but the least understood. It isn't hard, but it is different. For now, just know that there are three ways that cash flows in and out of your bank account:

1. Operations of your business—your P&L.
2. Investment in your business—purchase and sale of fixed assets. Fixed assets are items like buildings and equipment that cost a substantial amount and last longer than a year.
3. Financing your business—investments by owners, borrowing and repaying loans, and paying dividends (distributions) to owners.

If you purchase a car and finance it 100 percent with a loan, your BS is affected but your P&L is not. Why? GAAP dictates how transactions are recorded on your books. According to GAAP, when you buy the car, your assets (the car) go up and your long-term liabilities (loan to finance purchase of the car) go up. This transaction is recorded on the BS but not on your P&L. If you paid cash for the car, your assets (cash) went down and your assets (car) went up, but nothing is recorded on the P&L.

Your number-one priority in the operation of your business is to generate cash, which can be used to then purchase assets, repay loans, and make distributions to owners. Pre-tax net profits are nice, but cash is king. The P&L, BS, and cash flow statements will be discussed in more detail later. For now, just note the three determinants of cash flow: operations, investment, and financing.

Chapter Assignment

Prepare your own personal P&L and balance sheet. Initially, keep it simple and just organize items into the major categories of revenue, expenses, assets, and liabilities.

Below is an exercise. Organize the following items (accounts) and their amounts and assemble them into a P&L and a BS. Remember, assets are items you *own*, and liabilities are debts you *owe*. The answers are on the following page. Organizing things into financial statements isn't difficult, and with practice you will have no trouble doing it for yourself or your business.

My Personal Financial Statement Exercise	Asset, Liability, Rev, Exp	
Car Loan Balance		20,000
Cash – Money Market		5,000
Credit Card Balance Payable		3,000
Credit Card Payment		200
Dividends		100
Car – Insurance		150
Entertainment		200
Food		600
Home Maintenance		100
House		180,000
Insurance		200
Interest Income		50
Internet Access		50
Car – Fuel		250
Medical Expenses		200
Mortgage Balance		140,000
Mortgage Payment		1,000
Phone		200
Receivable – Loan to Friend		150
Restaurants		100
Car		30,000
Salary		4,000
Car Loan Payment		500
Utilities		300
Cash – Checking		600

Personal Profit & Loss Statement

Income:	
Salary	$4,000
Interest Income	50
Dividends	100
TOTAL INCOME	**$4,150**
Expenses:	
Mortgage Payment	$1,000
Utilities	300
Food	600
Phone	200
Home Maintenance	100
Insurance	200
Medical Expenses	200
Restaurants	100
Car Loan Payment	500
Car – Fuel	250
Car – Insurance	150
Credit Card Payment	200
Internet Access	50
Entertainment	200
TOTAL EXPENSES	**$4,050**
NET PROFIT OR (LOSS)	**$ 100**

My Balance Sheet

ASSETS:	
Cash – Checking	$ 600
Cash – Money Market	5,000
Receivable – Loan to Friend	150
Total Current Assets	**$ 5,750**
House	$ 180,000
Car	30,000
Total Fixed Assets	**$ 210,000**
TOTAL ASSETS	**$ 215,750**
LIABILITIES:	
Credit Card Balance Payable	$ 3,000
Total Current Liabilities	**$ 3,000**
Car Loan Balance	20,000
Mortgage Balance	140,000
Total Long-Term Liabilities	**160,000**
TOTAL LIABILITIES	**$ 163,000**
NET WORTH / EQUITY	**$ 52,750**

CHAPTER 45
ACCOUNTING CONCEPTS

"If you can't measure it, you can't manage it" – Peter Drucker

As we discussed, your financial statements are your historical scorecard, indicating whether you are winning or losing the "game" of business. As a business owner, you need to understand what GAAP requires for your financial statements. You may argue that no one manages a business using their GAAP financial statements, so why prepare them to conform to GAAP? Well, I suggest you do, because banks and investors expect to see GAAP financial statements. You need to understand GAAP principles to prevent misleading or misrepresenting your company to outsiders.

Knowing some key concepts will help you understand how and why GAAP financial statements are set up as they are. Following is a brief discussion of the most important accounting concepts.

Comparability

To understand if your financial results are improving or worsening, you need to compare those results to something—a benchmark of some sort. Suppose you were watching a football game and it showed your favorite team's score is 17, but you don't know the other team's score. Is your team winning or losing? You don't know, unless you know both teams' scores.

Similarly, you need to compare financial information to something. There are two primary yardsticks against which to compare your financial information: the past or what is forecast. Are your P&L and balance sheet financial results better or worse than in the past, or in relation to forecast expectations?

Matching

Where possible, match revenues with the expenses incurred to create those revenues. Suppose you sell T-shirts. You buy them in

January for $200 and sell them in February for $400. Your P&L would look like this:

	January	February	Year
Revenues / Sales	$ 0	$ 400	$ 400
Expenses	$200	$ 0	$ 200
Pre-Tax Net Profit / (Loss)	$ (200)	$ 400	$ 200

Do you see a problem here? The pre-tax net profit for the year is correct. But each month is badly distorted. Matching aligns revenues with the expenses incurred to generate the revenues. Your accountant can accomplish matching in several ways, but the important concept for you to know is that when you see a zigzag pattern to your profits you need to be asking your accountant why it's happening. If your business has this kind of zigzag pattern to profits and losses, you can't evaluate if your financials make any sense, and you certainly can't forecast the future.

Now, remember the rule. To manage the financial side of your business, you need to know where to look, what to look for, and how to use the information. In this example, where to look is at your P&L on a month-to-month basis. What to look for is patterns or anomalies that don't make sense. How to use the information is when you spot inconsistencies, analyze the details or have your accountant explain what is going on.

Double Entry

Accounting is a dual, or double, entry system. It was invented in 1494 by Luca Pacioli. (Remember that if you are ever in an extreme trivia game.) Double entry means every financial transaction is posted to two accounts. Accountants organize all items of revenues, expenses, assets, and liabilities into accounts. Think of them as "buckets."

For example, in the last chapter, the personal financial statement example had four accounts for expenses on the P&L: rent, utilities, food, and car. In every financial transaction two events occur, and dual entry records this.

Suppose you purchase a box of copy paper. Two things have taken place. First, you have incurred an expense that will be recorded on your P&L, probably as "office supplies." Second, you have an obligation to pay for the copy paper. If you pay cash, your cash balance will decrease. If you pay on credit, you have a liability or obligation to pay for the copy paper in the future. This transaction shows up in two places, as an expense on your P&L and as either a reduction of cash or an increase in liabilities on the balance sheet.

When selling a product to the customer, you have earned revenue and you have either received cash or the right to receive the cash in the future (a receivable).

As you examine the following examples of frequent types of "double entries," note that every entry on the P&L has a corresponding entry on the balance sheet. However, many entries only affect the balance sheet and never appear on the P&L, which is one reason why P&L pre-tax net profits are never equivalent to cash flow.

- Invoicing a customer creates:
    - Revenue on the P&L statement
    - A receivable, or cash increase, on the balance sheet
- Receiving cash from a customer creates:
    - A cash increase on the balance sheet
    - Accounts receivable decrease on the balance sheet
- Entering a vendor bill creates:
    - An expense on the P&L
    - A payable, or cash decrease, on the balance sheet
- Paying a vendor creates:
    - A decrease in cash on the balance sheet
    - Accounts payable decrease on the balance sheet

Cash Basis versus Accrual Basis

There are two methods for recording your financial transactions: cash or accrual.

Think of a child with a corner lemonade stand. If she purchases her lemonade and cups with cash and then collects cash when she sells the lemonade, she is using the cash basis of accounting. But what if she obtains the lemonade from her mom and agrees to pay her back later after selling the lemonade? Additionally, she extends credit to customers, some of whom agree to pay for the lemonade in the future. Now, she is using the accrual system.

Under the cash basis of accounting, revenues are recorded on the P&L when the cash is received and expenses are recorded when cash is paid out.

Under the accrual basis of accounting, revenues are recorded when they are earned, not when the cash is received. Expenses are matched with the related revenues and recorded when the expense occurs, not when the cash is paid. Accrual accounting does a better job of measuring profitability during a specific time period because it matches expenses with their corresponding revenues.

Can you use both methods? Many small businesses use the cash basis for preparing tax returns, because this offers some tax benefits. However, for internal reporting and financial management, I recommend the accrual basis. Your accountant and tax preparer can guide your selection of what is best for your situation.

Revenue Recognition

Revenue recognition refers to the point in time when you record revenues in your accounting records, or "books." GAAP dictates that you record revenues when they are earned, which is not necessarily when cash is received. Revenues are earned when the product or service is delivered to the customer, and the customer takes title or ownership of the product or service.

Ideally, revenues are recorded in the period (month) in which the product or service has been delivered to the customer, but that doesn't always happen. A landscaping company might provide weekly service to a customer but only invoice them once a month for the previous month's service. Assume the landscaper invoices customers on August 5 for services provided in July. Technically speaking, those revenues were earned in July as services were provided then. If the invoice is dated August 5, it will be recorded in August, which is not the month in which the revenues were earned.

Expense Recognition

Expense recognition refers to when you should record expenses. According to GAAP, expenses should be recorded in the period in which the expense was incurred. Expenses are incurred when the product or service is received. Like revenues, expenses may be recorded in a different period (month) than the period in which the vendor is paid, especially if the invoice terms are "payable in 30 days."

Chapter Assignment

Following is a brief summary of each of the accounting concepts discussed, to use as a quick reference. If you need further explanation, consult your accountant. Understanding these concepts will enable you to understand your business financial statements.

- Comparability: Compare financial results to either the past or to the forecast.
- Matching: Match expenses with the revenues they produced.
- Double Entry: Every financial transaction consists of two interrelated actions.
- Cash versus Accrual: In a cash basis system, financial transactions are recorded when cash is received or paid out. In an accrual system, financial transactions are recorded when revenue is earned or expenses are incurred, which may be at different points in time from when cash is received or paid out.
- Revenue Recognition: Revenues should be recorded when they are earned (in other words, when the product or service is delivered or passes to the customer).
- Expense Recognition: Expenses should be recorded when they are incurred, which could be at a different time period than the payment to the vendor.

CHAPTER 46

PROFIT AND LOSS STATEMENT

"You can tell a lot by looking." – Yogi Berra

Let's look at your business P&L in more detail and highlight some of the ways that it differs from your personal one.

The profit and loss statement is sometimes referred to as an income statement. The term "income statement" is not as explanatory as "profit and loss," which recognizes there can be either profits or losses, so we will use P&L. For this discussion, nct profits or losses are assumed to be pre-tax, or before paying state and/or federal income taxes.

Knowing your net profit is essential to making sound business decisions. Without understanding your profitability, how will you know whether you are charging enough to cover expenses—let alone whether it's feasible to expand or grow? Even if you hire a professional to prepare your financial statements, you still have to know how to read and understand them. You are liable for their content, regardless of who prepares them.

Many small business owners look at their P&L only on an annual or year-to-date basis. Review the P&L at least every month. Run the report for the past twelve months. By looking at line items of revenues and expenses for the past twelve months, side by side, you can spot inconsistencies and see items that don't make sense.

Your business P&L has some differences from your personal P&L. They are the same in that both record revenues and expenses. As a record of your revenues and expenses, the P&L's main function is to show how revenues become pre-tax net profit. To calculate pre-tax net profit, subtract your expenses from your revenues.

Revenues minus Expenses = Pre-Tax Net Profit/(Loss)

Every business will organize its P&L differently and have different subcategories of revenues and expenses.

P&L revenues stem from the sale of your product or service. For this discussion, the terms "revenues" and "sales" will be considered synonymous. If you borrow money from a bank or get cash from an investor, is that revenue? No. Cash receipts from a loan or an investor are not from the sale of your product or service, so they are not recorded as revenues. However, they will be recorded on your balance sheet, as I'll explain later.

P&L expenses are the costs incurred to operate the business day in, day out. They include any costs incurred in the production or sale of your product and any sales, marketing, administration, and research expenses incurred each month. Another characteristic of P&L expenses is that they are, in effect, used up each month. The electricity costs you incurred for the month can never be used again. Wages to an employee are for work they did during the month.

Now, here's where it can get a little tricky. Not all costs incurred are for the day-to-day operation of the business, and not all costs are used up immediately. Let's distinguish between *expenditures* and *expenses*. Expenditures are the total of all costs incurred and/or payments made. Expenses are a subset, or subcategory, of expenditures. Only expenses are recorded on the P&L. Following are examples of expenditures that are not P&L expenses.

Dividends/Distributions

A dividend, or distribution to owners, is not a cost incurred to operate the business on a day-to-day basis. Rather, it is a reward to the owners for achieving positive financial results. Therefore, a distribution is an expenditure but is not a P&L expense.

Loan Payments

If you make a loan payment to a bank, is that a P&L expense? Well, yes and no. Loan payments have two components: interest and principal. The principal of a loan is the amount borrowed. In a sense, the bank is renting its money to you. Eventually the bank expects its money back, and the rent the bank is charging you to use their money is called interest.

For each monthly payment, the bank applies part of it to interest and part of it to reduce the principal of the loan. When you make a loan payment, the interest part is recorded on the P&L as an expense, but the principal part is applied to reduce the loan balance on the balance sheet. The interest is the ongoing monthly expense for using the bank's money.

Purchase of Fixed Assets

If you purchase a large piece of equipment or vehicle for your business and the item has a life expectancy of more than a year, is that a P&L expense? Again, the answer is yes and no. It is not a P&L expense on the day of purchase, but will be in future months and years as you use it in the course of your business.

Assume you buy a truck costing $48,000 and it has a useful life of five years, or sixty months. Each year, you "use" one-fifth of the value of the truck. Each month, you use up one-sixtieth of the value of the truck. The monthly usage of the truck is called depreciation. Depreciation recognizes that the asset is used up gradually, over a period of time. In this case, the monthly depreciation expense would be $800 ($48,000 divided by sixty months). Your best practice is to record depreciation each month. Some owners and bookkeepers record depreciation only once for the whole year. That works for tax purposes, but it distorts the monthly comparison of pre-tax net profits. (Note: There are different depreciation methodologies and GAAP requirements for different types of fixed assets, so consult your accountant on the proper recording method.)

P&L Structure

The P&L is simply revenues minus expenses = pre-tax net profit/(loss). To understand better what is causing results, you need to classify revenues and expenses into categories. How you structure the P&L helps to get underneath the numbers and determine what is causing financial results.

Revenue Structure

If you have revenue from multiple types of sales or different locations, you want to determine the pre-tax net profits of each to determine which areas are most profitable. Espy Lumber could categorize revenues by lines of business such as millwork, siding, roofing, and decking. Espy could also categorize revenues by their two locations. Categorizing revenues helps determine the profitability of different types of products. You can create P&L subsets for each location or line of business, which requires knowing each one's revenues.

Expense Structure

There are three categories of expenses: cost of sales expense, sales and marketing expense, and administrative expense.

Cost of Sales Expense

Cost of sales (COS) expenses are expenses directly related to the generation of revenue. If you don't incur these expenses, you don't have any revenues. If you produce or manufacture a product, this would be the cost of goods sold. Every business has some cost of sales expense. Unfortunately, small business financial statements often don't reflect cost of sales. Some service businesses argue that they don't have cost of sales. That is incorrect. If you are a lawyer, CPA, financial planner, insurance agent, mortgage broker, etc., you have COS. All of these professions prepare documents for their clients. The time involved to prepare those documents is COS. If they don't prepare those documents, they can't invoice their client.

The salaries and wages required to deliver the service are part of COS. Reclamation By Design's COS are the building materials purchased to construct houses. If the company doesn't buy these materials, it has no revenues. UniSource Mortgage Services collects data from borrowers, researches the best lender, and prepares loan documents. No documents means no revenues.

It is extremely important for every business to calculate its cost of sales. You need to know your cost of sales so you can calculate your gross profit margin. Gross profit is the amount of profit you have before paying sales, marketing, and administration expenses.

Revenues minus
Cost of Sales = Gross Profit

Knowing your gross profit is important for several reasons. In many cases, COS tends to be variable in nature. As revenues increase or decrease, certain elements of COS do the same. Sales, marketing, and administrative expenses tend to be relatively fixed over time. They will vary a little each month but not drastically. Therefore, bottom-line pre-tax net profit is significantly affected by your gross profit margin. If gross profit as a percentage of revenue improves, virtually all of the increase goes directly to bottom-line pre-tax net profit.

If the prices you charge don't generate adequate revenue to cover your direct cost of sales, you have a major problem. What should your gross profit be as a percentage of sales? That depends entirely on the characteristics and nature of your business. Some say it should be 30 percent, and others say 40 percent. There is no hard and fast rule.

In one case, a company was going along at 45 percent and just breaking even for years. Gradually, they raised their gross profit percent a little each year getting to 57 percent. At that point, they made more pre-tax net profits than in the last ten years combined.

Let's summarize:

Revenues minus Expenses = Pre-Tax Net Profits
Revenues minus Cost of Sales = Gross Profit

Expanding it one step further:

Gross Profit minus Sales, Marketing, and Administration Costs = Pre-Tax Net Profit

Gross Profit minus Sales, Marketing, and Administration Costs = Pre-Tax Net Profit

Sales and Marketing (S&M) Expenses

Best practice is to separate sales and marketing expenses from administration expenses to better determine how much is spent for this category. By knowing your sales and marketing (S&M) expenses, you can calculate the cost of customer acquisition. Customer acquisition cost is your sales and marketing costs divided by the number of new customers.

You also want to determine the impact on revenues if S&M is increased or decreased. Also consider having subcategories under S&M so you can determine if changes in spending impact your revenues—for example, advertising, sales personnel, and travel and entertainment.

Administration Expenses

The number of administration expense accounts and categories of accounts is a matter of preference. My recommendation is as much detail as is practical, because some line items of expense may only occur once a year or quarterly. Practical means having enough data to manage the business and forecast future expenses. Some companies go overboard and have literally thousands of expense accounts, which makes their P&L so long they never review it.

Conversely, other companies have "black hole" accounts. Black hole accounts occur when businesses don't separate types of expenses and dump everything into one massive black hole. They do it to save the time it takes in determining which account (expense line item) the expense belongs, but then they have no idea on what they're spending the money. If you don't know where you are spending your money, you can't manage your business and find ways to reduce expenses or forecast future expenses.

The purpose of your accounting system is to gather financial data for decision making. It is better to have too many accounts than way too few.

Let's look at a hypothetical P&L for Mama's Banana Pudding Shop. When the owner prepared her P&L statement for 2015, her numbers for the year were as follows:

- Revenues for the year – $255,637
- Cost of sales for the year – $78,782
- Sales and marketing expenses for the year – $9,659
- Administrative expenses for the year – $146,715
- Other income and expenses for the year – $1,000

She plugged in the numbers, did the math, and created her P&L statement. Take a minute to study it, making sure you understand how she found the amount and percent of revenues, her gross profit, and pre-tax net profit. If you have forgotten or need a refresher, review the section that explains their definitions and formulas. Note the columns for both 2015 and 2014. P&L statements are more valuable when you can compare two or more years or a series of months.

P&L – Mama's Banana Pudding Shop

	2015	2014	Change $	% Change
Revenues	$ 255,637	$ 227,192	$ 28,445	12.5%
Cost of Sales Expenses	(78,782)	(50,128)	(28,654)	57.2%
Gross Profit	$ 176,855	$ 177,064	$ (209)	-0.1%
% of Revenues	69%	78%		
Sales & Marketing Expenses	$ (9,659)	$ (4,694)	$ (4,965)	105.8%
Admin Expenses	(146,715)	(144,204)	(2,510)	1.7%
Operating Profit	$ 20,480	$ 28,166	$ (7,685)	-27.3%
Other Income/Exp	1,000	1,000	-	0.0%
Pre-Tax Net Profit	$ 21,480	$ 29,166	(7,685)	-26.4%
% of Revenues	**8%**	**13%**		

By comparing 2015 to 2014, the owner of Mama's Banana Pudding Shop can draw some helpful conclusions about strengths and weaknesses that will affect decision making for the next year. This is what she learned:

1. There was a significant increase in sales and marketing, which may be why revenues increased 13 percent.

2. Cost of sales expenses increased 57 percent faster than revenues, and as a result gross profit as a percent of sales declined from 78 percent to 69 percent.
3. General administrative expenses increased 2 percent, probably with inflation.
4. Pre-tax net profit decreased by $7,685, or 26 percent.

So how does she now use this information? There are positives and negatives. Why did cost of sales expenses have such a large increase? This could have been caused by the mix of products or services sold (some have higher margins than others, and food costs are continuously changing). Perhaps a particular expense line within COS shot up, either due to a price increase or something posted to the wrong account. The sharp increase in COS alerts the owner to investigate and determine what caused the increase.

As Yogi Berra once said, "You can tell a lot by looking." With practice you will gradually improve your understanding of the P&L and recognize instances where the numbers don't make sense. By analyzing individual accounts within the broad categories of COS, S&M, and administration, you can identify items affecting expenses, enabling you to control, minimize, and in some cases eliminate expenses. That will give you a competitive advantage.

A client asked for help learning how to read her financials. She ran her *QuickBooks* P&L on a year-to-date basis, and it showed a very profitable business. She was then asked to run the P&L on a monthly basis, for the past twelve months. Scrolling down through the monthly P&L, one line item of expense jumped out. One account had expenses of $4,000 every month except one, and in that one month it was $16,000. What happened? She didn't know.

Looking at a transaction detail report for that account revealed a payment of $12,000. However, there was no description in the memo field to explain what was purchased. She then clicked on that transaction to show the vendor bill. Fortunately, it was a one-time expense that may never recur. By moving that one-time expense into its own account, she now knows not to include it in her forecast for the next year.

If a particular revenue or expense account makes a sudden jump or decline, then you need to determine the cause. Something may have been posted to the wrong account. Maybe a fixed asset purchase was posted to a P&L expense account in error. Maybe a new piece of business was acquired, and in the initial month revenues suddenly increased. There are numerous possibilities.

Sadly, there is one other possibility that you need to seriously consider: someone could be stealing from you. It happens all the time, and often by people you know well and trust. In one case, the chief accountant got a divorce, bought a BMW, and joined the country club. The owner got suspicious because divorce and an increase in lifestyle are mutually exclusive.

He discovered his longtime trusted friend was paying his personal credit card bills with company money and hiding it in a large black-hole account. The fraud was discovered by going through canceled checks. The owner discovered checks written to a credit card company but coded to "telephone expense," which didn't make sense because the company didn't have a credit card!

You can spot problems by quickly reviewing, on a monthly basis, revenue and expense items that might be hidden when looking at the entire year. Think of it this way. If you're in a submarine and the radar screen revealed a blip, what would it tell you? Nothing ... until you investigate further. It could be a warning, an opportunity, or a whale. Without information about where it was a minute ago, you don't even know if it's moving toward you, away from you, or if it's moving at all.

The P&L reflects more than numbers, revenues, and expenses. It also reveals the productivity and efficiency of your business. It tells you what needs improvement—and there is always room for improvement. Your P&L can help you spot where you need to improve. Here are some comments from the successful companies interviewed.

- "We prepare rolling twelve-month projections/forecasts of sales and expenses every month so we can better see what is ahead. We also prepare projections for each store." – Mike Reeves, Espy Lumber
- "You've got to know the numbers. Margins are thin and costs are constantly changing." – Damien Hayes, British Open Pub
- "I look at financial reports every day. The financial reports are not just for filing taxes. They tell me the health of the

business and enable me to figure out how to make it more profitable in the future." – Mike Covert, Covert Aire

- "Know your numbers on a daily, weekly, and month-to-date basis." – David Crenshaw, International Dunnage

GAAP Profit versus Taxable Profit

The P&L for Mama's calculates pre-tax net profit according to GAAP. You also need to be aware of "taxable net profit." The IRS calls this taxable income. The IRS does things differently from GAAP, and when it comes to paying income taxes, the IRS takes precedence.

According to IRS regulations, not all P&L expenses are deductible. When your tax preparer calculates your taxes, taxable profit will probably be different from what is on your financial statements. There may be expenses on your P&L that are not deductible for taxes. Some expenses are only partially deductible, such as travel and entertainment. Work with your tax preparer to determine the tax-deductible expenses for your business. This may affect decisions on what expenses to incur.

Chapter Assignment

With a little practice, you *can* understand your company's P&L even if you don't like working with numbers. After all, you are a DWIT. My e-mail signature at D. J. Powers says "Accounting is Fun (;>)." When I retired, my staff presented me with a T-shirt with "Accounting is Fun (;>)" on the front. You may never agree that accounting is fun, but hopefully you will agree that accounting is an indispensable tool in the quest for a competitive advantage.

Review your company P&L. If there are items you don't understand, insist that your accountant explain them to you. If needed, instruct your accountant to add line items to help you better understand the source of revenues and expenses.

CHAPTER 47

THE BALANCE SHEET

"Beware of little expenses. A small leak will sink a great ship." – Benjamin Franklin

The balance sheet is sometimes referred to as a "statement of assets and liabilities." That's what it is, with one difference. The BS also shows the company net worth or equity.

The profit and loss statement details what has been occurring in the operation of the business during a specific time period. The balance sheet reflects the financial condition, or health of your business, at a given point in time. The P&L covers a time period, like a month, quarter, or year. The balance sheet is a snapshot of a point in time. For instance, how much cash do you have in the bank on May 31, or how much is owed on your truck loan as of October 31?

Just like the P&L, the balance sheet is separated into categories. The three major categories are assets, liabilities, and equity. Assets are items you *own*, liabilities are debts you *owe*, and the difference between assets and liabilities is the equity, or net worth, of the business.

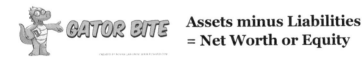

Assets minus Liabilities
= Net Worth or Equity

Within each of these major categories, there are subcategories to assist in understanding your financial health. Following is a quick summary:

ASSETS

- Current Assets
- Fixed Assets
- Other Assets

LIABILITIES

- Current Liabilities
- Long-Term Liabilities

EQUITY/NET WORTH

- Owner's Investment
- Retained Earnings
- Distributions/Dividends

Assets

Current Assets

Current assets are assets you own that can be converted into cash within a year's time or less. There are other current asset items, but these are the major ones:

- Cash or cash equivalents: Items that can be quickly converted into cash, like a CD.
- Accounts receivable: Invoices that you've sent to customers but for which you haven't been paid.
- Inventory: Merchandise you have purchased either for resale or for use in producing a product. Like food in your pantry, you want to either sell it or use it before it goes bad. (Note: Accounting for, and costing of, inventory is complicated and beyond the scope of this book. If you have physical inventory, work with your accountant to assure inventory is recorded properly on your BS, and as cost of goods sold on your P&L. There are several methods for determining the cost of inventory.)
- Prepaid expenses: A common prepaid expense is insurance. Suppose the premium for the year is $2,000, and at the beginning of the year you pay it all upfront. You have paid

for insurance that you have not yet used. Every month you use up one-twelfth of the annual policy. If you cancel the policy after six months, the insurance company will refund you $1,000, the unused portion of the policy. Consult your accountant on the proper way to record prepaid insurance. If you record the entire $2,000 in one month as insurance expense on your P&L, it could distort month-to-month pre-tax net profit comparisons.

Fixed Assets

Fixed assets are assets:

1. with life expectancy of more than a year, and
2. that exceed a cost threshold.

When a fixed asset is purchased, it is not recorded on the P&L because it will be used over several years. It is recorded on the BS and depreciated over time on the P&L as an expense depicting the ongoing use of the asset.

Let's say you buy a hammer in 1972 for $20. After forty years, you still have the hammer and it still works. The hammer meets both of the above criteria for a fixed asset. However, if you recorded that hammer as a fixed asset and depreciated it over forty years, the depreciation would be 4.1 cents a month. That would be ridiculous, of course, but I've seen it done.

A more sensible method is to establish a minimum dollar threshold before recording something as a fixed asset and depreciating it. Different size companies set different thresholds. One large company has a threshold of $2,500. Most small companies use something like $500, in which case the asset must cost $500 or more to qualify as a fixed asset. Check with your accountant to determine the appropriate threshold for your company, and what will satisfy an IRS auditor.

Fixed assets include things like land, buildings, vehicles, equipment, and leasehold improvements. If you are unsure whether to record an item as a fixed asset or an expense on your P&L, check with your accountant. The IRS takes a dim view of fixed assets improperly recorded as P&L expenses because it reduces taxable income, which in turn reduces income tax. The IRS does not like taxes understated.

Other Assets

Other assets could include a variety of items like intellectual property (patents, trademarks, copyrights, etc.), cash value of life insurance, investments in stocks and bonds, and investments in other companies. These aren't common for most small businesses. When in doubt, check with your accountant.

Liabilities

Current Liabilities

Current liabilities are debts you owe that must be paid within a year or less. The major types of current liabilities are:

- Accounts payable (bills received from vendors that haven't been paid)
- Credit card debt
- Payroll withholding taxes payable to the government
- Short-term loans due to be repaid within the next twelve months
- Insurance premiums payable (a year's insurance premium paid over a period of months)
- The current year's portion of long-term debt

Long-Term Liabilities

Long-term liabilities are debts to be repaid over a period of years. Major types of long-term liabilities are:

- Bank loans
- Long-term leases
- Loans from owners or shareholders

Other possible long-term liabilities exist but are unusual for small businesses.

Equity/Net Worth

In accounting terms, equity is the difference between assets and liabilities. You may have heard the term "book value." Book value is simply:

Assets minus Liabilities = Book Value

Whether you call it equity, net worth, or book value, it has several components.

- **Owner's investment**: Other names for this include "capital stock" or "member's investment." When a company is set up, the owner(s) may invest their personal money. On day one, the new company balance sheet may only consist of the asset cash, which is the owner's investment. If you invested $1,000 to get the business started, your balance sheet would appear as:

Assets— Cash	$1,000
Liabilities	$ 0
Equity – Owner's Investment	$1,000

- **Retained Earnings**: The accumulated profits and losses from your P&L for the length of time in business.
- **Distributions/Dividends**: If the business has done well, the owner(s) may decide to reward themselves by paying out a dividend or distribution. Distributions reduce equity (net worth).

Let's use Mama's Banana Pudding Shop once again to relate the basic elements of a balance sheet. Note that it compares two years to evaluate what has changed.

Mama's Banana Pudding Shop – Balance Sheet

	12/31/2015	12/31/2014	Change
Cash	$ 13,814	$ 10,530	$ 3,284
Receivables	38,103	32,766	5,337
Current Assets	$ 51,917	$ 43,296	$ 8,621
Fixed Assets	$ 70,717	$ 70,717	$ -
Accumulated Depreciation	(54,745)	(45,296)	(9,449)
Book Value – Fixed Assets	$ 15,972	$ 25,421	$(9,449)
TOTAL ASSETS	**$ 67,889**	**$ 68,717**	**$ (828)**
Total Payables/Current Liabilities	$ 960	$ 1,050	$ (90)
Bank Loan	$ 15,264	$ 25,481	$(10,217)
Long-Term Liabilities	$ 15,264	$ 25,481	$(10,217)
TOTAL LIABILITIES	**$ 16,223**	**$ 26,531**	**$(10,307)**
Investment	$ 5,000	$ 5,000	$ -
Retained Earnings	108,161	86,681	21,480
Owners Distributions	(61,495)	(49,495)	(12,000)
TOTAL EQUITY	**$ 51,666**	**$ 42,186**	**$ 9,480**
TOTAL LIABILITIES & EQUITY	$ 67,890	$ 68,717	$ (827)

What conclusions can be drawn from analyzing Mama's balance sheet?

1. Cash has increased $3,284. Increasing the cash balance is a positive indicator.
2. Receivables have increased by $5,337. Is that good or bad? You need more information to draw a conclusion. How old are the receivables? If you haven't collected on customer invoices over thirty days old, the odds of ever collecting decrease each day. If over ninety days old, the odds of collecting are slim.
3. Bank loan: The balance due on the bank loan has been reduced by $10,218. Remember, the repayment of principal on a bank loan does not appear on the P&L, so the fact that Mama's was able to substantially reduce the balance due on the bank loan *and* increase the cash balance is a positive.
4. Retained earnings increased by $21,480, which means that the company had a P&L pre-tax net profit of $21,480 for the year. Refer back to the P&L chapter and you will note that this is the pre-tax net profit on Mama's P&L.
5. Owner's distribution: The owners were able to pay themselves $12,000. Considering that the cash balance increased, the bank loan balance decreased, *and* the owners could take a distribution suggests that the business is succeeding.

Chapter Assignment

The balance sheet measures a company's financial health at a point in time. However, knowing the health of your business today is of little value if you don't compare it to what it was at some point in the past. As with the P&L, you are looking for anomalies—blips that don't make sense.

If receivables spike up, is it because sales have increased or because you aren't collecting receivables? If you aren't collecting receivables, you are working for free. Failure to collect receivables is a significant contributor to companies going out of business. Often owners are so busy "doing" the business that they don't make time to collect receivables.

Many small business owners understand a P&L, but fewer understand the balance sheet. Yet understanding the balance sheet is critical to understanding the health of your business. If you go to the doctor and have an EKG done that shows significant abnormalities in your heart, you would take steps to fix the problem. But if you never had the EKG done, you wouldn't know a problem existed. Your balance sheet is a kind of EKG for your company's financial health.

Review your company balance sheet. If there are items you don't understand, insist that your accountant explain them to you.

CHAPTER 48

THE CASH FLOW STATEMENT

"Opportunities come to those with cash." – Greg Crabtree, author, *Simple Numbers*

The most important, yet least understood, financial statement is the cash flow statement. Normally, if profits are increasing, the cash will probably also be increasing. However, this is not always true. Your cash flow statement reports the causes of changes in your cash balance. Many small businesses and some fairly good-sized companies (with $100 million in annual revenues) have never heard of a cash flow statement. The cash flow statement ties the P&L and balance sheet together by indicating from where cash is generated and where it is being spent.

Understanding the cash flow statement requires an understanding of the P&L and balance sheet that you learned in the last two chapters.

Why is the cash flow statement so important? The number-one priority for any business should be to increase cash flow and accumulate cash. Positive cash flow is essential for the growth, improvement, and survival of your business. As Greg Crabtree says in *Simple Numbers,* "Opportunities come to those with cash."

Gayle Humphries, the chief financial officer for JCB of Georgia, states, "Going into the 2008–2009 Great Recession, we had cash reserves that enabled us to avoid layoffs. However, the recession lasted so long for our industry that we finally had to lay off some people in 2011. Without those cash reserves, we might not have survived."

Tom Zombik of Hilton Head Glass puts it this way: "We didn't anticipate the savings & loan crisis of 1991. It killed the construction industry in New England and along with it the supporting subcontractors. We had to cut everything to the bone and lay off employees. Fortunately, we were personally debt free so that our house and car were paid for. We had to forego a paycheck in order to keep the business alive.

"There were a lot of hard choices, and we had two young daughters at the time. The business had a lot of debt because we had just bought a building and some expensive equipment. Everyone around us was going out of business, but we managed to stick it out. In the long run the experience made us stronger and better business people. We became highly focused on the numbers, because to survive we had to minimize or avoid every possible expense and find ways to run the business more efficiently. When the Great Recession of 2008–2009 hit, it hurt our business, but we were much better prepared. We saw it coming in 2006 and started building up cash reserves and paying down business debt, and we were personally debt free."

Before the Great Recession of 2008–2009, many businesses borrowed substantial amounts of money to buy equipment and improve facilities to keep up with the demand for their products and services. When the recession hit, they had fixed payments owed to banks and finance companies. Without the ability to pay both their loans and their employees, many businesses were forced to lay off employees. You can't "lay off" loan payments. If you don't make payments, the bank can foreclose on the loan and take possession of the asset used as collateral for the loan. Banks prefer not to repossess assets (they aren't in the business of selling equipment), but they won't permit loan payments to remain unpaid for long.

Businesses with ample cash reserves were able to weather the recession storm *and* keep their employees. Again, profits are not the same as cash—and cash is more important than profits. A business can have accounting (GAAP) losses but still have cash and operate for years. A business also can have accounting (GAAP) profits but no cash, and go out of business. Remember, GAAP statements are prepared on the accrual basis so revenues are recorded when earned (not when cash is received) and expenses are recorded when incurred (not when cash is paid).

No business can exist long term without positive cash flow. Understanding where your cash is coming from and going to is critical to the survival of your business, and this is why the cash flow statement is the most important financial statement.

The cash flow statement organizes cash flows into three categories:

- Cash Flow from Operations
- Cash Flow from Investing (purchasing or selling assets)
- Cash Flow from Financing (investments from owners, borrowing and repaying loans, and distributions to owners)

Total cash flow for the month is the difference between the cash on hand at the beginning of the month and the cash on hand at the end of the month. If your personal checking account has $2,000 at the beginning of the month and $1,000 at the end of the month, your cash flow for the month is negative $1,000. The pertinent question is: What caused the drop in cash? Perhaps it went down because money was spent on regular monthly living expenses, because a new refrigerator was purchased, or because loans were repaid.

All you need to know to understand the cash flow statement is the three categories of cash flow—operations, investing, and financing—and what comprises each. Cash flow from operations is the most important because it indicates whether the operation of the business is generating cash. If not, big problems are on the horizon.

Few accounting systems are set up to classify or "tag" individual cash transactions as being operations, investing, or financing. Therefore, you must indirectly calculate cash flow from operations. There is an easy way and a more detailed way to calculate cash flow from operations. Let's start with the easy way.

Method 1

Cash flow from operations is total cash flow minus cash flow from investing and cash flow from financing. Cash flows from investing and financing are easy to calculate.

Total Change in Cash minus Investing Cash Flow minus Financing Cash Flow = Cash Flow from Operations

<u>Cash Flow from Investing</u>

Cash flow from investing comes primarily from buying and selling fixed assets such as vehicles, equipment, buildings, or property. Add up these transactions during the time period.

If you purchased a fixed asset, it used cash (cash went out of the bank) and that would be a negative cash flow item (in other words, cash *outflow*). If you sold an asset, that would add cash (in other words, cash *inflow*).

How can an asset purchase use cash if you borrowed the money to buy the asset? When you borrowed the money, you deposited money into your bank account, which increased the cash balance (cash flow from financing). Subsequently, you withdrew money from the bank account, decreasing the cash balance, to pay the vendor for the asset (cash flow from investing).

Cash Flow from Financing

Cash flow from financing is primarily borrowing money and repaying loans. It can also include investments by owners in the business or distributions/dividends to owners. Total these transactions during the period.

Borrowed money increases the cash balance and long-term liabilities (debt) but does not affect the P&L. Repaying the loan principal on borrowed money reduces cash and long-term liabilities but does not affect the P&L.

This is important because you want to know if the operation of the business is increasing or decreasing cash. In your personal checkbook, if your salary and other income do not cover normal monthly living expenses, you don't have adequate money to purchase a new appliance. If the deficit continues, you may have to make drastic cuts in your normal living expenses or borrow money to cover the deficit.

When a business doesn't generate enough cash from operations to cover regular monthly expenditures, it has to increase sales revenues, reduce expenses, or borrow money (which creates more fixed expenses). If too many of those expenditures are fixed and can't be reduced, jobs may have to be eliminated.

Twice in my career I've been involved in having to lay people off. Both times it was a horrible experience. Seeing the look of pain, fear, and rejection on their faces was heartbreaking. In both cases there was no choice. If there were no layoffs, the company wouldn't have survived and everyone would have been out of a job. This is why I'm so passionate about cash, what it is, how to track it, and how much it matters.

Method 2

This method is used by your accountant to calculate cash flow from operations. It is important to understand this method because there are several components affecting cash flow from operations, and you need to manage each component. This method starts with P&L and backs out non-cash expenses on the P&L. It then adds or subtracts changes in working capital.

P&L Profits or (Losses)
+/– Non-Cash Transactions on the P&L
+/– Changes in Working Capital (Receivables, Inventory, Prepaid Expense, Accounts Payable)
+/– Other (write-offs, gain/loss on sale of equipment)
= Cash Flow from Operations

<u>Non-Cash Transactions on the P&L</u>

How can there be non-cash transactions on the P&L? Again, profits are not equal to cash. There are non-cash transactions on the P&L. The most common is depreciation. When you buy a fixed asset like a truck, you record it as an asset on the balance sheet. If you pay cash, this reduces cash on the balance sheet. If you borrow the money, it increases long-term liabilities (debt). However, at this point nothing is recorded on the P&L. You will use that truck for a period of years, so that usage is recognized and recorded as depreciation on the P&L over time. Each month you record depreciation on the truck. Depreciation is a non-cash transaction, so it must be "backed out" of net profit to get to cash flow from operations.

<u>Changes in Working Capital</u>

Working capital is the difference between current assets and current liabilities. Current assets are the most liquid of your assets, meaning they are cash or can be converted to cash in the next twelve months. Current assets are primarily cash, receivables, inventory, and prepaid assets. Current liabilities are obligations (debts) due within one year and are primarily vendor accounts payable where payment is due in thirty days.

Receivables

Refer to the example of Mama's Banana Pudding Shop in the last chapter. At the end of 2013, Mama's company had receivables of $38,103 compared to $32,766 at the end of 2012, for an increase of $5,337. What is the effect of the increase in receivables? When you invoice a customer, you record revenue on the P&L even though you haven't been paid yet. You have, however, earned the right to be paid. That revenue on the P&L is a non-cash transaction because you haven't been paid. If receivables are increasing, there is non-cash revenue on the P&L, so you subtract the difference ($5,337) from pre-tax profits. Conversely, if receivables are decreasing, you are collecting more from customers than you are invoicing, so you need to add the change in receivables to pre-tax net profits.

Inventory

Inventory works the same way as receivables. If inventory increases in the period, you subtract the change from pre-tax net profits. If it decreases in the period, you add the change to pre-tax net profits.

Prepaid Expenses

Prepaid expenses work the same way as receivables. If prepaid expenses increase in the period, you subtract the change from net profits. If they decreases in the period, you add the change to net profits.

Accounts Payable

Accounts payable works the opposite of receivables and inventory. When a vendor bills your company, an expense is recorded on the P&L and a liability on the balance sheet because you must pay the vendor at some point in the future. Accounts payable on the balance sheet represent expenses you have incurred but not yet paid. The expense on the P&L is a non-cash expense and needs to be backed out (eliminated) from pre-tax net profits. Mama's had payables at the end of 2013 of $960, which was down from $1,050 at the end of 2012 by $90. Since payables decreased, you know she paid more money to vendors than she recorded in expense on the P&L, so you subtract $90 from P&L earnings.

To summarize what has occurred so far with Mama's:

Pre-Tax Net Profits	$21,480
Plus	
- Depreciation	9,449
Minus	
- Increase in Receivables	(5,337)
- Decrease in Payables	(90)
Cash Flow from Operations	$25,502

Method 2 Recap

Cash flow from operations is the amount of cash generated by the operation of the business. To calculate it, start with pre-tax net earnings on the P&L and then back out (eliminate) any non-cash transactions contained in the P&L. Start with pre-tax net profits on the P&L and then:

1. Deduct all non-cash transactions on the P&L (normally depreciation and amortization, but there can be other non-cash transactions on the P&L).
2. Add or subtract changes in working capital (receivables, inventory, prepaid expenses, and payables).
3. The result is your cash flow from operations.

Once you have calculated cash flow from operations, the rest is easy. The sum of cash flow from operations plus cash flow from investing and cash flow from financing equals total cash flow. Below is Mama's cash flow statement.

CASH FLOW STATEMENT – Mama's Banana Pudding Shop	12/31/2015
Pre-Tax Net Profit	**$ 21,480**
Less Depreciation	9,449
Adjusted Pre-Tax Profit	$ 30,929
Changes from Operating Activities not included in Pre-tax Profit	
Change in Accounts Receivable	$ (5,337)
Change in Current Liabilities	(90)
Changes from Operating Activities not Included in Net Income	(5,427)
Net Cash Provided/(Used) by Operating Activities	**$ 25,502**
Cash Flows from Investing Activities (Purchase of Capital Assets)	
Equipment Purchases	$ -
Vehicle Purchases	-
Net Cash (Used) Provided by Investing Activities	**$ -**
Cash Flows from Financing Activities (Borrowing & Repaying Loans)	
Bank Loan Payable	$ (10,218)
Distributions to Owners	(12,000)
Net Cash (Used) Provided by Financing Activities	**$ (22,218)**
Net Increase/(Decrease) in Cash	**$ 3,284**
Proof	
Beginning G/L Cash Balance as of:	$ 10,530
Ending G/L Cash Balance as of:	$ 13,814
Net (Decrease) Increase in Cash	$ 3,284

Mama's total cash flow is the sum of cash flows from operations, investing, and financing. How do you know if you've calculated the cash flow statement correctly? If correct, the total change in cash on the cash flow statement should equal the change in cash on the balance sheet from 12/31/2012 to 12/31/2013. Cash in the bank on 12/31/2012 was $10,530 and on 12/31/2013 was $13,814, so cash increased by $3,284.

Five Categories of Cash Flow

I believe there should be five categories of cash flow rather than three. I would add "non-recurring events" and "distributions to owners."

Non-Recurring Events

GAAP has a strange definition of Cash Flow from Operations. GAAP includes everything not in the "Financing" or "Investing" categories as "Operations." Cash Flow from Operations becomes the catch-all, or *default* category, in which to put everything else. It is a "black hole" type of category for everything that doesn't fit into the definition of "Financing" or "Investing." What if your business has a large expense to settle litigation? Suppose you make a large payment to a pension plan or merger-related expenses? Another example would be proceeds from insurance claims. These, and many other non-recurring items, appear on the P&L and get lumped into Cash Flow from Operations. If non-recurring items are large, they distort both the P&L Pretax Net Profit and Cash Flow from Operations. It is critical to know how much cash is being generated by the operation of your business, so I recommend putting non-recurring events in a separate category to improve management decision making.

Owners Distributions/Dividends

According to GAAP, owner distributions/dividends are classified as cash flow from financing. In a sense, they are. You invested money in your business initially and now you are taking it out, plus (hopefully) a return on your investment. As stated before, owners have crippled the future growth and improvement of their business by taking large distributions to fund lifestyle. However, if these distributions are highlighted on the cash flow statement, the owners would be more aware of how much cash is being withdrawn and the effect on the future of the business and its employees.

The most common reason for owners to take distributions is to pay taxes. Most small businesses are either LLCs or S Corps, and those legal entities do not pay income taxes. Instead, the owners include their share of pre-tax net profits on their personal income tax return. In effect, the owners pay the company's business income taxes. Owners may need to take distributions to pay taxes associated with the business. However, if owner distributions are many times what is necessary to pay the taxes on the business—which often happens—those distributions can cripple the business.

Excessive distributions deprive the company of money to make improvements to equipment, productivity, efficiency, or provide a Just-In-Case (JIC) cash cushion for recessionary times. When the Great Recession of 2008–2009 hit, many businesses succumbed and disappeared, and the owners' high-flying lifestyles came to an abrupt end.

As a small business, you can create a "management" cash flow statement for internal use with as many categories of cash flow as you deem appropriate. Work with your accountant to develop an internal report that best helps you manage your business.

Chapter Summary

The cash flow statement analyzes the change in the company's cash balance on the balance sheet to determine what caused the change in cash from the beginning of the period to the end of the period. The cash flow statement separates inflows and outflows of cash into three categories:

- Operations
- Investing
- Financing

The most important category is operations. If the business isn't generating cash from its operations—the conduct of its primary business function—money will not be available to grow and improve the company, repay debts, or make distributions to owners.

An excellent book on the subject is *Creative Cash Flow Reporting: Uncovering Sustainable Cash Flow* by Dr. Charles W. Mulford and Dr. Eugene E. Comiskey. Although somewhat technical in places, most people without an accounting background can still understand the material. The book relates true stories, which makes for interesting reading.

Insist that your accountant gives you a cash flow statement every month. If your accountant doesn't know how to prepare a cash flow statement, and many don't, then you have the wrong accountant.

Following is a reference guide to use when reviewing the cash flow statement if prepared using Method 2:

- Receivables or inventory going up—revenues on P&L not paid for; net profits adjusted down
- Receivables or inventory going down—collections exceed revenues on P&L; net profits adjusted up
- Payables going up—not paying out as much as expenses on P&L; net profits adjusted up
- Payables going down—paying more payables than expenses on the P&L; net profits adjusted down

Chapter Assignment

Examine your company's cash flow statement. Does it makes sense? If you've never done this, or if you don't have a cash flow statement, now is the time to act. Work with your accountant so you have a full understanding of the cash flow statement.

CHAPTER 49
INTERNAL CONTROLS

"What separates people is not the presence or absence of difficulty, but how they deal with the inevitable difficulties of life." – Jim Collins

No one likes to think of trusted employees stealing from their business. But in reality, it happens quite often. Setting up internal controls can save you money, time, and heartache. Even good people can do bad things contrary to their values, if they are under enough stress. Churches are particularly negligent in setting up internal controls, and sadly, church employees and volunteers do steal from their church as well.

Internal controls are procedures to minimize fraud or theft. Although impossible to completely prevent, you can minimize the threat. As we saw in chapter 47, even longtime trusted employees can act contrary to their values if their financial situation is desperate. *QuickBooks* is an accounting software commonly used by small businesses. It is relatively inexpensive, extremely versatile, and comprehensive. However, its internal controls need improvement. If you are a sole proprietorship, there is no problem since you won't steal from yourself (I hope!). The potential for problems increases as more people have access to your accounting software.

There are several versions of *QuickBooks*. Most are designed for a single user. *QuickBooks Enterprise* is designed for larger companies with multiple employees entering transactions. However, *Enterprise* has some of the same internal control flaws. The major problem is that someone can change the date of a transaction, reclassify a transaction to another account, or delete it entirely, with little audit trail to determine who made the change.

QuickBooks does have some limited audit reports to help detect who did what. For example, in one business, all employees with access to *QuickBooks* used the same user ID and password to access the system. It wasn't possible to determine who actually posted the transaction. A check could be written and dated twenty years prior, in the present, or fifty years in the future. *QuickBooks* does warn you that you are about to post a transaction to a date outside the current period, but it does not stop you if you click OK.

Your accounting software should never allow changes to an original entry. If a mistake is made and something is posted to an incorrect account, the change should be accomplished using a journal entry. A journal entry shows from where something is being moved and to where it is going, so you can see what happened.

For two years, one company had no cash receipts—only checks or electronic transfer receipts from the customer's bank. When the front desk employee, a longtime trusted "friend," became ill and couldn't come to work for a couple weeks, suddenly there were cash receipts. When investigated, they estimated that over $25,000 had been stolen over the past two years. Unfortunately, there wasn't adequate evidence to prosecute this employee.

How did it happen? When a customer paid in cash, the employee created an invoice in *QuickBooks* to the customer for the cash received. The customer could enter this invoice into their accounting system. However, when the customer left, the front desk employee deleted the invoice and pocketed the cash. Perhaps an expert could discover the customer invoice had been deleted, but most business owners would not know how.

Another common fraud is called "check washing," which can be done in the backseat of a car. Suppose you write a check for $50 and somewhere along the line that check is intercepted by the fraudster. The fraudster changes the name of the payee to their name, changes the amount of the check to $500, and cashes the check. Often it is extremely difficult to tell that the payee and amount have been changed. Reconciling your bank statement will uncover the problem.

Similar to check washing is fraudulently signing the check as another person. When I was treasurer for the John R. Hay House in Kingsport, Tennessee—a halfway house for convicted felons—a resident was cleaning the office and discovered some blank checks in the bottom of a drawer. He wrote checks payable to cash and signed my name, Roy Austin. He was caught for two reasons:

1. The Bank of Tennessee contacted me when these checks started showing up because the account had been closed for years.
2. I never sign the checks Roy Austin because that isn't my full legal name.

Internal controls are difficult for small companies with limited personnel and resources. Even so, there are some ways to protect the assets of your business.

Separation of Duties

Ideally, split up accounting duties for bookkeeping, deposits, check writing, paying bills, reconciling bank statements, and reviewing the general ledger. If fraud occurs, it then requires the collusion of two or more employees. The more people involved, the harder it is to execute. If full separation of duties isn't possible, then sharing responsibilities so that critical tasks are performed, or reviewed, by more than one person is a viable option. One procedure is:

- Employee A—invoices customers
- Employee B—pays vendor bills
- Owner—receives and deposits checks, or has customers pay via electronic transfer directly to company's bank account
- Outsource accountant—reconciles the bank statement
- Owner and outsource accountant—review general ledger transactions

Access Controls

Hopefully, your software has the capability to control access to respective parts of an accounting system. For example, the employee invoicing customers cannot access the accounts payable section, and therefore cannot write checks.

The most common method is through the use of user IDs, passwords, and lockouts. If multiple employees are accessing your accounting system, you want the capability to identify who posted a transaction. Most accounting software has tracking reports that can show who posted a transaction. Never, ever provide someone your user ID and/or password. If you do, you could be accused of a fraud they committed.

Physical Audits

Physical audits include hand-counting cash and any physical assets tracked in the accounting system, such as inventory, materials, tools, and equipment. If the physical count doesn't match what the accounting system reports, there is a problem. If the accounting system says $500 is in petty cash but a count only comes up with $150, what happened to the other $350? Inventory items can often "disappear," so regular physical counts are important.

The plant manager at one company told me he caught an employee filling up a five-gallon pail with chocolate milk from the production line. Items, particularly small ones, can "accidently" fall off a retail store's shelf and into a tourist bag.

One manufacturing company did an inventory every quarter. A review of the accounting system inventory report revealed an item stored in bin "CNF." Inventory items were stored in bins, with each bin having a number and location so forklift drivers knew where to retrieve or store an item. The bins were not in alphabetical order. An investigation revealed that a forklift driver who could not locate the bin where something was to be stored used his handheld device to *create* bin CNF in the system. CNF stood for "Can Not Find."

Small tools are particularly vulnerable to being "lost." Make physical counts a part of your internal control procedures.

Documentation

Standardizing, and numbering, documents used for financial transactions, such as customer invoices, purchase orders, bills of lading, internal materials requests, inventory receipts, or travel expense reports, can help maintain consistency in record keeping. Using standard document formats can make it easier to review past records when searching for the source of a discrepancy in the system. A lack of standardization causes items to be overlooked or misinterpreted in such a review.

Transaction Detail Reports

Run a transaction detail report each month. Most business owners can scroll through this report in about fifteen minutes. As CFO for D. J. Powers, I scrolled through thousands of transactions each month to find transactions in the wrong account code, all in one hour. By doing this each month, you'll become more proficient in detecting what does and does not make sense, because you will be aware of what to look for.

If you see a vendor bill in a revenue account, you know something is wrong. Conversely, a customer invoice in an expense account doesn't make sense. A quick method to find transactions in the wrong account is to export the report to a spreadsheet and then do a search for "invoice" and "bill."

You also want to review what is in an account. What if the monthly office rent bill shows up in the electricity account? You will soon learn to spot anomalies.

Bank Reconciliations

This is an extremely important control that is often neglected. A bank reconciliation compares the transactions on the bank statement to the cash transactions in your accounting system and identifies differences. The most common difference is outstanding checks where you've written a check to pay a vendor who either hasn't cashed it, or, if they have, it hasn't been received by your bank. A bank reconciliation also reveals deposits the bank received that aren't on your books, or conversely, deposits on your books that the bank hasn't received. There could be a deposit on your books but the money has not yet been deposited in the bank. (Did someone pocket the money?)

A bank reconciliation also reveals withdrawals from your bank account that aren't on your books. Remember the "check washing" story. An electronic hacker could withdraw money from your bank account, and you would never know if you don't reconcile the bank statement to your accounting records.

It's important to understand that the cash on your books rarely equals what is in the bank. A common practice is for a business owner facing payroll tomorrow to call the bank to determine available cash. The problem is that a number of checks may not have cleared the bank. When payroll checks are issued tomorrow, those outstanding checks could clear before the payroll checks. Your employees won't be happy when their paychecks bounce. Post your cash transactions in your accounting system every day so you always know exactly how much money is available.

The bank has limited liability if fraudulent transactions siphon money out of your account. It is your responsibility to notify the bank on a timely basis of a discrepancy. Contact your bank regarding their policy.

Approval Authority

Requiring specific employees to authorize certain types of transactions adds a layer of responsibility to accounting records by proving that transactions have been seen, analyzed, and approved by appropriate personnel. Requiring approval for large payments and expenses can prevent unscrupulous employees from making fraudulent transactions with company funds. A good practice is to require checks to have two signatures so that no one person writes checks. A variation of this is to require two signatures on checks above a certain dollar amount.

Never use a signature stamp, which a fraudster can easily use to sign your name to a check.

Positive Pay

Most banks provide what is called Positive Pay. With Positive Pay, each day you upload to the bank a file that contains all the checks written that day. As people cash checks you've written, the bank's system compares the file you uploaded to the checks that are clearing and notifies you of anything not on the file.

Electronic Funds Transfer

Electronic funds transfer (EFT) is bank terminology for "pay bills online." You should limit the authority of who can initiate EFTs. Even though I have Internet access to a number of client's bank accounts, enabling me to download transactions and reconcile their bank statements, I am blocked from initiating any type of cash transfer.

Chapter Assignment

Review your internal control procedures, making a list of what you have in place. Work with your bank and accountant to strengthen them and determine if additional controls are needed.

SECTION 8

SWAMP SURVIVAL SKILLS

CHAPTER 50
TIME MANAGEMENT

"Time Management is not managing time. It is managing ourselves."
– Steven Covey, author, *The 7 Habits of Highly Successful People*

Being responsible for the survival of a business can be overwhelming. You get phone calls, e-mails, and texts all day every day. How do you assign enough time to learn to manage all the various functions of your business, pay attention to them, use them effectively, keep improving yourself, and devote time to your family? In other words, how do you manage your time effectively?

Small business owners constantly state, "I don't have time." If you've been in business for long, you know that your most valuable resource is time. Like all resources, there is a finite supply, and once it is used, you can't get it back. The challenge then is to use it wisely. However, it is imperative to allocate time to work *on* the business. Owners often push back, saying they are so busy working *in* the business that they don't have time to work *on* the business and also be able to devote time to their families, friends, or church activities. We all face the same dilemma.

When interviewing Don and Dave Sergio of Calfkiller Brewing, I asked what their greatest challenge had been, expecting them to mention all the legal issues involved in obtaining approvals for a brewery in a "dry" county. Their answer was, "Focusing on bringing more balance to the time we spend with our families outside of work hours." Obviously, there needs to be a balance between your work life and your personal life. If not, you will burn out at work or suffer negative consequences in your personal life.

One owner, who worked "night and day" for four years, saw annual revenues gradually declining. The business was in danger of going under, and he was depressed about what to do if his business failed.

Part of the problem was that his business had become a tedious job, and he was so stressed that he didn't enjoy the job or the business anymore, which affected his customer relationships and the quality of his work. What began as a fun and exciting adventure had become drudgery. He was working almost nonstop. Fortunately, he was able to re-focus and make necessary changes, and the business is now doing well and growing.

You have to manage all the various aspects of your business, but that doesn't mean you have to do everything (micromanage).

How should you satisfy all the demands on your time, while maintaining your sanity and balance in your life? There are a multitude of books on time management, and different systems work for different people. Here are a few strategies:

1. Do the most important thing first.
2. Delegate, but supervise.
3. Schedule your time.
4. Plan your tomorrow, today.
5. Have a strategy for small amounts of idle time.

First Things First

Do you have an "action list," or a to-do list, of various essential tasks? If you don't, create one. Tasks can easily be forgotten. You never want to have a customer call and complain that you haven't done something you promised to do. Not only is it embarrassing when things fall through the cracks, but it may be the difference between gaining or keeping a customer.

Having the action list is just the first step. Identify the most important task on the list and work on that before you tackle other items. As the day progresses, you will be pulled this way and that as you "fight fires" and manage your business. I know it happens to you because it happens to me and every business owner I know. When you have put out the immediate fire, continue working on the most important task on the list.

Work on the most important task until it is done.

Don't pick out the easiest item on the list or the task that you most enjoy doing. Work on the most important thing. If you can't get the most important task done, then the other tasks don't matter.

Delegate, but Supervise

When first starting the business, you may be the only person involved, and you have to do everything. As you grow, you realize that you can't do everything. Your time is best spent utilizing your best skills and talents. Focus on tasks and projects that fit your core expertise and delegate, but *supervise*, the rest. You can delegate, hire part-time people, and/or hire independent contractors to do many functions, but make no mistake—although you can delegate responsibility for a set of tasks, you cannot delegate *accountability*. You alone are responsible for checking the work done to ensure it is done correctly.

A common excuse for not delegating is, "I can do it faster myself. It takes too much time to train someone." While this may be true, you limit the growth of your business if you try to do everything yourself.

Even if you hire the CPA or bookkeeper with the most experience and best reputation to perform your accounting, always remember that *you* are accountable for checking their product to make sure it makes sense. You must have at least a basic understanding of accounting. You don't need to be an expert in accounting, marketing, or logistics, but you do need to know enough to manage and supervise these functions, and that simply means knowing where to look, what to look for, and how to use the information so you can ask intelligent questions.

Once you have a working knowledge of each subject, you then decide which to focus on personally and which to assign to someone else. Remember, as a leader you can delegate the authority to complete a task, but you cannot abandon the responsibility of making sure the work is done properly. That responsibility will always rest squarely on your shoulders.

Delegate, but supervise.

In *The E-Myth Revisited*, Michael Gerber discusses the problem of "management by abdication." As he says, you can't just hire or contract with someone and then walk away. It is your business and your responsibility. Ultimately, you are the only one accountable for its growth and success. And you are also accountable for its backward slide and failure.

Schedule Your Time

You may be groaning by now. Yes, I know it takes thought and discipline to schedule effective use of your time, but the rewards are substantial. The fact is that if you don't control your calendar, your calendar will control you.

If you don't control your calendar, your calendar will control you.

Controlling your calendar means controlling every facet of your life. Schedule personal time as well as your time in the business. Probably 98 percent of e-mails aren't emergencies and don't need to be acted on immediately. Yes, there are exceptions. Bob All of Custom Security Specialists prides himself on 24/7 rapid response when his customers call or an alarm is triggered. But since he can't possibly do it all himself, he has employees who monitor their customers night and day.

Schedule your time and watch how you use it or abuse it. Be aware of a few of the pitfalls of running a business that erode your time and progress. For example, being busy and being productive are two different things. Just because you've had a busy day, met with numerous people, and completed paperwork, that doesn't mean you've been productive. Cut back on unproductive activities as much as possible. As the leader, you're setting the example. If that example has your employees believing that being busy is the same as being productive, how do you think they will behave? When you comprehend the difference between being busy and being productive, you can spot the employees who are being busy but not productive and redirect their efforts.

If you are self-employed, you know how dangerous it is to choose busy over productive. In the end, you're the only one who produces, so the work must be done, even if it's after midnight and the next day starts early. Owning a small business frequently necessitates overtime. However, overtime needs to be productive; otherwise, it's not worth it. The best use of overtime is developing systems and methods that will eliminate the need for future overtime.

You have to control your calendar from working *in* the business and working *on* the business, to working overtime, and to having time for life away from the business. Refer to, and work with, your calendar as much as possible, until you're completely on top of it and there are no surprises or panic attacks when you look at it.

Scheduling your time includes making appointments with yourself to work *on* the business every week, for at least half an hour. Pick a time when you know you will not have any interruptions. This may mean getting to the office earlier or staying late. During that time, turn off your phone and don't look at e-mail. There are few situations that can't be delayed for thirty minutes. Make sure you can be reached in an emergency, but otherwise this time is sacred. Do whatever it takes to protect it.

You may have to train your employees to leave you alone during this period. If your door is usually open, close it. If it's usually closed, put a sign on it stating when you will be available again. If people drop by "for just a minute" or with "a quick question," tell them you will come find them or invite them back when you are finished. Refuse to be drawn into anything less than an emergency. Keep in mind that while you are teaching others to respect this time, you are also teaching yourself to respect it. If you don't respect your own boundaries, you'll never be able to prioritize properly.

This practice is important, because just half an hour a week adds up to twenty-six hours a year devoted to improving your business, and the cumulative effect is even greater. When you improve one aspect of your business, you free up time and resources to improve other areas. Half an hour a week will have a significant cumulative impact on your business. Imagine what ten to fifteen minutes a day can do.

If your action list is out of control, step back and re-evaluate. Return to what you now know: do the most important task first. Get the list out of your head and onto paper or into your computer and number each item in order of importance. People tend to take the power of this simple act for granted, but it's important to give each item on your action list enough thought to delegate its place.

Think of building your business the way you would build a house. Imagine an empty lot filled with grass, bushes, and mounds of dirt. Working on yourself and your leadership skills, and organizing the way you work *in* and *on* your business, is similar to clearing away the dirt, removing the grass, and pulling stumps to prepare the site. It is hard work, but the results make way for an exciting and beautiful future.

Plan Your Day before It Starts

Have you ever started your day committed to getting through a list of tasks, but then the phone started ringing, the e-mails wouldn't stop, and texts got out of control? At the end of the day, you never accomplished half of what you intended. This happens to all of us, and sometimes it can't be avoided. However, you can minimize the distractions by planning your day before it starts. Don't wait until alligators are nipping at your heels.

Having the plan for tomorrow written down the day before will give you peace of mind, and may even help you sleep better. Life is stressful when you are being torn apart by numerous, conflicting demands. Have you ever heard someone say, "When things settle down, I'll get to that"? Let me tell you—things *never* settle down, and if you're leading an active and productive life, it will always be hectic. When you have a plan and a sense of direction for what you want to accomplish, life becomes less stressful.

Don't Waste Time on People Who Waste Yours

We all know this person. They're chronically late for meetings and appointments, or totally forget them.

I understand that everyone has emergencies. Occasionally, but hopefully rarely, we forget an appointment. When someone is chronically late, it is a waste of your time. Why are they always late? Don't accept, "That is just the way I am." Everyone makes time to do what they want to do. If an activity is important enough, they will be on time or get the job you asked for done.

Besides being rude and inconsiderate, what are these people *really* saying? That you are not important enough to be for them to be on time. They are saying that their time is more valuable than yours, so you just have to wait.

What do you do with these people? Don't waste your valuable time with them and, if possible, drop them from your business network. You have better things to do than sit around and wait on people who waste a limited resource—your time.

Have a Strategy for Using Small Amounts of Idle Time

Do you ever find yourself with five, ten, or fifteen minutes of idle time? Maybe you're in between appointments, or someone cancels or is late to an appointment, or the meeting ends early. It happens to all of us. Even though there is not enough time to work on a significant project, you don't want to waste time either. The question is, what are you going to do with that idle time? Do you play games on your phone, idly surf the web, or do you have a list of mini-tasks to work on when this happens?

You can make a courtesy call to a customer, answer a LinkedIn invitation, enter contact information in your phone or address book, clean your tools, or take on any other task that needs doing. Have a strategy for using these short intervals to avoid or minimize wasted time. Sometimes an appropriate use of these short intervals is just to chill out, relax for a few minutes, and reflect on all the positives in life. When life is really hectic and stressful, part of your time management plan may include downtime for meditation and relaxation.

Chapter Assignment

1. Create an action list.
2. Prioritize the list to identify the most important task.

3. Work on the most important task first.
4. Delegate where possible.
5. Schedule time on your calendar to work *on* the business and your personal life.
6. Make a list of things to do during short intervals when you are between tasks or appointments.

CHAPTER 51
CONTRARY OPINIONS

"To better avoid errors, you should talk to people who disagree with you and you should talk to people who are not in the same emotional situation you are." – Daniel Kahneman, 2002 Nobel Memorial Prize in Economic Sciences

In many ways, this topic fits in with the planning and preparation for your business. However, I've given it a separate chapter because it is an extremely important skill. How do you react when someone disagrees with you? If people always agree with you, just what have you learned?

I was having dinner one evening with my friend Robert Elsner, who is an extremely intelligent engineer. I mentioned an idea I had for this book. He looked me in the eye and said, "Roy, I don't agree with you." He then explained his rationale.

Internally, my first reaction was defensive. I thought I had a pretty good idea. But instead of arguing my position, I listened to his perspective and tucked it away in the back of my brain. Over the next few days, I thought about what he had said and tried to think of some logical reason why my idea was a good one.

The point is that by disagreeing with me, Robert *forced* me to think and re-evaluate. Had he simply agreed with me, I would have learned nothing. I trust Robert. He was not disagreeing with me to criticize me personally. He simply had a different opinion, and he voiced it diplomatically out of friendship.

Find someone who disagrees with your idea.

Small businesses are often started on the premise that because we like a product or service, everyone will like it. Just because people need something doesn't necessarily mean they want it. If you bounce your business idea off friends and family, the vast majority will tell you it's a great idea even if they think it isn't. Why? Because they don't want to discourage you or hurt your feelings.

In the initial auditions for the TV show *American Idol*, there are contestants who simply can't sing, and in some cases are horrible. They often complain bitterly about not being sent through to Hollywood and accuse the judges of not being able to recognize their great talent. Why do they think they have such great talent? Is it because their parents or friends told them they had such talent? Is it possible that those friends and family were merely being polite or didn't want to discourage them?

When someone agrees with you, you learn nothing.

If you are planning to go into a new business or make significant changes in your existing business, find a friend who is willing to disagree with you in a loving and caring manner. Just because someone disagrees with you doesn't make them right, but it should force you to think and re-evaluate your position. If you do not have a positive logical argument why you are right, then you need to make a change.

A businessman asserted that in forty years he and his partner had never had an argument. How can that be any good? Compare that to the following story about Grant Teaff, who I heard speak in Knoxville, Tennessee.

Grant Teaff, an All-American football player and head football coach at Baylor University from 1972 to 1992, understood the value of contrary opinions. He won two Southwest Conference titles, and his teams played in eight bowl games. Coach Teaff believed in loyalty, and in diverse and contrary opinions.

I can still hear him say that when the coaches had their planning sessions to devise a game plan, the feathers flew. There were disagreements over what the plan should be, and often voices were raised. But when the team went on the field—no matter whose plan was adopted—that plan was the team's plan, and everyone, players and coaches alike, committed 110 percent to it. Coach Teaff understood that getting everyone's candid input made the team, and the plan, stronger.

When you find someone whom you can trust and respect and who will offer up divergent opinions and contrasting views, you have found a valuable ally.

Chapter Assignment

Identify friends you can trust to give you honest, candid, and thought-provoking feedback about your ideas. Discuss your ideas with these people.

CHAPTER 52
SINGLE FOCUS

"When you discover your mission, you will feel its demand. It will fill you with enthusiasm and a burning desire to get to work on it."
– W. Clement Stone

Have you heard the story about the guy who jumped on his horse and rode off in all directions? You can't accomplish everything at once, and you can't accomplish ten things at the same time. Obvious, right?

All too often, small business owners try to accomplish too many things and wind up not doing anything well. Varying the products and services your company offers is fine, but there is a time and place for diversification.

Image by Pixabay

When a lion stalks its prey, it picks one animal out of the herd and focuses solely on it. Other animals can run right in front of the lion, but its eyes will stay focused on the one it picked out. When the lion has finished its meal, it can then focus on something else.

Many companies try to ride off in all directions. They have so many ideas that they keep skipping from one to another and finish none of them.

One man, a brilliant engineer, solicited my advice about one of his ideas. His ideas are really big; no one will ever accuse him of thinking small. His head is filled with ideas for products. Unfortunately, staying focused on one idea at a time is a problem for him. We discussed the "lion focus" concept. His response was, "Yeah, yeah, I get it!"—but then he immediately launched off on another tangent. I declined to work with him because I knew it would be a waste of his money since he never finishes what he starts.

Another example of a lack of focus is trying to run too many businesses at the same time. I've met people who try to run two, three, or even four businesses in different industries at the same time. That may work if you are a large conglomerate with thousands of employees, but it doesn't work well for a small business.

You've heard the adage "jack of all trades, master of none." Build one business that operates at peak efficiency, profitability, and cash flow first, and then consider other ideas and businesses.

Calfkiller Brewing Company in Sparta, Tennessee, is a prime example of executing one idea, and one business, really well, and then gradually adding more varied products. Don and Dave Sergio love beer. They first learned to brew beer in their kitchen for personal use. Friends liked their beer, so the brothers converted a barn into a larger-scale brewing operation. Gradually the operation expanded, and they began brewing larger quantities for sale to local area bars and restaurants. Initially, they had only one beer, Grassroots Ale. Then they added J. Henry Original Mild, and they continue to add new beers to their product offering.

They have perfected their craft and now have a five-year plan to open their own inn, restaurant, and brewery on the Calfkiller River, providing a dock for kayaks and canoes. The brothers are progressing one step at a time and realistically planning each step. They are DWITs. DWITs have "lion focus."

Be a DWIT with lion focus.

Another example of focusing on one business or idea until it is perfected and then moving on is Olio Tasting Room. In 2011, Penny Williman opened with one store in Alexandria, Virginia, offering olive oil products.

With the first store operating at peak efficiency and profitability, she opened a second. Gradually, Olio expanded its product lines to include pastas, sauces, teas, sea salts, tapenades, specialty condiments, and more. Penny did one thing well—olive oil in one store—before graduating to other stores and products.

Focus on the one product, service, store, or idea until it is perfected and successful in the market. When you do that, you will make some money, and that money will enable you to offer other products or services.

Chapter Assignment

Think of a time in your life when you were lion focused on getting a particular project done or in reaching a particular goal—where even if something interrupted your focus, you went right back to working on that goal.

CHAPTER 53
MISTAKES

"Learn from the mistakes of others. You can't possibly live long enough to make them all yourself." – Eleanor Roosevelt

One of my favorite movies is *Avatar*, the 2009 epic tale of a former marine, Jake Sully, who is thrust into hostilities on an alien planet. As an "Avatar"—a human mind in an alien body—he finds himself torn between two worlds in a desperate fight for his own survival and that of the indigenous people, the Na'vi.

In one scene, the spiritual leader of the Na'vi probes Sully (who is referred to as one of the "Sky People") as to why he is on their planet.

"I came to learn," he says honestly.

"We have tried to teach other Sky People," the spiritual leader says, scoffing. "It is hard to fill a cup which is already full."

Your life is not a blockbuster movie taking place on a distant planet 140 years in the future. However, your life is an adventure and includes mistakes and problem-solving challenges that require being open to new information and changing strategy in the face of failure.

We all make mistakes. Then we have to choose whether to perpetuate them or correct them. And we must deal with other peoples' mistakes. Just never forget that you can overcome your mistakes.

No one possesses a full cup of knowledge. Those who think they have it all figured out are usually the ones who have the most to learn. They're so busy thinking they know it all that they miss what's in front of their face. In the business world, as in life, you should always be striving to learn and improve.

GATOR BITE

When you are finished learning and changing, you are finished.
– Don Brashears, Chair, Bluffton (South Carolina) Chamber of Commerce

Always be open to learning new ideas and concepts. Today's world is extremely fast paced, with technology changing at an amazing rate. Those who are not constantly learning, growing, and improving will be left behind. Whatever competitive advantage they had will evaporate.

Think of growth in two contexts. In one, growth means the business is becoming larger in some way—more revenues, employees, locations, and/or assets. Not everyone wants expanded business. Some prefer to keep to a certain size, which is an acceptable choice. However, you must constantly grow the business in the context of continuous improvement. If not, your business will lag behind the competition and ultimately lose customers to businesses that stay at the forefront and learn to do things better, cheaper, and faster.

Recognizing that everyone makes mistakes, I encouraged my staff to admit theirs. They were also instructed to present a plan for preventing a mistake from happening again. They were not penalized if they made a mistake unless they tried to hide it. You lose the opportunity to learn and improve if you hide, ignore, or deny a problem you have created.

Step 1: Learn from your mistakes.
Step 2: Prevent them from recurring.

Allocate time for improvement and learning. Take time to read books and articles, even if it is only one page a day. Those who say they don't have time to read err in the assumption that they know everything they need to know. People with different knowledge, skills, and perspectives are an invaluable resource for your business.

Mistakes are inevitable, but intelligent business decision-making practices minimize how often and on what scale those mistakes occur. Making a sound business decision is difficult even when you have all the information. However, it is impossible to make a good business decision when you have incorrect (or no) information.

Chapter Assignment

List the major mistakes you have made, and reflect on what you learned from them and what actions you took to prevent future occurrences.

CHAPTER 54
ADAPT

"There is nothing to be learned from the second kick of a mule."
– Mark Twain

To survive in the Business Swamp, you must be able to adapt. The buzz word today is "pivot." The old saying that "the only certainties in life are death and taxes" isn't true. You can add "change" to that list.

Today, change occurs at an accelerated pace, making it virtually impossible to catch up. But here's the good news: your competitors have the same problem.

Adapting is a never-ending battle for all businesses. Our friend the alligator has managed to adapt, survive, and succeed despite over 150 million years of dramatic climate changes. Change can be dramatic and sudden (technology) or occur gradually over a long period of time (continuing minor changes to a process that slowly make it more efficient).

The president of marketing for a large manufacturing company fell in love with a new product. Initial market acceptance was outstanding, and he was convinced it was the key to the company's future growth. He enthusiastically advocated for this product and convinced the company to build additional factories to produce it. The first year was a stunning success, reinforcing the president's confidence in the product. Then the problems began.

The product had some quality problems when used in a clothing application. The clothing did not wear well or last. Additionally, this style of clothing went out of fashion. Each year the forecast was for higher sales volume and rising prices, but each year the opposite occurred. This major corporation supported the product for twenty years even though it never made money and finally dropped it when the president retired.

Clearly, this marketing president's obsession with the product was driven by denial and a fear to admit failure. The obvious fix appeared to be to dump the product and cut losses.

The moral of the story is that all ideas are not successful. Decision makers and those in leadership roles must concede when a project fails—even if initially successful—and move on and minimize losses.

A sound business decision today might not be viable in the future. Factors such as interest rates, inflation, economic cycles, geo-politics, whims of society, ecological changes, and technology can totally change the environment in which a business operates. You can either acknowledge you have stepped into quicksand and take steps to get out, or you can deny it and slowly sink into oblivion.

Develop the ability to be an impartial judge of your own decisions. If emotion, ego, or politics guide your decision making, you may be setting yourself up for future problems. As David Crenshaw with International Dunnage says, "Keep emotion and politics out of decision making, and make decisions that are in the best interest of the company as a whole, not just a particular department or division."

Keep emotion and politics out of decision making, and make decisions that are in the best interest of the company as a whole.

Chapter Assignment

What would you have done in the same situation if you were the president of marketing? What information would you rely on to let you know that something isn't working? Do you know exactly where to look? What would it take for you to dump a failure? Think of a time when you pivoted and went in a different direction. Were you right, or did you pivot too soon or too late?

SECTION 9

SWAMP BEST PRACTICES

CHAPTER 55
SECTION INTRODUCTION

"We simply attempt to be fearful when others are greedy and to be greedy only when others are fearful." – Warren Buffett

We've all heard the expression "experience is the best teacher." Usually, it is the negative experiences that teach us the most. However, there is a big drawback with experience as a teacher. Experiences, especially bad ones, chew up your life. They drain your time, emotion, and sometimes your money. A better teacher is somebody else's experience. Learning from the experiences of others saves time and heartache. Extracting ideas and concepts from others can help avoid business quicksand.

Avoid the temptation to say, "This doesn't apply to me. My situation is different." Everyone's situation is unique. But what is important is extracting the concept and adapting it to improve your individual situation. The cap you bought with your favorite sports team logo on it may not have fit when you bought it, but after you adjusted the Velcro strap, it did fit. You can also adjust the following ideas to fit your circumstances.

CHAPTER 56

TAX STRATEGY VERSUS BUSINESS STRATEGY

"However beautiful the strategy, you should occasionally look at the results." – Winston Churchill

Generally speaking, it is a good idea to minimize taxes. There are legitimate strategies for doing so. However, if tax strategy becomes more important than business strategy, you have a problem.

Most small businesses are set up as LLCs or S Corps. Both LLCs and S Corps are referred to as "pass-through entities" because the company itself doesn't pay income taxes. Instead, the taxable profits from the business are allocated to each owner, who then pays the tax on his/her personal federal tax return. No one wants to pay a dime extra in income tax, but paying taxes is one of the costs of doing business.

Max (not his real name) owned a business. He proudly stated that he didn't pay *any* income tax. Now how did he accomplish this? At year end, the business gave a bonus to all managers calculated to bring the pre-tax income of the business to zero. Sounds clever, doesn't it? The managers loved this strategy.

There is merit to giving a bonus to people who deserve one. However, does giving bonuses just to reduce income taxes align with the company's business strategy? In this case, many of those managers didn't deserve a bonus and some should have been fired. Giving some of them a bonus sent the message to other employees that it is acceptable to be late for work, do sloppy work, and have a negative attitude. If you are taking money out of the business to pay bonuses just to reduce taxes, where is the money to reinvest in future growth and improvement of the company and its operations? How do you buy new equipment if there is no cash? How do you build up a cash reserve fund in case of a recession or some other cash-requiring event that might put the existence of your business in peril? Money spent in one place can't be spent somewhere else.

Never let tax strategy trump business strategy.

Another tactic for minimizing federal income taxes is buying unnecessary items that qualify for bonus depreciation in the year purchased. The key word here is "unnecessary."

Let's say your business needs a pickup truck, and a used one for $15,000 would meet your needs. Instead, you purchase a new one for $50,000. It's a tax write-off, right? So why not get the top of the line?

Business owners often overspend under the guise of saving taxes. What is the tax savings on that $50,000 truck? It is not $50,000. If you could deduct the full $50,000, would that reduce your taxes by $50,000? Since tax laws change constantly and your situation is unique, you should coordinate with your tax preparer. In virtually all situations, your taxes will not be reduced by the full amount of the purchase.

Let's analyze a hypothetical situation. Suppose your business has pre-tax profits of $50,000. You buy the truck for $50,000, and in that particular year, there is a special tax provision allowing you to deduct the full price of the truck. Your pre-tax profits are zero: $50,000 minus the $50,000 deduction. How much did you save in taxes? This depends on your tax bracket, but for simplicity and discussion, let's assume you would have owed taxes of $12,500 on the $50,000 pre-tax income. Now your pre-tax profit is zero, so you saved $12,500 in taxes. That is a nice saving, but it isn't the full cost of the truck, and now you are obligated to pay for that $50,000 truck.

If you borrowed money to buy the truck, you now have monthly payments that include interest on the loan. If you paid cash for the truck, then you have depleted your bank account by $50,000 that could have been used for future business needs.

Chapter Assignment

What is your tax strategy? Think about any of the "creative solutions" suggested to you or that you have tried. Picture the long-term implications. Does it really save you money? Will it end up costing you something more important than money, like your business culture or the risk of not having enough cash? Does your tax strategy compromise any of your fundamentals—purpose, values, or operating principles?

Taxes are a part of business. Look for ways to minimize taxes, but do so in a manner consistent with your overall business strategy for the long-term success of your business.

CHAPTER 57

BAD DEBTS AND COLLECTIONS

"Even if you're on the right track, you'll get run over if you just sit there." – Will Rogers

What is your procedure when you realize a customer you invoiced is never going to pay you? You should do everything possible to collect from customers prior to this point. The reality is that every business will have some bad debts at some stage. One option is to give the invoice to a collection agency specializing in collecting bad debts. If the agency is successful, you may recover a small portion of what is owed.

How is a bad debt recorded on your accounting books? Small business owners frequently simply reverse, or cancel, the original invoice. Suppose you invoice a customer for $1,000 and eventually realize they will never pay. The original invoice created revenue on your P&L, which in turn created pre-tax profits, and you created a receivable on the balance sheet. Reversing the invoice took revenue off of the P&L, which reduced pre-tax profits and eliminated the receivable.

So what's the problem? The problem is that you have no historical record of the amount of bad debts. Do you have more bad debts now than in the past? Is the bad debt situation improving or getting worse? How do you improve your bad debt problems if you don't know their magnitude?

Instead of canceling or deleting the invoice, write off the receivable as a "bad debt expense." This eliminates the receivable, places bad debt expense on your P&L, and in turn the bad debt expense reduces pre-tax profits. Whether you cancel the invoice or write the receivable off as bad debt expense, pre-tax profits are the same. Now you have a record of your bad debts.

One client did not have any bad debt expense on their P&L in years. When asked why, she said, "Sure, we have customers that never pay. When that occurs, we just cancel the original invoice." Investigation revealed significantly large bad debts relative to the size of the company, with the problem getting worse every year.

Write off bad debts so you can track them.

Collecting Receivables

One company was terrible at collecting receivables. It did the work and invoiced the customer, but did not pursue receivables. Consequently, the partners were constantly loaning the company money to keep it afloat. By not collecting receivables, they were effectively working for free.

Develop a procedure, and either assign responsibility for collections to current staff or hire someone to help. Alternatively, use a collection agency. Try to make sure the collection agency will not damage your relationship with the customer.

Another possible solution is to hire part-time help with collections. Retired business people with collections experience are often happy to help a small business and normally work for a lot less than they were paid when working full time.

Most accounting programs have their receivable aging reports set up to capture whether a receivable is thirty, sixty, or over ninety days past due. If your program will allow it, set these "buckets" to twenty-five, fifty, and seventy-five. Why wait until the invoice is past due to call the customer. Instead, when an invoice hits twenty-five days, make a courtesy call and ask the customer if they are satisfied with the product or service provided. "And oh, by the way, this invoice will be due in a couple days," slides nicely into the end of your conversation. This procedure dramatically improves collections.

Chapter Assignment

Review your accounts receivable aging report every week. Identify the oldest and get to work collecting. If some of those receivables are uncollectible, write them off as bad debts.

CHAPTER 58

RECORDING VENDOR BILLS

"Real knowledge is to know the extent of one's ignorance."
– Confucius

When should you record vendor bills in your accounting system? Should you record them when you *receive* them or when you *pay* them? Many businesses do the latter. The most common reason is that "it saves time." It does save time, but is it the best practice? If you record a vendor bill and three weeks later go back into the system to pay it, you've gone into the system twice. However, if you enter the bill and pay it at the same time, you are only in the system once.

A better practice is to enter vendor bills when you receive them and pay them later when they are due. Yes, this procedure takes slightly more time, but there are benefits to doing it this way. You now have a record of who you owe and when the bill is due. You can run an accounts payable aging report showing all the vendors you owe, all the invoices for each vendor, and when each invoice is due.

If your company is in financial trouble, review the payables aging report and the amount of cash available to decide if the company could pay any vendors, and if you can, how much. You need to know to whom you owe money and when payment is due. In addition to managing your payables, you want to properly state your financial position. If you enter bills and pay them on the same day, the payables on your balance sheet will probably be close to zero.

Is that true when a stack of bills is sitting in your inbox waiting to be entered? If you provide financial statements to your bank or anyone else, including owners, you are responsible for presenting an accurate statement of where your business sits financially.

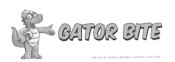

Record vendor bills when they are received.

In some cases, it may be appropriate to record a payable if you have incurred the expense but haven't received the vendor bill. If you have a vendor estimate that will be close to the final invoice price, enter it as a payable and adjust the bill in the system when the invoice arrives. This will enable better matching of expenses to revenues.

Chapter Assignment

Establish a procedure for timely recording of vendor bills. Review your accounts payable aging report each week to determine which vendors have priority for payment.

CHAPTER 59
PAYING OFF LOANS

"One reason why some are always in debt is because they cannot do without the things they do not need." – Roy L. Smith

An owner asked what procedure should be used to pay off loans incurred by the company. The company had some excess cash, and one of the owner's goals was to be debt free. An interesting question.

Before deciding which loan to pay off, decide if paying off a loan early is in alignment with your business strategy and fundamentals (purpose, values, and operating principles). Our old friend opportunity cost kicks in again. Paying off a loan early uses money that could be used for another purpose. In addition, there may be tax benefits in not paying a loan off early. Talk with your accountant before making a decision.

Assuming that paying a loan off early is part of your business and tax strategy and is in alignment with your fundamentals, there are options. No one option is right for everyone. If you have multiple loans and are determining which one to pay off first, consider the following:

1. Pay off the loan with the highest interest rate.
2. Pay off the loan with the highest monthly payment.
3. Pay off the loan with the lowest monthly payment.
4. Pay off the loan with the smallest remaining balance.

Many years ago, I was approached by a young couple in desperate financial trouble. They had bank loans, school loans, car loans, and credit card loans. Their monthly payments on these loans exceeded their take-home pay.

Declaring bankruptcy violated their religious beliefs, so that wasn't an option. Some of their lenders would not renegotiate the terms of the loan such as the interest rate or the repayment period. One banker said, "There is no hope for them, so we'll just repossess their car when they stop making payments."

However, the couple did entirely eliminate the debts, keep their car, and avoid bankruptcy. The strategy was to pay off the loan with the smallest balance first. They contacted all of their creditors and informed them that they would pay each one every month, but only enough to cover the interest due on the loan. This prevented the loan balance from growing. When the loan with the smallest balance was paid off, it freed up cash flow to start applying to the next loan. As each loan was retired, they had additional money available to pay down the next. They cut their living expenses to the bone and added part-time jobs to their full-time employment. In three years, they were debt free.

The best option for you will depend on your own situation, cash on hand, and business strategy. Unless the situation dictates otherwise, I recommend paying off the loan with the smallest balance first.

Pay off the loan with the smallest balance first.

Chapter Assignment

Make a list of all your loan debts. For each one identify the monthly payment amount, interest rate, and number of remaining payments. Use this information to establish a procedure for paying off your debts.

CHAPTER 60

DEBT FREE?

"History tells us that leverage (debt) all too often produces zeroes, even when it is employed by very smart people." –Warren Buffett

Should you and/or your business be debt free? Again, this is a question that needs to be answered in the context of your fundamentals and long-term business strategy. Many "experts" counsel using other people's money to grow your business. Now, there are situations where borrowing is appropriate; however, if your business moves in sync with economic cycles, then you probably should be debt free. Companies that have significant debt when the economy (or their industry) declines have a high failure rate. The views of several of the successful companies interviewed follow:

> "In 2004 we decided to buy a building in order to increase capacity. We had to go into debt to do it, which goes against our beliefs. Even so, the building enabled us to increase capacity to do three more kitchens a month, which more than covered the monthly payments. We paid off the loan long before it was due. We started debt free and remain debt free."
>
> – Terry Peacock, Peacock Cabinetry

> "When we moved to the larger facility, we had to borrow heavily to buy new equipment. To do that, some of the investors had to personally guarantee the loans, placing them and the company at greater risk. The board meetings were intense! However, they stuck with us, and at the end of 2012 the company was debt free. At the end of 2013, the equity investors were debt free. We could not have achieved debt-free status without meticulous attention to the financial side of the business. We are engineers by background, not financial people. We had to learn the finance and

accounting side of the business in order to survive, grow, and prosper. Along the way there were sleepless nights, significant problems, and hurdles to overcome. Without those challenges, we wouldn't be poised for the exciting future in front of us. Those challenges honed and shaped us and helped us grow as individuals. They made us who we are today. We've learned that you never stop learning. We know the future will bring its own set of challenges and problems, but after what we've been through, we are confident that we are up to the task."

– John Curry, Sweetener Solutions
(Note: One of the fundamental operating principles of Sweetener Solutions is "Be debt free.")

"We believe in being debt free. We couldn't have survived 1991 or later recessions if we had been laden down with onerous debt payments."

– Tom and Veronica Zombik,
Hilton Head Glass/Veronica's Art Glass

"One of my top priorities was to be debt free so we can provide health insurance for employees. My partners and I agreed that we would not take any dividends/ distributions from the company until we were debt free."

– Berry Edwards, Island Tire

"My partner and I each kicked in $5,000, and we operated initially out of our houses with our own cars. We started debt free, and the company is still debt free. We didn't get paychecks for the first six months. That was tough on our families, but fortunately we had some savings to draw on. Being debt free helped us weather the 2008–2009 Great Recession. When we need to buy equipment, we can negotiate better prices because we pay cash. And being debt free gives us peace of mind that enables our families to sleep better."

– Bob All, Custom Security

Borrow only when absolutely necessary and then repay as fast as possible.

Chapter Assignment

Evaluate your philosophy on using debt. Is it in alignment with your fundamental purpose, values, and operating principles? Is it in alignment with your strategy to grow the business? Develop a plan to bring your debt in alignment with your fundamentals and your business strategy.

CHAPTER 61
JUST IN CASE

"There's not a lot you can do about the national economy, but there is a lot you can do about your personal economy." – Zig Ziglar

I strongly recommend having a Just-In-Case, or JIC, fund. Having ready cash provides opportunities to negotiate and buy at better prices as well as withstand economic downturns. There will be another recession. It is not a question of if, but when. One of the most significant causes of business failures is a lack of cash reserves. The successful companies interviewed cite "maintaining adequate cash reserves" as one of their fundamental operating principles.

Gayle Humphries, CFO at JCB of Georgia says the following about having cash reserves: "At the depth of the recession, there was a lot of equipment from many manufacturers sitting idle and that had been financed. Companies with this equipment were drowning in debt payments and looking for a way out. We sent our salespeople out to look for grass growing up around equipment. We offered to buy the equipment, which helped the company get out from under their debt, and we could buy it at really good prices. We then resold the equipment at good prices. Now that the economy has recovered, many of those companies whose equipment we bought have come back to us to buy new equipment, because we helped them out when they really needed it. We couldn't have done that without our cash reserves and good line of credit."

Good times never last and bad times never last. Be prepared for both with a JIC fund.

Chapter Assignment

Do you have a JIC fund? How much cash should be in your JIC fund? Every business is different, so there is no correct answer as to the size of your cash reserves. Total up all of your expenditures and compare that to cash on hand. How many months could you operate if customers stopped paying or revenue drastically declined? Determine the number of months' worth of cash reserves needed for your business and implement a plan to reach and sustain that level of cash reserves.

CHAPTER 62
BUDGETS VERSUS FORECASTS

"Chance favors the prepared mind." – Louis Pasteur

Is there a difference between a budget and a forecast? Should you be doing either? The terms "budget" and "forecast" are often used interchangeably, and indeed the two are similar. The difference is primarily in the mind-set people have.

Budget Mind-Set

The mind-set in most large organizations, particularly government, is that if you don't spend all of your budget this year your budget next year will be cut. With this type of thinking, spending decisions are made that are not in the best interest of the organization as a whole. They are made to protect someone's little fiefdom.

Small businesses generally do not have this mind-set because, due to their size, they focus more readily on what is best for the entire company, not an individual department. Hopefully, your company is going to grow and become increasingly successful. As that happens, be mindful of this potential problem.

Forecast Mind-set

You should be forecasting your financials, particularly cash flow, to anticipate obstacles in the Business Swamp. While the mind-set of a budget is often, "What are my spending limits?" the mind-set of a forecast is, "What do I need to spend in order to accomplish my goals?"

To adapt to changing climates and conditions in the swamp, you need to envision what is coming and adjust accordingly. If new conditions require spending money in a different place to accomplish a goal, then that is what your business should do rather than spending money needlessly just because it is in the budget.

Mike Reeves of Espy Lumber says the following about forecasts: "We prepare rolling twelve-month projections/forecasts of sales and expenses every month so we can see better what is coming. We also do projections for each store."

An important aspect of succeeding in the swamp is cutting through the fog to see the potential obstacles, and being prepared to avoid or overcome them. A forecast with the mind-set of, "What do I need to do to accomplish my objective?" will help you meet your objective.

Forecast Mind-set:
What do I need to do to accomplish my goals?

Chapter Assignment

Develop a forecast for the next twelve months and update it every month.

CHAPTER 63
CONTROLLED GROWTH

"A company should limit its growth based on its ability to attract enough of the right people." – Jim Collins

What is a Goldilocks growth rate? Not too slow, not to fast—but just right. Can you grow too fast? Absolutely. Remember WorldCom? WorldCom grew from virtually nothing, and in a few years became a huge corporation with sales revenues in the billions. They were the darlings of Wall Street, and sophisticated investors were throwing money at them. Then they crashed and their CEO went to jail. What happened? One problem was that they grew so rapidly that they couldn't manage it all.

Contrast WorldCom with Southwest Airlines. For over forty years, Southwest has been profitable while other airlines have gone through bankruptcy, been acquired, or gone out of business. One of Southwest's fundamental operating principles was to grow only 20 percent a year (Source: *Great by Choice* by Jim Collins). Southwest rejected opportunities to grow faster so they did not exceed their ability to manage their growth, and it continues to grow and prosper.

Scott Slawson, CFO for The Greenery, states, "We want to grow, but not faster than we can manage and still provide the quality our customers know us by. It is one of our fundamental operating principles."

Establish a targeted maximum growth rate and stick to it.

Chapter Assignment

Set a target maximum growth rate that is aligned with the fundamentals of your business.

CHAPTER 64
PROFIT CENTERS

"An investment in knowledge pays the best interest."
– Benjamin Franklin

Do you know what respective departments or other locations cost?

One company had a small warehouse operation for the convenience of its customers. How much did the warehouse operation cost? Did it make any money? The owner said it wasn't necessary to determine its cost because the goal of the warehouse was not to make a profit. If the cost were $5,000 a year, then maybe that would be acceptable. However, what if it were $500,000 a year? Is that still acceptable?

The warehouse was set up as a cost center with its own P&L. The result of an analysis was that the loss on the warehouse operation was acceptable. If you don't know the costs of a department, location, or product line, you cannot make a sound decision.

Know the costs and profitability of departments, product lines, and locations.

Chapter Assignment

Work with your accountant to develop reports that identify the costs, profitability, and cash flow for all your business segments.

CHAPTER 65
LEASE OR BUY?

"If you don't know where you're going, you'll probably end up somewhere else." – Lawrence J. Peter

How should you pay for the acquisition of new equipment, vehicles, buildings, or building improvements? There are three options:

1. Pay cash and buy the equipment outright.
2. Get a bank loan and make repayments.
3. Lease it and make payments.

Let's look at each of these options.

Paying Cash

Paying cash is straightforward. You plop down your $30,000 and drive the car home. You own it outright, and you have no future monthly payments. The disadvantage to buying an asset outright is missing out on what you might have been able to earn had the money been invested elsewhere. As an investor, you may be able to earn a higher rate of return on the money than the interest rate on a loan or lease. You may also have been able to use that $30,000 for another business opportunity.

Borrowing

A loan from a bank or finance company is an alternative method to buy the equipment. Typically, but not always, a down payment is required. The bank charges an interest rate based on your credit worthiness and current market rates. Based on the interest rate, the term of the loan (how long it runs), and the price of the equipment, the bank calculates monthly payments. The bank retains the title to the asset until the loan is paid.

For instance, you purchase a car for $30,000 using a loan with a 7 percent interest rate and a repayment term of five years. The monthly payments would be $594 per month. To reduce monthly payments, you can negotiate for a lower cost of the asset, a lower interest rate from the bank, or a longer loan term. Upon final payment, the car is yours. Should you fail to make payments, the bank can take possession of the asset, after which they can sell it to recover some of the money loaned to you.

Leasing

Leasing is more complicated. A lease is a contract between the entity/person that will buy/use the asset (the lessee) and the entity that is selling/owns the asset (the lessor). Just like a bank loan, every lease is based on an interest rate. If you lease a car, the dealer is legally obligated to divulge the interest rate on which the lease is based. This isn't the case with other types of equipment. Salespeople for various types of equipment argue passionately that there is no interest rate, just a monthly payment. How did they determine the monthly payment? It was determined based on an interest rate and a repayment period.

Leases are popular because the monthly lease payment is usually less than that of a bank loan. With a lease, you are in effect renting the equipment for a specific period of time. At the end of the lease, you may or may not own the asset depending on the type of lease.

For example, you lease a car for two years. The original cost of the car (which is negotiable) is $30,000. You make a down payment of $2,000. At the end of two years, the car has a residual value of $20,000—the estimated worth of the car at the end of the lease. In effect, you are borrowing $8,000 for two years: $30,000 minus the down payment of $2,000, minus the residual value of $20,000, is $8,000. What are the monthly payments for this vehicle? Assume the interest rate is 7 percent, the same as our example with the bank loan. The payments would be $358 for the two-year lease, or $236 less than the bank loan. One way to look at it is that you bought two-fifths of a car and after two years you will give the other three-fifths back to the dealer. Sounds like a good deal, right?

In most cases, the interest rate on a lease will be *higher* than that on a bank loan because the lessor needs to make a profit. The bank's profit is the interest on the loan. The lessor purchased the asset originally and has a variety of costs associated with that purchase, which must be covered to realize a profit.

There are two types of leases, an operating lease and a capital (or finance) lease. Each is recorded on your books differently, and each has different tax implications. Your accountant and/or tax preparer should review the lease agreement prior to signing to advise you. NOTE: As of this writing, there are new rules governing how leases are recorded that will be going into effect in the future.

Operating Lease

Operating leases are for a fixed period of time, at the end of which you return the asset to the vendor. The vendor can then resell or re-lease the asset. When you return the asset, it still has what is called "residual value." In effect, you are really just renting the asset. On your books you record the amount of the monthly lease payment as a P&L expense.

Whether an operating lease is a good deal depends on your situation and philosophy. Compare the interest rate on the lease to what you can obtain from a bank loan.

In one situation, a company leased a fax machine for three years. Then they re-leased it for two more years and then again for two more years. They paid for that machine many times over. Buying the machine with a bank loan would have been much more economical.

Capital Lease

A capital lease results in your owning the equipment when the final lease payment is made. From a GAAP perspective, you bought the asset, and therefore are required to record an asset on the balance sheet for the value of the asset and a liability for the future lease payments. The asset would be depreciated over time as a P&L expense, just like any other fixed asset. The monthly lease payments are split into two parts, interest and principal, just like a loan. The interest is recorded as a P&L expense, and the principal portion reduces the amount of the liability on the balance sheet. A capital lease is actually a financing arrangement similar to a loan.

GAAP has a complicated set of criteria for determining if a lease is operating or capital, and the accounting for leases on your books can be complicated. Always consult your accountant before signing a lease.

Lease Drawbacks

Leases have three drawbacks: interest rates, early repayment, and property taxes.

Interest rates on leases are generally higher than you would pay for a bank loan.

Early Repayment: When you borrow money from a bank, you repay the loan in monthly installments. Each payment includes an amount to pay interest on the loan and an amount to repay the loan (reduce the balance on the loan). Assuming there is no penalty for early repayment of a bank loan, if you want to pay it off early, the payoff is the remaining balance on the loan. By doing so you save interest expense that you would have incurred had you made monthly payments for the life of the loan. With a lease, should you choose to pay it off early, the payoff is the sum of the remaining monthly payments, which includes interest. In other words, you pay the full amount, including interest, regardless of whether you pay off the lease early or make all the monthly payments for the life of the lease.

Property taxes, assessed by many states and localities, are usually higher with a lease than if you buy the asset with cash or a bank loan. Property taxes are usually based on the depreciated value of fixed assets. This means that each year the property taxes on an asset go down as the value of the asset depreciates. In the lease agreements, property taxes are usually the same for every year of the lease, resulting in the lessor keeping the difference.

Lease or Borrow

On my website, www.rockwellbusinesssolutions.com/diagrams, you can download a guide indicating the pros and cons of buying versus leasing.

If you prefer the latest technology and equipment and are strapped for cash flow, then leasing might be a reasonable idea. However, from a strictly dollars-and-cents perspective, leasing is almost always more expensive.

One business owner said he leases all his heavy equipment because as the assets age, the maintenance costs increase, so long-term higher lease payments are offset by lower maintenance. Maybe that is true if the asset will be in poor operating condition at the end of the lease. However, depending on the terms of the lease contract, you may be required to pay the lessor for repairs when you return the asset. While a lease may have lower upfront costs than purchasing via a loan, leasing generally has the following disadvantages:

- Higher interest rate than a bank
- Higher property taxes
- Early payoff does not save future interest expense
- At the end of an operating lease, you own nothing
- Vehicle leases have mileage restrictions (if you exceed the limits, there is a per-mile charge)

Depending on the tax laws in effect, there may be tax incentives for buying assets that would allow deduction of all, or a substantial portion, of the purchase on your tax return. Include your accountant in the decision process before buying or leasing, because tax laws regularly change and GAAP requirements can also change.

The decision to buy or lease depends on your situation and the fundamentals of your business, particularly your fundamental operating procedures.

The best solution isn't always the lowest monthly payment.

Chapter Assignment

Download the Lease vs. Buy Decision Guide from my website: www.rockwellbusinesssolutions.com/diagrams. Refer to it when faced with a lease-versus-buy decision.

CHAPTER 66
FACTORING

"Just because you can do something doesn't mean you should."
– Sherrilyn Kenyon

"Factoring" is when a business sells its accounts receivables (invoices) to another company (factor) at a discount. The factor pays the business a percentage of the face value of the invoices and then attempts to collect the receivable from the customer who was invoiced. In effect, the factor is a collection agency that takes some of the risk of collecting from the customer.

For example, you sell a $1,000 invoice to a factor named Wegotcha, Inc. Wegotcha pays you $800. You get paid immediately, which improves your cash flow. Depending on the terms of the contract with the factor, you may receive additional money back. How much is refunded may depend on how long it takes for Wegotcha to collect from your customer.

Read the contract carefully, and get advice before signing. In this example assume that if Wegotcha collects in less than thirty days, you get an additional 15 percent of the original invoice back, or another $150, so now you have received $950. If it takes Wegotcha thirty to fifty-nine days to collect, they may refund only 10 percent, or $100. If it takes sixty to eighty-nine days, they refund you 5 percent, or $50.

What if the invoice can't be collected in ninety days? In some cases, the factor then sells the invoice back to you minus their fee. In this example, the most you can expect for that $1,000 invoice was $950, assuming Wegotcha can collect in less than thirty days (the $800 they paid you when they bought the invoice plus the $150 when they collected in less than thirty days). Is it worth it to sell your receivables for 95 cents, or less, on the dollar? If you are desperate for money and have no alternative, factoring may be worth considering.

Be cautious before entering into a factoring agreement. Not only is this decision a matter of cost, but you also need to take into consideration how the factor may treat your customers. The factor may be more interested in collecting from your customer than in sustaining your business relationship with that customer. Factoring is the last possible alternative to consider for financing your business.

Be very careful before entering into a factoring agreement.

Chapter Assignment

If you are considering factoring as an alternative for financing your business, consult with your accountant and legal professional. Factoring contracts can be very complicated, and you must understand everything to which you agree.

CHAPTER 67
BARTERING

"Good judgment comes from experience, and a lot of that comes from bad judgment." – Will Rogers

A barter group enables you to sell a product or service to members of the group and purchase products or services of other member companies. No cash changes hands. You are trading, or bartering, your product or service for another company's product or service. Transactions can be with entirely different companies.

For example, as a landscaping company, you mow lawns for other members of the barter group. Over the course of a month, you provide lawn mowing worth $1,000 but you get no cash payment. The barter group now owes you $1,000 (in other words, you have a receivable balance from the barter group). How do you receive your $1,000? You can purchase products or services of other members using your "barter dollars." Perhaps you need your office cleaned, so you spend your barter value with a member who provides cleaning services. Sounds good, right? You sell your product or services and buy other products or services without using cash. In some cases, especially when just starting a business, a barter group may provide products or services you need when you don't have the cash to buy them.

However, there are precautionary considerations.

1. All barter transactions must be recorded on your accounting books and have tax consequences, even though no cash changes hands. Consult your accountant.
2. Barter clubs often say you can trade your services for personal (non-business) expense items, such as bartering for family vacation trips at member hotels. Before doing this, consult with your tax preparer. If you pay cash for personal expenses, these are not deductible as business expenses, so why would paying for personal expenses with barter dollars be deductible? You may be able to use barter dollars for personal expenses, but you probably cannot count them as business expenses.

3. Often companies build up large receivable balances with a barter group and then find no productive way to spend their barter dollars. Be sure other members of the barter group have products and services you need. One barter group will limit the size of your receivable balance and then help you spend it on things you need so that the situation doesn't get out of balance.

   Barter groups may be a way to help you obtain products or services that you cannot otherwise afford. Set limits on how much you are willing to provide (sell).

Set limits on how much you are willing to provide (sell) to barter club members.

Chapter Assignment

Carefully evaluate all the potential products and/or services you could receive through the bartering group you are considering. Do they fulfill legitimate business needs? Have your accountant review the barter group contract.

CHAPTER 68

OPEN BOOK MANAGEMENT

"The biggest cowards are managers who don't let people know where they stand." – Jack Welch

I want to introduce you to a concept called "open book management." Some companies practice it in part, others embrace it totally, and others reject it entirely. You need to decide what is best for you.

Open book management means sharing the company's financial information and results with employees, the idea being that when people know how the company is doing they perform better and will be more invested in company success.

Arguments against Open Book Management

Companies whose stock is publicly traded on a stock exchange are required by the Securities and Exchange Commission (SEC) to publicly report a vast amount of their financial information. Small privately held companies are exempt from this type of reporting, and many small business owners are opposed to opening their books to employees. Let's examine the main reasons:

1. My competitors would know how well I'm doing and could gain a competitive advantage.
2. If things are going badly, my employees will resign and seek other employment.
3. If things are going well, my employees will want raises and bonuses.

Arguments for Open Book Management

First, let's examine the competitive advantage argument. Consider Southwest Airlines. It has been a publicly traded company since 1971. As such, it is required by the SEC to publicize financial statements. Southwest has been profitable for over forty years. Did knowing Southwest's financial performance give their competitors an advantage? Every other airline has gone out of business (remember Pan Am and TWA?), experienced bankruptcy, or merged with another airline in order to survive. If knowing Southwest's financial information had given TWA a competitive advantage, it might still be around today.

If your business financial information leaked to a competitor, how could they use it against you? If you knew a competitor's revenues and profits, how could you use it to your advantage? What about your prices? Once you give a customer a quote, your prices are out in the open. Sharing financial results with your employees is unlikely to give competitors a useful advantage.

Second, will there be employee turnover if they are privy to financial results? In his book *The Great Game of Business,* Jack Stack explores the benefits of open book management. His compelling point is that if you don't share financial information with your employees, they will just make it up. Their assumptions regarding profits and losses are usually unrelated to reality. Employees often assume the business is making a fortune and the owner is lining his basement with gold bars. Have you ever driven by a restaurant with a full parking lot, yet within a few months the restaurant is gone? Looks can be deceiving.

If the financials aren't looking good, will everyone jump ship? In my experience, the answer is no. Most employees are loyal and want to see the company succeed. Your star employees can leave anytime; mediocre to poor performers will rarely leave. If you are playing on a sports team and the game isn't going well, do you quit and walk away or do you become closer as a team and work harder to be successful? Good teams come together and work all that much harder.

Here's an example. In January 2014, the Indianapolis Colts were down by 28 points late in the third quarter against the Kansas City Chiefs in an NFL playoff game. The players knew the score and the huge deficit they were dealing with. Did they start to leave? Did the Chiefs try to recruit them? No. The Colts increased their effort and rallied, winning the game 45 to 44. What happens if an employee does leave because they think the business is doing poorly financially? Ask yourself if you really needed someone who wasn't a team player.

How does an owner deal with the anticipation of raises and bonuses if the company is doing well? Isn't that the goal? If you really value your employees—the people who are making you successful—why wouldn't you want to share the prosperity with them?

I believe in open book management as opposed to a secret-society business culture, in which only a handful of people know what's actually occurring in the business. How can employees understand how to help the company reach its goals if they don't know what the score is? The financial reports are the scorecard for the business.

A prime example of open book management is Whole Foods. In 1986, John Mackey introduced the policy of sharing everyone's salary information. Mackey is quoted in the book *The Decoded Company: Know Your Talent Better than You Know Your Customers* by Leerom Segal, Aaron Goldstein, Jay Goldman, and Rahaf Harfoush, saying, "If you're trying to create a high-trust organization, an organization where people are all-for-one and one-for-all, you can't have secrets."

Some of the successful companies interviewed for this book did not practice open book management, some did to a degree, and some had never heard of this philosophy. Here are some of their comments.

> "We definitely practice open book management here at The Greenery. Each department manager gets their respective income statement after each month closes, and is asked to share it with supervisors and staff. Within our accounting department, we look at each department's income statement and the consolidated statements at our monthly accounting meetings. Twice a year, we have larger supervisor/manager meetings and go through all our department financial results. Additionally, each year after our company is valued and our share price is calculated, it is posted at each of our facilities. Every employee understands that the better our financial performance is, the higher our share price, the higher our ESOP value, and the higher their retirement account value."
> – Scott Slawson, The Greenery

Scott also says employees with access to the accounting software can look at the general ledger. That helps the staff make sure things are coded to the right account. In their ESOP communications meeting, they review the financials. There is a "why and what" segment on the agenda, where people can ask why certain things are being done and what is being done. Transparency of financial information enables management to learn what employees are thinking and what questions they have, which in turn helps the company educate everyone on how they can all be better owners.

> "We share financial information with managers and department heads. Each one is responsible for their own P&L. We don't share financial information with all employees." – Billy Robinson, Port City Logistics

> "We are pretty open about sharing financial information because we have some profit-sharing programs, and people need to know how we are doing." – Mike Covert, Covert Aire

> "We share financial information with managers and key employees at our weekly Friday meetings."
> – Gayle Humphries, JCB of Georgia

> "We share financial information with management and employees at weekly and monthly meetings."
> – Mike Reeves, Espy Lumber

Chapter Assignment

What is your opinion of open book management? It may or may not be appropriate for your company. Do your own research to determine what is best for you, and to what degree you might want to practice open book management. Many companies find it to be a valuable tool to improve performance.

Of course, if your financial records are replete with inaccuracies, open book management would be detrimental. Remember, you can't make a good business decision with bad information, and neither can your employees.

CHAPTER 69
NEGOTIATING

"For me, relationship is very important. I can lose money, but I cannot lose a relationship. The test is, at the end of a conversation or a negotiation, both must smile." – Sunil Mittal, entrepreneur, philanthropist

Most people dislike and are not accomplished at negotiating. They see it as a confrontational situation. However, if your business is going to be successful, you must learn to negotiate. The book *Getting to Yes* by William Ury, Roger Fisher, and Bruce Patton can teach you the intricacies of negotiating. Negotiating should be nonconfrontational. Negotiating is coming to a mutually beneficial agreement that is a win-win for both parties. Here are some personal experiences.

Prior to a meeting with the Tennessee Department of Corrections, a colleague, John Baber at Eastman Chemical Company, advised, "If you are right and reasonable, you will usually get what you want."

The John R. Hay House in Kingsport, Tennessee, where I volunteered, was seeking additional funding from the Tennessee Department of Corrections. Hay House had a residential facility housing twenty-four convicted felons who were either on parole from prison or on probation. Hay House wasn't a jail; there were no bars, and residents were free to come and go.

At night, there was only one staff member on duty. The problem with only one staff member, besides his being alone all night with a house full of convicted felons, was that in an emergency there was no one else available to cover the house if the staff member had to leave to assist another resident.

The Tennessee Department of Corrections funded the majority of the operation of Hay House through a community corrections grant. We requested additional funding to hire a second staff person for the night shift. The executive director of Hay House, Chuck Walsh, and I went to Nashville to negotiate with the commissioner of the Department of Corrections. The commissioner's position was that as the steward of the people of Tennessee's money, additional funds could not be allocated. We stressed that, according to American Corrections Association guidelines, two staff members were required for this many residents, plus the safety issues with only one staff person on duty. In the end, he said no.

As we were getting up to leave, I said, "The safety issues and being out of compliance with ACA standards create significant liability for the Hay House Board. If an incident occurred, Board members could be held personally liable, which is a great concern to all of us."

The commissioner frowned and swung his chair around to face the window for a couple seconds, then turned back and said, "Okay, Roy. What do you want?" He knew we were right and we were reasonable. We weren't asking for more money than necessary. If you are right and you are reasonable, you will usually get what you want.

Obtain Three Bids

Get three bids for purchases of any significance, including borrowing money from a bank. Frequently there will be a high bidder, who really doesn't want the job but will do it if the price is high enough; a low bidder, whose quality may be suspect; and someone in between.

When asking a bank for a loan, don't unquestionably accept what they offer. A client wanted to refinance a multimillion-dollar mortgage on their property. Interest rates had come down substantially, and they wanted to take advantage of lower rates. The bank holding the existing mortgage offered to refinance at 4.75 percent, not a bad rate.

For comparison, we met with several other banks. Ultimately, three banks bid for the mortgage. When they learned bids were being obtained from other banks, the interest rates offered started to fall. The winning bid was 3.0 percent, which on a multimillion-dollar loan saved the client hundreds of thousands of dollars over the life of the mortgage.

- **Get three bids.**
- **Everything is negotiable.**
- **If you are right and reasonable, you will usually get what you want.**

Chapter Assignment

Resolve to improve your negotiating skills through reading books and articles, attending seminars, and practicing.

CHAPTER 70

SECTION SUMMARY

"Life is not a matter of holding good cards, but sometimes, playing a poor hand well." – Jack London

Use best practices and constantly be looking for new ones. A fundamental operating principle for Damian Hayes of British Open Pub is, "Learn from others, particularly other restaurants." In your business, consider learning from others, especially those also in your industry.

To share your best practices with other small business owners, e-mail me at Rockwell@hargray.com, and I'll post them on my website blog and give you credit for them. You can post comments at:

http://www.rockwellbusinesssolutions.com/gator-bites/

SECTION 10

INTERPRETING THE SWAMP

CHAPTER 71

SECTION INTRODUCTION

"If you do what you've always done, you'll get what you've always gotten." – Tony Robbins

In the preceding sections, you learned how to build your business house in the Business Swamp, and how to operate the business. You are ready to combine this knowledge in the Interpreting the Swamp section. Here you will develop SMARTS in the swamp. Additionally, you will be provided with some tools to help you better understand how to move your business toward its vision. Finally, you will learn the key metrics that indicate if you are on the right track.

In this section, you will explore the following:

1. SMARTS goals
2. Fishbone business model
3. Trend analysis
4. Key performance indicators

CHAPTER 72
SMARTS

"If I only had an hour to chop down a tree, I would spend the first forty–five minutes sharpening my axe." – Abraham Lincoln

To survive in the swamp, you need SMARTS. Yes, you have to be intelligent about what you do and the decisions you make, but you also need the right tools. One of those tools is SMARTS goals. I've added the letter "S" at the end because the concept of SMART goals is incomplete, hence "SMARTS" goals.

Achieving your vision is about having goals and making decisions that are aligned with your fundamentals. In addition, goals need alignment with each other. As your business grows and has more functional departments, locations, and lines of business, keeping everything aligned is increasingly difficult. Making sure everyone is working toward what is best for the entire organization requires that everyone focus on the same target.

There are three aspects of goal setting and SMARTS goals:

1. Goals—deciding on the goals
2. Alignment—aligning the goals with the fundamentals of the organization and with each other
3. Commitment—without commitment, a goal is just a wish. A committed decision is essential to reach any significant goal.

Goals

Goals—true goals—have several characteristics. Without these characteristics, they are merely hopes and wishes.

S	Specific
M	Measurable
A	Attainable
R	Relevant
T	Time Bound
S	Strategy

Specific

A goal must be specific; otherwise, you cannot determine if the goal has been accomplished or how to develop a plan to achieve it. On an ocean cruise, the first thing the captain needs to know is the destination. Without a destination, the captain can't plot a course. Increasing revenues is not a goal because it is not specific. Increasing revenues 15 percent is specific. Why is being specific so important, as well as so powerful? Simply put, you can't hit a target you don't have. Your goals need to be very clearly defined and specific as to what you want to accomplish.

Measurable

There has to be some measure to determine if progress is being made toward attaining a goal and whether the goal has been reached. The goal of increasing revenues by 15 percent can be measured by examining the organization's P&L statement and comparing current period revenues to a prior period.

Attainable

Goals should be realistically attainable and yet a stretch. If they're too easy, no one feels a sense of achievement. If unrealistic, employees won't be motivated to work toward their accomplishment. Growing revenues by 15 percent is probably attainable for most companies but also a bit of a stretch. However, a goal of growing revenues 400 percent may be unrealistic or even undesirable (remember controlled growth) for most firms. Conversely, a goal of increasing revenues by 2 percent is too easy and could happen by luck.

Relevant

Relevance addresses the question of alignment. Is the goal in the best interest of the overall success of the organization? Often, goals for different functional areas of the business conflict with each other and with the fundamentals of the organization. Growing revenues 40 percent may be attainable, but what is the effect on the company as a whole? Do compromises need to be made that aren't in the best interest of the entire company? Does 40 percent violate a fundamental operating principle of only growing 20 percent a year? Growing revenues 40 percent might be accomplished by over-selling some customers by convincing them to buy products that they don't need. This could sour long-term relations with that customer.

Time Bound

What is the target date for accomplishing the goal? In the example of growing revenues 15 percent, it is one thing to say 15 percent for this year over last year and quite another to say the 15 percent will be realized in ten years. Without a deadline for accomplishing the goal, there is no sense of urgency to get it done and no commitment to its accomplishment.

Strategy

Now, the all-important "S." How are you going to achieve your goal? What is the plan? Many times, business owners state their goals, but when asked what their plan is for reaching them, they just shrug their shoulders.

A goal without a plan for its accomplishment is just a wish and is rarely accomplished. Achieving any goal takes work *and* a plan. How are we going to grow revenues 15 percent? If there are several product lines, on which ones will you focus your efforts? What target market of new customers will you try to reach? *How* will you reach them? If the goal wasn't reached, was it a bad strategy or were there unforeseen factors? In the movie *Peter Pan*, Wendy asks where they are going, and Peter says, "Second star to the right and then straight on till morning." Achieving your goal will require a more specific plan.

Alignment

Your organization may have multiple goals. Each functional area, or location, may have its own goals. The key questions for all of them are: Are they in alignment with each other and also with the fundamentals of the firm? The larger the organization and the more goals, the easier it is to get out of alignment. The accomplishment of a goal in one area can negatively impact another area.

Increasing revenues 15 percent may be a fine goal, but if the plan for reaching the goal violates the organization's fundamental purpose, values, or operating principles, it will probably do more harm than good. Costs could be reduced by using inferior materials, resulting in a product of inferior quality. Is low quality consistent with who you are and your beliefs?

Commitment

As discussed in chapter 7, nothing is more powerful than a committed decision to do whatever it takes to reach a goal. Are you a DWIT? DWITs decide to Do Whatever It Takes. Being a DWIT doesn't mean ignoring your family or spiritual life. Your life must be balanced. DWITs simply develop a plan and are committed to accomplishing their goals.

SMARTS Goals Decision Grid

The SMARTS Goals Decision Grid is a tool for setting goals and making sure they are in alignment with your fundamentals. At the top of the grid, enter your fundamental purpose, values, and operating principles. This will keep them visible in the goal-setting and planning process. Also, having all the goals on one page makes it easy to determine if they are in alignment.

Set one goal in each area in the left column, such as revenues, expenses, collecting receivables, etc. There may be several goals for each area, but too many gets messy. If you have more than one goal for a particular area, pick the most important one and work on that.

When that goal is accomplished, you can work on the next most important goal.

Below is a condensed version of the SMARTS Goals Decision Grid. You can download a spreadsheet version of the SMARTS Goals Decision Grid on my website at www.rockwellbusinesssolutions.com/diagrams/.

For each goal, ask yourself two questions:

1. Is the goal in alignment with my fundamentals?
2. Are the goals for each area in alignment with each other?

Does one goal conflict with another? For instance, you might have a goal to collect receivables faster, and the strategy is to use a third-party agency, or factor. However, that could conflict with a fundamental operating principle or value on how to treat customers. Keeping your fundamentals in front of you at all times can pay rich dividends.

Have you ever been in a meeting where the discussion went off topic and in all different directions? It's easy to go off into the weeds. As chair of the Volunteer Advisory Board for the Tennessee Department of Corrections, I had a large banner made listing our fundamentals. Whenever the discussion went off track or an idea was proposed, we would point to the banner and ask, "Is this in alignment with our fundamentals?" This kept our focus in the right direction.

SMARTS Goals Decision Grid

FUNDAMENTAL PURPOSE	
FUNDAMENTAL VALUES	
FUNDAMENTAL OPERATING PRINCIPLES	

	Specific Goal	Measure	Attainable?	Relevant?	Time/ Deadline	Strategy
Revenues						
Expenses						
Quality						
Productivity/ Efficiency						
Collecting Receivables						
Paying Payables						
Inventory						
Equipment Needs						
Loan Repayment						

Chapter Assignment

Complete the SMARTS Goals Decision Grid for your company and update it as goals are attained or conditions change. Be sure and fill in the "Strategy" section for accomplishing each goal.

After you've filled in the entire grid, ask yourself if the goals and strategies are in alignment with your fundamentals and with each other.

CHAPTER 73

CAUSE AND EFFECT FISHBONE

"Happy is he who has succeeded in learning the cause of things."
– Virgil, Roman poet and philosopher

The Fishbone Diagram at the end of this chapter is partially completed with examples to provide a better idea of how it works. You can download a blank Fishbone from my website at www.rockwellbusinesssolutions.com/diagrams/. Since the diagram at the end of this chapter may be somewhat small to read, I recommend downloading the full page version for reference as you work through this chapter.

The purpose of the Fishbone business model is to present an overview of your entire business so you can examine what factors are driving, or causing, your financial performance, thus enabling you to devise an improvement strategy. Use the Fishbone model in conjunction with the SMARTS Goals Decision Grid. At the end of the day, if a strategy doesn't increase revenues, decrease costs, improve PEQ (productivity, efficiency, quality), or increase cash flow, is that strategy of value?

The ultimate goal for every business should be to have cash available for owners. All too often business owners withdraw cash in the form of distributions or dividends to fund their lifestyle at the expense of the future well-being of the business. Yes, you want to have a return on the investment of your time and money in the business. Why else would you go through all the effort and take all the risks of having a business? The key is to know when to reward yourself. You can reward yourself when all of the present and future needs of your business have been met.

Reward yourself only after all your business needs have been met.

You might think, *Well, I've got profits on my P&L and cash in the bank, so now I can reward myself.* Maybe, maybe not. The cash in the bank can be used for multiple purposes besides rewarding yourself. Any excess cash represents cash available for business opportunities (CABO). Before paying yourself, are there business opportunities you need to consider to move you toward your vision and the accomplishment of your fundamental purpose? There are four major categories of business opportunities:

1. Capital Equipment Needs: Money used to buy or construct a new building, purchase land, and leasehold improvements and new equipment or vehicles.
2. Purchasing Another Business: This could include opening a new location, adding a new product line, merging with another company, or buying a company.
3. Repaying Loans: If you have debt, you are making required monthly loan payments. If one of your fundamental operating principles is to be debt free, you could make additional loan payments to accelerate retirement of the debt.
4. Just-In-Case Fund: Do you have adequate cash available if the economy crashes, a major customer leaves, there is a major equipment failure, or there is some other emergency need?

Certainly, there are other categories and subcategories of business opportunities unique to your business. The point is that before you reward yourself, you must assure the long-term success of your business is addressed adequately.

What creates CABO? It is generated by three main sources:

1. Business profits (P&L)
2. Working capital management (collecting receivables and paying payables)
3. Required loan or equipment lease payments

Business Profits

Section 7 discussed your financial statements. Your business profits are reported on the P&L and are affected by revenues and expenses. If you increase revenues or decrease expenses, then profits rise. There is, however, a third factor that can significantly affect both revenues and expenses: PEQ (productivity, efficiency, and quality).

Poor quality can affect future revenues. Inefficient delivery times can affect revenues if customers don't get the product or service on time. Inefficiencies can slow down the production process.

You may be thinking, *I have a service business, so I don't have to worry about a production process.* Every business has a production process. If you provide a service, that includes time and effort to provide the service.

Likewise, productivity improvements can have a positive influence on revenues and expenses. Maybe some new equipment or technology will enable you to produce more goods or services in the time you have available, and often that new equipment is less expensive to operate.

PEQ

How do you improve productivity, efficiency, and quality? It starts with understanding how your business works. You are probably saying, "But, Roy, I know how my business works. It is my business." The issue is that as your business grows it becomes more complex. Woven into that complexity are processes and procedures that have evolved. Some of those processes and procedures were by design and others gradually accumulated. No matter what the business, you must look at how you can make any process better, cheaper, or faster. What about administrative processes? They too can be improved. Refer to the discussion of process improvement in chapter 17 and the SIPOC (Source, Input, Process, Output, Customer). A SIPOC is an effective tool to improve PEQ.

The SIPOC can identify processes that are duplications, could be done in a different way, are creating bottlenecks that slow production down, or are causing waste. A SIPOC can also reveal handoffs. It is common, as the business grows, for one person to hand off something to another person, who hands it off to another, and that person to another, and so on. Each time there is a handoff, there is a chance for a mistake. Ideally, you only want to enter data once. The more times the same data is entered, the greater the chance for mistakes.

Often, processes evolve because of the way a particular person liked to do things. As the business grows, that may not be the most efficient or productive way to do things anymore, but the process has become ingrained and the original reasons for it have been forgotten.

As discussed earlier, every business has some type of work-in-progress inventory. If you can process the work faster and more accurately, you save time and provide better service to your customers. By analyzing the work you do using a SIPOC, you can determine how to improve your work in progress.

Working Capital Management

Working capital is a function of how fast you can collect receivables and how long you can delay paying payables. Improvements here are short term in nature. Collecting receivables quicker, and paying vendors slower, improves cash flow in the short run, but improvement becomes increasingly more difficult beyond a point. You can only delay paying vendors for so long before they start screaming and possibly cut you off. Your vendors have a business to run, and if they go out of business, your business may be adversely affected.

The faster you collect your receivables, the more cash you will have. What actions can you take to improve collection of receivables? As mentioned before, this is a major problem for many small businesses. Certainly there is a limit on how quickly you can collect. Like you, your customers are trying to retain their cash for as long as possible. Refer to section 9, chapter 57 for ideas on improving collections.

Required Loan and Lease Payments

While these payments are fixed, in some cases you may be able to negotiate better terms (interest rates or pay-back period) or refinance the loan to make it more affordable. Of course, repaying the loans sooner with CABO will ultimately result in increasing CABO by reducing these cash payouts.

Using the Fishbone

In the Fishbone, identify all of the possible factors that could cause revenues to go up, expenses to go down, PEQ to improve, collection of receivables to speed up, or payment of vendors to slow down (within reason). This is a brainstorming exercise, so it doesn't matter whether or not a factor is one you would consider using. The more possibilities you list, the more ideas you generate. Once the Fishbone is completed, you and your team should decide on the most important factors for improvement. Pick one factor in each area for improvement:

- Revenues Increase (profitable revenues)
- Expense Reduction
- PEQ Improvement
- Working Capital (faster collection of receivables, slower payment of payables)
- Loan Repayment (reduce required loan payments)

Improvement in these areas will generate more CABO.

As a result, you have five goals to work on to improve cash flow. Each goal should have one employee responsible for its accomplishment, either individually or as the leader of a team. If no individual is designated, the result is that, usually, no one takes responsibility for any of them. Limit yourself to five goals. Having too many can be confusing, and you want to focus on the most important goals.

Chapter Assignment

Fill in the Fishbone for your company. Use the Fishbone in conjunction with the SMARTS Goals Decision Grid to make sure everything is in alignment. Have a target for how much CABO your business should have.

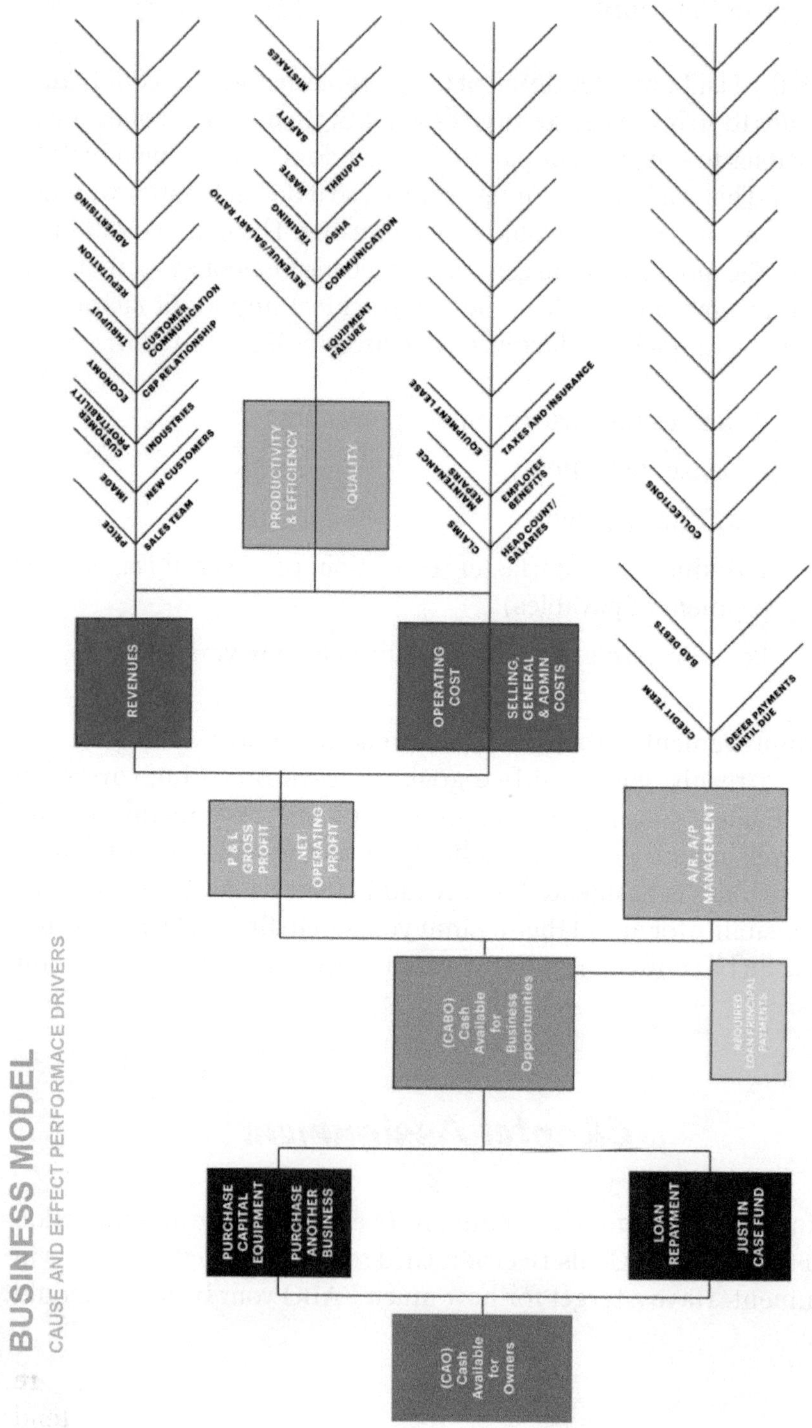
BUSINESS MODEL
CAUSE AND EFFECT PERFORMACE DRIVERS
PRICE
IMAGE
CUSTOMER PROFITABILITY
ECONOMY
THRUPUT
REPUTATION
ADVERTISING
SALES TEAM
NEW CUSTOMERS
INDUSTRIES
CBP RELATIONSHIP
CUSTOMER COMMUNICATION
REVENUE/SALES/SALARY RATIO
TRAINING
WASTE
SAFETY
MISTAKES
EQUIPMENT FAILURE
COMMUNICATION
OSHA
THRUPUT
PRODUCTIVITY & EFFICIENCY
QUALITY
CLAIMS
MAINTENANCE REPAIRS
EQUIPMENT LEASE
HEAD COUNT/ SALARIES
EMPLOYEE BENEFITS
TAXES AND INSURANCE
COLLECTIONS
BAD DEBTS
CREDIT TERM
DEFER PAYMENTS UNTIL DUE
REVENUES
OPERATING COST
SELLING, GENERAL & ADMIN COSTS
P & L GROSS PROFIT
NET OPERATING PROFIT
A/R, A/P MANAGEMENT
(CABO) Cash Available for Business Opportunities
REQUIRED LOAN PRINCIPAL PAYMENTS
PURCHASE CAPITAL EQUIPMENT
PURCHASE ANOTHER BUSINESS
LOAN REPAYMENT
JUST IN CASE FUND
(CAO) Cash Available for Owners

CHAPTER 74
TREND ANALYSIS

"I expect to spend the rest of my life in the future, so I want to be reasonably sure what kind of future it is going to be. That is my reason for planning." – Charles Kettering

Two of the easiest techniques for spotting errors are trend analysis and a review of the transaction detail report. Reviewing transactions was covered in chapter 50. Trend analysis helps you spot anomalies in your financial transactions and determine the general direction your business is heading.

Most accounting software makes trend analysis relatively simple. Run your P&Ls and balance sheets by month, choosing any number of months. Generally, the last twelve months is sufficient, but you could opt for thirty-six or seventy-two months. Also, most accounting software enables exporting data to a spreadsheet from which you can create a graph.

To spot things that don't make sense, look for blips. Normally, most revenue and expense codes will be relatively constant over time. However, when a line item suddenly shoots way up or drops way down, it needs to be investigated. Sometimes blips or anomalies occur and are correct, especially if your business is seasonal. Otherwise, they usually indicate something is wrong. In five to ten minutes, you can scan the last twelve months and spot any blips. If there are any, have your accountant investigate what caused them.

If you want to monitor key elements of revenue or expense, have your accountant plot the months on a graph. Some people like charts and graphs and others prefer looking at data. My preference is charts and graphs because they more readily reveal both anomalies and trends at one glance.

When asked about trends in their business (let's say revenues), most people will state the trend for the last few weeks. Yet, when charting the data over the last couple of years, the actual trends are almost always different from what the owner thought. People tend to remember the most recent past. Chart the data by months over a couple of years to reveal the true trend. Sometimes the last four to six weeks is a temporary blip. When preparing forecasts, the past is helpful, but be aware that the future won't necessarily behave like the past.

See if you can spot the anomalies in the following data:

	Rent Expense	Cell Phone Expense
Jan	$ 3,000	$ 212
Feb	$ 3,000	$ 250
Mar	$ 3,000	$ 235
Apr	$ 3,000	$ 205
May	$ 3,000	$ 242
Jun	$ 3,000	$ 256
Jul	$ 3,000	$ 210
Aug	$ 10,000	$ 260
Sep	$ 3,000	$ 227
Oct	$ 3,000	$ 248
Nov	$ 3,000	$ 712
Dec	$ 3,000	$ 231

What happened to rent expense in August and cell phone expense in November?

What does an anomaly look like on a graph? Following is a graph of water usage.

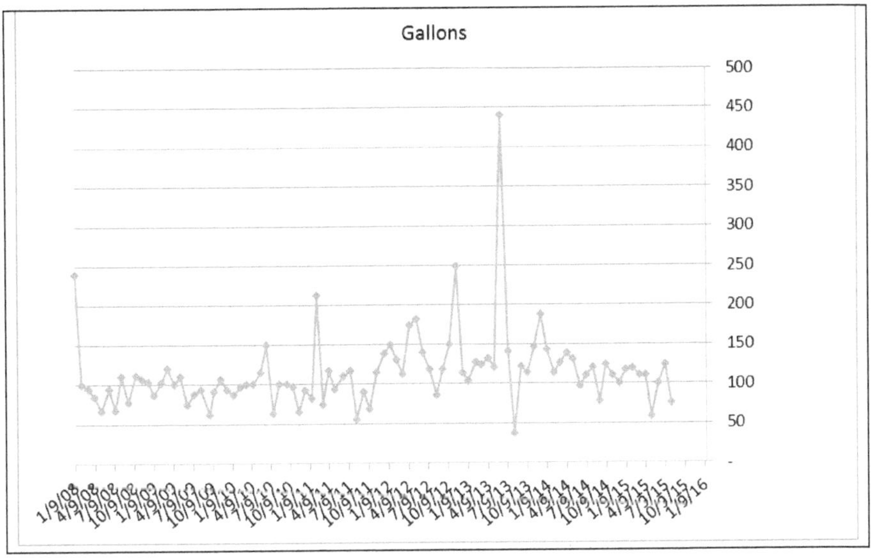

What happened in June of 2013? An investigation revealed a leak in some underground pipes, which was repaired with minimum digging. A significant jump in the water bill would have alerted the owner *if* they were reviewing vendor invoices each month. Unfortunately, most accounts payable employees simply pay the bill without question.

Sometimes charges that don't belong can appear on your vendor invoices and are hard to detect. If you fail to question these, they can remain indefinitely, and you continue to pay unnecessarily.

As CFO at D. J. Powers Company, I reviewed and approved all invoices for payment. One of those invoices was for telecom services from MCI and was one and a half inches thick. Not having the time or expertise to assess the bill's validity, I hired a contingency fee consultant to review the invoices for overcharges or improvements that could reduce our telecom expense.

Contingency fee consultants are a win-win for everyone. They analyze the vendor invoices and are paid a percentage of any savings they discover. If they don't find anything, they get paid nothing. Generally, they will get 30 to 50 percent of the savings for a period of time. Their percentage is usually negotiable. In my case, the consultant found numerous phone and fax lines that had been discontinued years before but were still on the MCI invoice. In addition, we were being billed for services we didn't need and never requested. This practice is called "cramming." A vendor adds an item or service to the invoice, either by accident or on purpose. If the customer pays, it stays on the invoice month after month.

The consultant was able to recoup past overpayments, eliminate ongoing expenses, and place us with a carrier less expensive than MCI. We paid the consultant 35 percent of the refunds and the ongoing savings for three years, which meant we kept 65 percent of savings. Cramming, whether by accident or on purpose, is common. Trend analysis helps you spot such problems early on and can save you substantial money.

Trend analysis also reflects strengths or weaknesses in specific products or services, or even with a particular customer. If your business sells multiple products or services, which ones are contributing the most to revenues and profits? Which business customers are growing and which are declining? If you notice that the revenues for a major customer are gradually declining, you want to investigate and determine why. Don't simply rely on gut instinct as to what is occurring with a customer. Maybe your gut instinct is in line with the data, but more often it is not. How many new customers are you obtaining each year? How many customers do you lose each year? Trend analysis provides a picture of what is going on in your business.

Chapter Assignment

Trend analysis, whether in data or graphic format, helps you detect problems before they get out of hand. You can track both financial and non-financial data. You can track waste or defective products, customer complaints, vendor delivery times, overtime hours, or any other area to enable you to better manage your business, thus improving its profitability and cash flow. You can develop the reports and graphs yourself, or instruct your accountant to do so.

Using the SMARTS Goals Decision Grid and the Fishbone Diagram, chart the key causal factors contributing to the success of your business.

CHAPTER 75

KEY PERFORMANCE INDICATORS

"Mike, how do you have time to track all this stuff?"
"How can you not take time? How do you know where you stand if you don't track your KPIs? You have to make the time."
– Mike Reeves, President, Espy Lumber

Key performance indicators (KPIs) indicate the health of your business from a financial standpoint. KPIs also indicate how well you are positioned for the future.

A performance metric is similar to statistics in sports. In football there are statistics such as time in possession, passing yards gained, rushing yards gained, penalties, turnovers, etc. Those statistics give an indication of how well the team did—and is likely to do in the future. Improving on those statistics increases the likelihood that the team will win in the future. They are causal factors that can impact the final score. However, having the best statistics doesn't mean you will win the game.

As in football, a lot of fluke things can happen in the Business Swamp. KPIs are important, but in the end the only thing that matters is who wins the game, as long as winning is done within the rules and with ethical and moral standards.

In your business, what is the equivalent of a final score that determines if you've won? If a business isn't generating cash from its primary operations, it won't survive for long in the swamp. You win if you have cash available for owners after you take care of cash available for business opportunities. Following are some KPIs, which, if maximized, will enable most businesses to accumulate cash from the operation of the business. Certainly, your business is unique, so you may have other KPIs that drive/cause cash flow in your business.

1. Gross Profit as a Percentage of Revenues
2. Pre-Tax Profits as a Percentage of Revenues
3. Average Day's Receivables Outstanding
4. Current Ratio

5. Debt-to-Equity Ratio
6. Cash Flow from Operations as a Percentage of Revenues
7. Number of Months' Expenditures Cash on Hand (NoMC)

Gross Profit as a Percentage of Revenues

In chapter 47 on the P&L, you learned the importance of having gross profits sufficient to cover sales, marketing, and administrative expenses. Gross profit is calculated by taking revenues and subtracting cost of sales.

Gross Profit = Revenues minus Cost of Sales

Cost of sales is any expense that must be incurred to generate revenues. Using that definition, all businesses have some amount of cost of sales. What should gross profits be as a percentage of sales? Well, that depends. In the book *Accounting for the Numberphobic*, Dawn Fotopulos advocates at least 30 percent. For many businesses, that may be adequate. One company was breaking even at 45 percent.

To determine where your gross profit percentage should be, play some "what if" games with your P&L. Your accountant can help you. If your gross profit is 40 percent, what will be pre-tax profits? What will pre-tax profits be if gross profits are 30 percent or 50 percent? If you are at 30 percent but need to be at 50 percent to generate sufficient pre-tax profits, what can you do to improve your gross profit percentage? Are you selling low-margin products that contribute little gross profit? Could you add some higher margin products or services to your offerings? Can the production process be improved? Can you find materials of the same quality costing less? There are endless possibilities for improving gross profits.

Pre-Tax Profits as a Percentage of Revenues

Virtually all improvements in gross profits will increase pre-tax profits. What should your pre-tax profits be as a percentage of revenues? Greg Crabtree argues in *Simple Numbers* that 10 percent is the absolute minimum because at that level your business will be treading water in terms of generating cash. Remember, profits are not equal to cash.

There are cash expenditures not on the P&L that need to be paid, like fixed-loan repayments. In addition, there may be old receivables not collected. Greg recommends, and I agree, to strive for at least 15 percent and preferably 20 percent.

At that level of profitability, you should be generating sufficient cash to have CABO. Reaching 20 percent will be assisted by increasing your gross profit margin, but that doesn't mean you can ignore sales, marketing, and administrative expenses. Part of the strategy for increasing your gross margin may be to increase marketing expenses to promote products or services that have a higher gross profit percentage. However, the higher margins must offset the increased marketing expenses. Administrative expenses tend to be relatively constant over time, but often there are some ways to reduce these expenses without sacrificing quality.

The two KPIs of gross profit as a percentage of revenues and pre-tax profit as a percentage of revenue go hand in hand. Higher gross profits contribute higher pre-tax profit, but this is not the only factor to consider.

Average Day's Receivables Outstanding

Collecting receivables is critical to the financial health and cash flow of the company. Average day's receivables outstanding is a good KPI for measuring how proficient you are at collections. The concept is simple. On average, how many days does it take for you to collect your receivables? If the terms on your customer invoice is for the customer to pay in thirty days, then you want this metric to be close to thirty days. Some authorities recommend no greater than 37.5 days (25 percent beyond the due date). If the customer mails its check on the exact payment date, it takes a few days to receive. However, if you use the technique of a courtesy call five days before the invoice is due (see chapter 58), you may be able to get much closer to thirty days.

Every company and industry is different, so you need to decide what is appropriate for your company to set your target. If you aren't collecting receivables on a timely basis, then you are in effect financing the operations of your customers. They have been able to purchase your product and use it in their business for free until they pay you.

To calculate average day's receivables outstanding, you need two pieces of data:

1. Average accounts receivable
2. Annual revenues

The formula is to divide average accounts receivable by annual revenues and then multiply the result by the number of days in the year.

You can calculate this each month by using average receivables and revenues for the past twelve months. Your accounting software should be able to provide this information. Average day's receivables outstanding might look like the following chart.

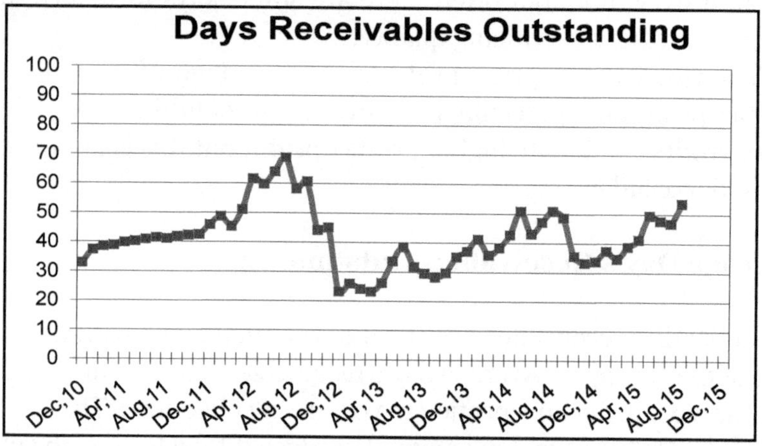

Days Receivables Outstanding = Average Receivables divided by Revenues times number of days in a year

What can you conclude from this chart? Receivables were getting out of hand in 2012 and then a concerted effort was made to collect them. However, since December 2012, receivables have been getting older and older. This company needs a collections policy and a procedure to execute each week so it can begin receiving cash on a regular basis.

What does all this mean in dollars? If annual sales are $500,000, then thirty days' receivables would be $41,096 ($500,000 divided by 365 days and then times 30 days). If receivables are forty-five days old, how much of your money are the customers holding? The answer is $61,644 ($41,096 times 1.5 months). At that level, you have over

$20,000 sitting in customers' bank accounts that you could be using. If receivables are an average ninety days old, you would have $123,288 owed to you, which is $82,192 sitting in your customers' bank accounts that you could be using. What could you do with all that money?

Current Ratio

The current ratio is a liquidity ratio. Liquidity, in this sense, is the company's ability to pay short-term obligations. In other words, does the company have enough cash, or current assets that can be turned into cash in the near future, to pay its current liabilities? The primary current assets are cash, accounts receivable, and inventory. Current liabilities are primarily accounts payable (vendor bills due to be paid in the next thirty days). The formula for calculating a company's current ratio is:

Current Assets divided by Current Liabilities

What should the current ratio be? This will vary based on your industry and the types of products and services you provide. To provide a benchmark as to where your company aligns with other companies in your industry, search the Internet for "current ratio benchmark." Your bank can probably help you determine what is appropriate for your industry because liquidity is important to them. They want to know that you can repay loans. In general, financially healthy companies are between 1.5 and 3.0. What are your conclusions from the following current ratio chart?

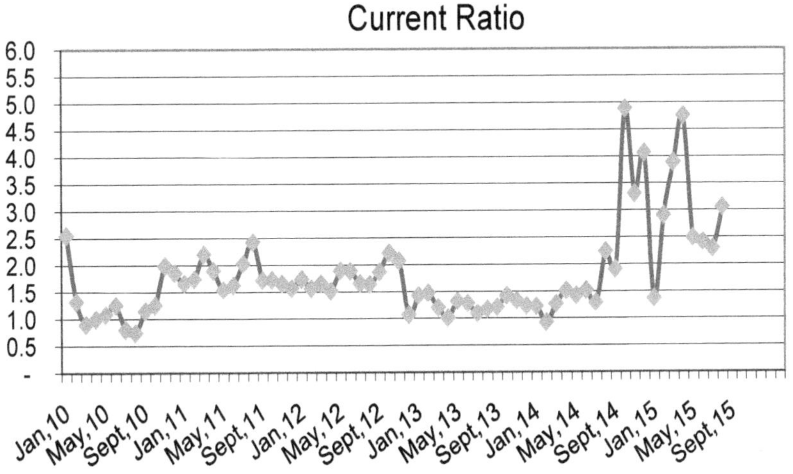

At face value, liquidity has really improved in 2015. However, don't stop there. It is important to know why something looks good or bad. Maybe the ratio is good because accounts receivables, or inventory, are abnormally high. Another possibility is that many vendor bills haven't been posted. Hopefully the current ratio has improved because the company is flush with cash. Whenever you see any metric get out of a normal range, investigate and find out why.

Debt-to-Equity Ratio

The debt-to-equity ratio measures a company's financial leverage. Financial leverage is the degree to which a company uses long-term debt. The more debt financing a company uses, the higher its financial leverage. A high degree of financial leverage (debt) means high interest payments, which negatively affects the company's bottom-line earnings and cash flow. The debt-to-equity ratio is a measure of financial risk. Higher debt means higher risk to owners and lenders. If debt gets too high, the risk of a company defaulting on paying its loans increases.

The debt-to-equity ratio is calculated by dividing a company's long-term liabilities by its equity. Recall from chapter 48 that equity is total assets minus total liabilities. The debt-to-equity ratio indicates how much debt a company is using to finance its assets relative to the amount of value represented in equity. Equity is composed of the investment that owners made in the company, accumulated P&L earnings, and distributions/dividends to owners. The formula for calculating the debt-to-equity ratio is:

Debt-to-Equity Ratio = Long Term Liabilities divided by Equity

An alternative formula is to use total liabilities (short-and long-term) instead of just long-term liabilities. The result may be expressed as a number or a percentage. What conclusions can you draw from the following debt-to-equity ratio chart? What is a good ratio for your business?

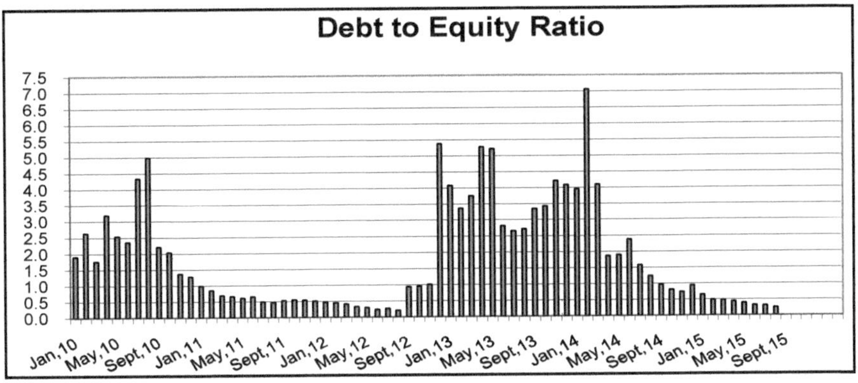

In 2010, and again in 2013–2014, the ratio was dangerously high. Without more information, you can only speculate as to what caused these increases. The increase in 2010 may have been the result of the recession, which could have caused P&L losses that thereby reduced equity. In 2011 and 2012, the ratio continued to drop and was below 0.5. The improvement may have been due to improving P&L profits, not incurring new debt, and paying down existing debt. In 2013–2014, it appears the company decided to take on some new debt, possibly to acquire new equipment. After February 2014, the ratio dropped rapidly to healthier levels below 0.5.

Is there an ideal ratio for your business? What is considered high or financially unhealthy will vary by industry. Some industries by their nature have to utilize more debt. Owners need to examine the historical trend to know if the ratio is outside a "normal" range. A higher ratio could show that a company has been aggressive in financing growth with debt, which may be okay as long as future earnings can provide the cash flow to pay the debt. A high ratio can also show that the company is at risk of defaulting on its debt obligations.

You have to decide the right level for your business. As with the other KPIs, the underlying causes for changes in the debt-to-equity ratio need to be determined. The ratio only provides an indication of *what* is occurring, but you need to find out *why*.

Cash Flow from Operations as a Percentage of Revenues

The last two KPIs are geared toward cash. An underlying theme of this book has been the importance of cash and the generation of cash or cash flow. Cash flow from operations is the amount of cash that the operation of the business is generating. As you saw in chapter 49 on the cash flow statement, cash flow from operations is P&L profits adjusted to exclude non-cash expenses on the P&L, such as depreciation, and then adjusted for changes in working capital (receivables, inventory, and payables). You may want to review that chapter. The formula for this KPI is:

Cash Flow from Operations as a % of Revenues = Cash Flow from Operations divided by Revenues

Cash flow from operations can fluctuate significantly from month to month due to fluctuations in P&L earnings and changes in working capital. This is particularly true if the business is seasonal in nature. To better evaluate the underlying trend, I recommend using a rolling twelve months of cash flow from operations and revenues. Calculate this by adding up the cash flow from operations and revenues for the past twelve months.

For instance, May 2012 would be the sum of June 2011 through May 2012, June 2012 would be July 2011 through June 2012, and so forth for each month. The result can still fluctuate substantially from month to month, but the underlying trend is what is important. Look at the following chart of cash flow from operations as percentage of revenues.

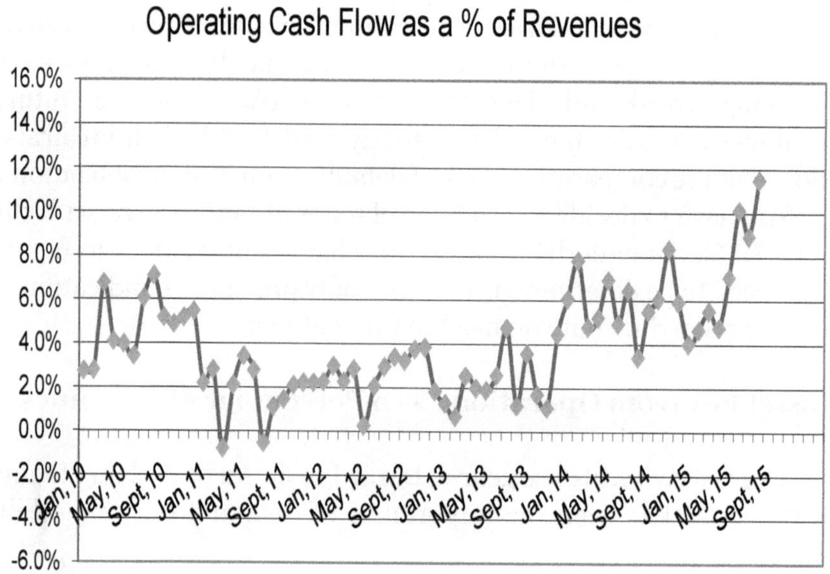

What conclusions can you draw from this chart? This KPI is showing how many dollars of cash flow from operations are being generated by each dollar of revenue. At 6 percent, each dollar of revenue is generating 6 cents in cash flow. The chart shows that the trend is for each dollar of revenue to generate increasing cash flow from operations. Each dollar of revenue is approaching generating 12 percent or 12 cents. Is 12 cents good? As before, it depends on the company and industry. Certainly, in this case the trend is going in the right direction.

A variation of this KPI would be to include required loan payments in the calculation. As you recall, there are three types of cash flow on the cash flow statement: operations, investing, and financing. Loan payments are not included in cash flow from operations but are considered part of cash flow from financing. Still another variation would be to include purchases of fixed assets, which is included in cash flow from investing. Including loan payments and/or fixed asset purchases would recognize that these are important aspects of your business. The method you choose to calculate this metric will depend on your goals and overall business strategy.

Number of Months' Expenditures Cash on Hand

ING (now Capital One) used to have a television ad that asked, "What is your number?" In the ad, people were walking around carrying numbers. By your "number," they meant the amount of money needed in order to be able to retire. For your business, what is your safety net number?

A good KPI for your safety net would be enough cash on hand to pay all the company's expenditures for a certain number of months. Let's call it number of months' cash on hand (NoMC). How many months' expenditures could you pay with the cash you now have in the bank? Expenditures include all of the regular monthly cash P&L expenses plus any required loan payments (or any other required monthly payments).

A business may have receivables and inventory that can be converted into cash to pay the bills, but what if the economy crashes and receivables can't be collected and inventory can't be sold? How long could your company survive with just the cash reserves you have right now? To calculate NoMC, divide your cash balance by the sum of all your cash expenditures for the month.

NoMC = Cash divided by Cash Expenditures for the month

What are your conclusions from the following chart?

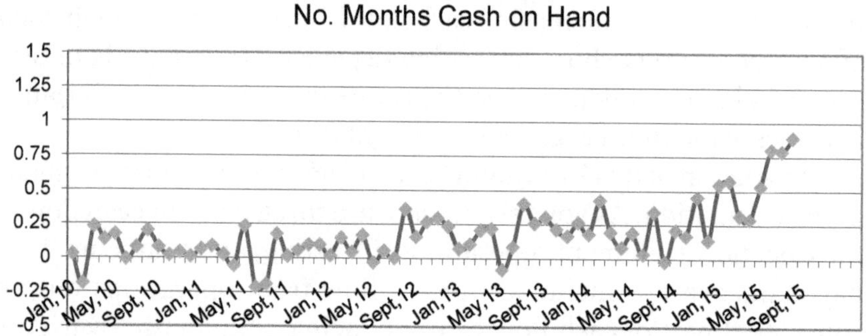

In this example, the company has cash on hand equal to 0.9 months or about twenty-seven days. Is that enough? This depends on your business and future growth plans. You need to determine a number and set a target level with which you are comfortable.

In Jim Collins' book *Great by Choice*, he writes that Bill Gates wanted to have cash in the bank equal to a year's worth of expenditures. Why a year? Because Gates was concerned that some company could come along with a new technology that would eclipse Windows and he would need a year to catch up. In order to catch up, he needed to retain and pay his employees.

How much do you need? That's a question that only you can answer. When the Great Recession of 2008–2009 hit, many companies didn't really feel the effects and start taking action until six to nine months after it started. They didn't immediately recognize its severity. By the time they recognized how badly they were being affected, they were forced to lay off employees, which further deepened the recession.

The number of months' cash you need will depend on your industry, the seasonality of your business, your geographic location, and other factors. It may also depend on your ability to perform. Many small businesses are dependent on the owner to perform much of the work in addition to managing the business. If an owner is hurt in a car accident or has a serious health issue and can't work for six months, the business is particularly vulnerable. Often there are only a few employees to pick up the owner's work. There may not be enough hours in the day to do the owner's work too. In many cases, the employees may not be certified or qualified to do what the owner does. All these considerations need to be factored into deciding your NoMC.

Set up a separate JIC fund with some of your cash on hand as both a safety net and an opportunity fund. If your business is highly cyclical, like construction or housing, it is even more crucial to be prepared for the worst. Cyclical businesses can be in a recession even when the economy as a whole is not.

In addition to being prepared for the worst, you want to be prepared for the best. You never know when business opportunities are going to present themselves. You want to have the cash, or leverage, to take advantage of those opportunities. Have you ever heard someone say something like, "If I'd only had the money to buy that piece of property thirty years ago, I'd be on Easy Street today." Think back to some opportunities you've had but couldn't take advantage of due to lack of cash. Your business must accumulate adequate cash to provide for adverse contingencies.

Chapter Summary

Seven key performance indicators reflect the health of your business. All are directly or indirectly related to cash and cash flow.

1. Gross Profit as a Percentage of Revenues
2. Pre-Tax Profits as a Percentage of Revenues

   If you aren't sufficiently profitable, you probably aren't generating sufficient cash flow.

3. Average Day's Receivables Outstanding

   If you aren't collecting receivables on a timely basis, then cash flow will be adversely affected.

4. Current Ratio

   If you don't have sufficient current assets to cover your current liabilities, you will need to either dip into that JIC fund or take on more debt, which creates more cash outflow in the form of monthly loan payments.

5. Debt-to-Equity Ratio

   If you have too much debt, you may not be able borrow money when necessary. Remember, banks are only interested in two things when it comes to making loans:

   a. Do you have the cash flow to make the monthly payments? and

   b. Do you have collateral the bank can take if you can't make the monthly payments?

6. Cash Flow from Operations as a Percentage of Revenues

   The operation of your business must generate sufficient cash flow to provide for the future needs of the business and a return on investment for owners. Increasing revenues is important, but you want those revenues to be producing cash.

7. Number of Months Expenditures Cash on Hand

   Are you prepared for both the best and the worst? Remember, good times never last and bad times never last, so you need to be prepared for both. If you have cash, you can take advantage of opportunities in the best and worst of times.

A good reference book for ratios and metrics is *The Vest-Pocket Guide to Business Ratios* by Michael R. Tyran.

Chapter Assignment

Meet with your accountant and develop these KPIs and any other key indicators driving profit and cash flow in your business.

SECTION 11

DRAINING THE SWAMP

CHAPTER 76

COMPETITIVE EDGE

"The basic philosophy of an organization has far more to do with its achievements than do technological or economic resources, organizational structure, innovation, and timing." – Thomas J. Watson Jr., CEO, IBM

The Alligator Business Solution is both a business philosophy and an attitude. It is your blueprint for draining the swamp of obstacles to building a successful business.

Your company's competitive edge is the combination of all that your business does and represents. It culminates in decisions in the best interest of customers, employees, vendors, and owners. A single factor, although significant, cannot alone provide a competitive advantage. It must be supported by the entire organization. Superior marketing can recruit customers, but poor product quality, slow delivery times, inaccurate invoicing, or any of a host of operations or administrative functions can quickly drive them away.

In this book you have learned how to build a solid foundation, improve management of employees, streamline operations, focus on marketing, understand accounting, use best practices, and employ swamp survival skills.

You have learned how to utilize tools to understand what causes performance and to align decision making with your fundamentals. Your competitive edge is the result of all these things working in concert with the positive attitude to do whatever it takes. Ultimately, you becoming a better *you* permeates throughout your organization, defining your competitive edge.

Inch by inch anything's a cinch. – Robert Schuller

Alligator Mentality and DWIT Attitude

I invite you to adopt the "Alligator Mentality."

- Success starts with *me*.
- I am the leader.
- I envision what I want.
- I decide to do what it takes (DWIT).
- I establish the fundamentals to succeed.
- I systemize operations.
- I learn what works and what doesn't (best practices).
- I develop needed skills.
- I obtain tools to improve success rate.
- I process and use all the information.
- I make better decisions.
- I gain a competitive advantage.
- I enjoy lunch.

If you adopt the Alligator Mentality, sign the pledge to become a full-fledged, committed Alligator DWIT.

"I, ____________________________, am an Alligator DWIT. I will Do Whatever It Takes to realize my vision, fulfill my fundamental purpose, live up to my fundamental values, and execute my fundamental operating principles. I will learn whatever is necessary to manage and improve every aspect and function of my business."

____

Your signature

Picture created by Roman Larionov, PCSAVED.COM

My hope is that *The Alligator Business Solution* has provided you with the knowledge and tools to drain the swamp and build a bridge to your long-term success. Rocky and I wish you every success in your life and in your business.

"We have each been given a bag of tools, a formless rock and a book of rules. And each must make ere life is flown, a stumbling block or a stepping stone." – Walt Whitman

APPENDIX I

PROFILES OF SUCCESSFUL BUSINESSES

Custom Security Specialists– Bob All, Owner and CEO

Photo by Paul Nurnburg

Custom Security Specialists installs and maintains residential and commercial security solutions. Keeping customers and communities safe and free from fear is a way of life at Custom Security, and employees are available 24/7, no matter what the customer needs. Currently the company has fifteen employees and does about $2 million in revenues.

From 1981 to 1986, Bob managed Home Safety Equipment Company on Hilton Head Island. In 1998, he formed Custom Security in order to continue providing the integrity, professionalism, and personal service that has become their trademark and foundation for success. A family culture has developed over the years and continues now with daughter Robin All Blair as the company continues to grow. It is set apart as the company that cares for its customers and teammates as a family cares for each other.

British Open Pub – Damian Hayes, Owner and CEO

British Open Pub is a family-friendly pub-style restaurant featuring authentic English food with additional American favorites. It offers the finest ales and single malt scotches from the United Kingdom, in an atmosphere of good cheer surrounded by plenty of golf memorabilia. Blarney is invited, singing encouraged, and good humor admired.

Espy Lumber – Mike Reeves, President

Espy Lumber has been providing quality building materials for the Low Country since it was founded in 1958 by Wesley Espy. Initially, its primary business was to furnish concrete to the emerging resort developers.

In the 1960s, the population of Hilton Head grew and the business was broadened to include lumber and building materials. As a result, the company outgrew its original location. In the 1970s, Espy sold the concrete operation and continued to expand the lumber and building materials business. In 1979, Espy was acquired by Rodman A. McLeod and H. Ross Arnold III from the Wesley Espy estate. During the next thirty-four years, until his passing in 2013, Rod guided Espy into becoming a leader of building supplies in the Low Country.

Rod instilled in each and every employee the importance of honesty, integrity, and hard work. The 1980s and 1990s brought continued growth and expansion. In 1998, a twelve-acre site was acquired in Okatie, South Carolina, and a second location opened for business in January 2001, with their headquarters being moved to this location.

Since the company's founding in 1958, there have been many recessions, and the building industry has had recessions when the general economy did not. But Espy has weathered them all, including the Great Recession of 2008–2009.

Hilton Head Glass/Veronica's Art Glass – Tom and Veronica Zombik, Owners

Tom and Veronica moved to the Hilton Head/ Bluffton, South Carolina area in 1998 from the small town of Chicopee, Massachusetts. In Chicopee they were co-owners of a family-run glass business. After a very hard recession in the early 1990s, they concluded that bringing the company back on top would be difficult and that there really was little growth potential in that area. They visited the Hilton Head area and loved it, so on the return trip they decided to sell their interest in the business in Chicopee, pull up stakes, and move to Bluffton, South Carolina, with their two young daughters, Jessica and Christine, despite neither of them having a job.

Tom quickly found work in the glass business because of his experience and expertise in that field, and Veronica started establishing her art glass business. Ultimately, they set a goal to start a custom glass and fabrication company like they had in Chicopee.

For four years they planned and did their due diligence about the area market, the location of the company, and the customers they wanted to target. They felt that Bluffton was the right place to start their new business due to its rapid growth and significant upside potential. In 2002, they bought a building and called it Hilton Head Glass and Veronica's Art Glass Studio. They specialize in all the fields of the glass industry.

Tom does all the mirror, glass, table tops, shower enclosures, and commercial custom glass. They focus on the residential market because people are always upgrading their homes. Veronica does stained glass, leaded glass, etched glass, and more. Tom and Veronica believe strongly in having a company that is diversified in order to survive in today's market.

International Dunnage, LLC – David Crenshaw, Owner and CEO

International Dunnage is an American and Turkish joint-venture company with sales offices based in Savannah, Georgia, and Istanbul, Turkey. All products are manufactured at International Dunnage's state-of-the-art production facilities in Istanbul.

Quality is the highest priority, and International Dunnage has a full range of quality control processes. All L2 to L5 dunnage airbags are 100 percent tested and approved. International Dunnage offers excellent service with rapid and prompt delivery, as well as creative solutions for customer requirements. The fully integrated production consists of extrusion, weaving, coating, and bag conversion, utilizing the latest technology and equipment. Quality control is carried out at every stage of production under strict conditions of ISO 9001, and all products are made to comply with AAR and RAC standards.

Island Tire & Automotive Services – Berry Edwards, Owner and CEO

Island Tire & Automotive represents a forty-year-and-growing Hilton Head Island tradition of family ownership. The company was founded in 1973 to serve the automotive needs of the rapidly growing island community and was founded on the basic principles of providing quality products, honest service, and exceptional customer convenience, and making a reasonable profit in order to sustain and provide for all of the Island Tire team. Those same principles guide the owners and staff in everything they do today.

Island Tire believes that the customer is number one. The company is run by Berry Edwards III, who bought Island Tire in 2011. He previously owned an engineering and design firm with another partner. In 2009, the partner bought him out, and he began looking for another business, finding Island Tire for sale in 2010. Island Tire is proud to be a part of the American Tire Distributors Protection Plan Plus network, which is a network of locally owned tire dealers who uphold the highest degree of integrity, personal service, and technological innovation. Island Tire also offers a nationwide parts and labor warranty as well as a nationwide road hazard warranty on tires.

JCB of Georgia – Gayle Humphries, CFO

JCB of Georgia is your dealer for new JCB and used equipment for construction, agriculture, compaction, industrial, waste, and recycling industries in Eastern Georgia and Southern South Carolina. As a JCB equipment dealer, the company carries a full line of backhoes, wheel loaders, excavators, skid steers, track loaders, Vibromax compactors, industrial forklifts, telehandlers, Fastrac tractors, off-highway dump trucks, utility vehicles, and attachments. JCB also rents out equipment, provides maintenance services, and sells parts for JCB and other manufacturer's equipment at highly competitive prices through their Grid Iron Parts Solutions subsidiary.

The company started in 2001 with fourteen employees servicing the Coastal Georgia and the Augusta, Georgia regions. As the business continued to grow and expand, it moved into its new facility adjacent to the JCB North American Headquarters in Pooler, Georgia, just outside of Savannah.

Gayle Humphries joined the company in 2004, and today it has twenty-four employees and annual sales of $11 million. Tony Reardon is owner and CEO. The company's motto is, "We take pride in our ability to provide complete equipment solutions to our clients while upholding the highest standards for customer service and support."

The Landings Club – Jesse Ruben, CFO

The Landings Club on Skidaway Island is a private club dedicated to serving members with an active lifestyle and resort-class amenities in a vacation setting. Located twelve miles from historic Savannah, The Landings Club offers members access to six golf courses, two marinas, thirty-three tennis courts, seven restaurants, five swimming pools, and an innovative fitness and wellness center.

Covert Aire – Mike Covert, Owner

Covert Aire is a family-run business, owned and operated by Michael and Theresa Covert, that is local to the Bluffton/Hilton Head, Beaufort, and Savannah market. The Coverts have four daughters. Covert Aire covers the entire South Carolina Low Country and Midlands, the Sea Islands, and the Sand Hills of Georgia, and has recently expanded to northern Florida beaches. Factory trained staff are nationally certified by organizations such as NATE, EPA, NIULPE, ACCA, ASHRAE, and other certifying organizations. Covert Aire says that if it "heats, cools, or refrigerates, we fix it!"

National Interstate Insurance – Alan Spachman, Founder (retired)

In 1989, National Interstate Insurance opened its doors with the idea that customer service and personal attention mattered. Clients were more than mere claim numbers; they were people, with real lives, real questions, and real needs. The company was built around its customers, and in the process became one of the leading specialty property and casualty insurance companies in the country.

Today, National Interstate has more than 570 employees, including operations at VanLiner Insurance Company in Missouri, each of whom is committed to providing the highest level of personal service, the most efficient claims processing, and the best products.

As a leading specialty property and casualty insurance holding company, it offers more than thirty different insurance products, including traditional insurance, innovative alternative risk transfer (programs for commercial companies, and insurance for specialty vehicle owners). These products are available through a variety of distribution channels, including independent agents and brokers and affiliated agencies. Its insurance subsidiaries are rated "A" (Excellent) by A.M. Best Company. Headquartered in Richfield, Ohio, National Interstate also has operations in Kapolei, Hawaii; Mechanicsburg, Pennsylvania; and Fenton, Missouri; and offers customized insurance options for:

- Passenger transportation companies
- Truck transportation companies
- Moving and storage companies
- Alternative risk transfer insurance programs for commercial risks
- Recreational vehicles
- Transportation and general commercial businesses in Hawaii and Alaska

Alan Spachman founded the company after spending a year developing the business plan for NIC and raising $5.2 million from thirty investors. He invested $600,000 of his own money, which was his total life savings.

Reclamation By Design – Pat and Ron Strimpfel, Owners

Reclamation By Design is a custom home builder located in Bluffton, South Carolina. Pat and Ron have been building in the South Carolina Low Country since the early 1980s. Their goal is to provide clients with a pleasant building experience at a cost-effective price. Ron is a master carpenter and a builder with extensive background and history in the construction business. Their motto is, "Crafted by hand, inspired by history."

Pat had her first business at age fifteen, back in a small town in Ohio. Ron was one of ten children and has worked from a very early age. They got married out of high school and started a construction business, building their first spec house at aged twenty. However, they didn't like the cold and snow, so they moved to the Hilton Head/ Bluffton, South Carolina area in 1978 when they were twenty-two years old. They used the profits from that spec house to buy a lot in Palmetto Dunes on Hilton Head and built another spec house. They made $30,000 on that house, and, as they say, the rest is history.

Today, they have a crew of six, and their company grosses about $4 million in annual revenues. While Ron is the artistic design person, does the work, and supervises the crews, Pat takes care of the administrative side of the business. What is unique is that they have been both business partners and husband and wife for forty years, which is a great testament to them that they have worked and lived together successfully for so long.

Port City Logistics – Billy Robinson, Owner and CEO

Port City Logistics was founded in 2001 and provides strategic warehouse space and transportation services. It is a leading logistics company in the Southeastern United States. Billy Robinson and his partners bought the company in 2004, when the company had $1 million in revenue and five employees. In 2013, it had grown to $22 million in revenues, 164 employees, and 1.6 million square feet of warehouse space in six buildings. Over the years, there have been plenty of challenges and problems, but, as Billy says, "those problems made us better and stronger." Their motto is, "On time, on budget—the perfect logistics fit."

Sweetener Solutions – John Curry, President and Owner

Sweetener Solutions, which manufactures high-intensity sweeteners (HIS), started in 2002 with three employees and $200,000 in sales the first year. Backed by a group of investors and equity partners, it gradually grew to reach $1 million in sales in 2012. In 2013, its patience and perseverance paid off as sales jumped to $6 million. It now has eleven employees. The future looks bright, with sales projected to reach $20 million in the next five years. Initially, the company was in a small 1,000-square-foot space but has now moved to a 15,000-square-foot facility.

Each of today's high-intensity sweeteners has taste and function limitations. Sweetener Solutions sources the world's best-quality HIS to manufacture sweetener blends using proprietary, state-of-the-art technology. When compared to any stand-alone sweetener, its blends provide superior taste and functionality. The unique sweetener blends provide the taste profile and desired functionality to match customers' food ingredient needs. Each of its sweetener blends is offered in bag-in-a-box quantities or can be portion-packed to customers' exact batch specifications.

The product development of recipe-specific HIS blends provides improved taste, reduced carbs and calories, and significant cost savings for customers. Sweetener Solutions enables customers to reduce sugar/high fructose corn syrup, reduce calories, save money, and reduce commodity risk, all the while maintaining great-tasting products. Most of the company's applications work well in liquid applications (fruit drinks, flavored milk, yogurt, and tea are the easiest). The HIS can save customers 15 to 35 percent of their total sweetener costs, and HIS production requires significantly less water and carbon dioxide than sugars and can shrink customers' carbon footprint.

Peacock Cabinetry, Inc. – Terry Peacock, Owner

Peacock Cabinetry, Inc. is a full-service design firm, specializing in custom cabinetry and space planning, and committed to superior personal service with the goal of exceeding expectations. Terry is originally from the Eastern Shore of Maryland but calls Savannah, Georgia, her home. She started in the cabinetry industry thirty-four years ago with Wilmington Cabinet Company, earning $5/hour and helping customers with their cabinet selections. Over time she learned to make design drawings and moved into sales. During this time, she went to art school and also had a part-time stained glass business. She blends her artistic talents with her technical knowledge and has become a kind of "kitchen architect."

Prior to starting Peacock Cabinetry in November 1999, she worked on commission selling cabinetry for eleven years. Her first customers came from builders who she knew since she had worked in the industry for so long. She went to SCORE, and they helped her write a business plan. To get started she needed a line of credit and approached numerous banks, all of which turned her down because at that point the company had no collateral and no track record. Finally, she found a local bank willing to help and got a $5,000 line of credit. She only used it twice in that first year and immediately paid it back. It helped that her initial customers, the builders, were willing to give her a 50 percent down payment on the job order.

Her husband, Hunter, has been instrumental in helping her shape her business philosophy, particularly in staying debt free. Peacock Cabinetry also has a division that sells and installs security safes, and Hunter handles this side of the business. Terry attributes a lot of the company's success to Hunter. As she says, "I certainly could not have made this business what it is without his hard work." Her company now employs eleven people and has four install crews with whom it subcontracts. Annual gross sales are about $3 million.

The Greenery – Scott Slawson, CFO

The Greenery provides a full range of landscaping, maintenance, and construction services for both residential and commercial customers. It also has a garden center and sells gift items.

The company was first established on Hilton Head Island in 1973 by Ruthie and Berry Edwards. After vacationing on the island, the couple became enchanted with the area, decided to live the island life, and moved to Hilton Head. When the couple relocated, they bought a small landscape nursery (Hillside Landscape Nursery) with a staff of six employees, a couple of old pickup trucks, and the desire to do something different. Ruthie and Berry focused on growing their business by hiring the most knowledgeable and experienced landscaping and gardening staff in the Low Country. That commitment to providing the highest-quality customer service in the area has helped The Greenery grow into one of the largest and most highly respected landscaping companies in the Southeast.

Lee Edwards, son of Ruthie and Berry, started his career at The Greenery as a young boy, spending his afternoons and weekends helping out in the garden nursery. Lee, now The Greenery's CEO, is providing new leadership at the helm of this employee-owned corporation. The Greenery recently celebrated its fortieth anniversary in February 2013. Founder Berry Edwards, now retired, comments, "Who would have thought our little landscape company back in the 1970s would be what it is today?"

The company has grown from a small family-owned business to a 100-percent-employee-owned company poised for growth in South Carolina and Georgia. In the peak season, the company employs over 750 employees and has annual sales of over $40 million.

Olio Tasting Room – Penny Willimann

If you visited the home kitchen of Olio Tasting Room proprietor Penny Willimann, you would discover her counter is barely visible under all the bottles of olive oils and balsamic vinegars lined up in neatly organized rows. This obsession in her kitchen grew over many years and ultimately inspired her to open her first Northern Virginia tasting room in Old Town Alexandria in 2011 and her second in Middleburg, Virginia, a year later.

"I wanted my friends and neighbors, cooks and novices alike, to discover what I already had—that quality oils and vinegars are a game changer for your diet, your taste buds, your health and, of course, for your dinner parties. I wanted them to try the products in the store before they buy so they could truly understand the difference." This notion inspired the tasting room concept.

These days Penny splits her time between her "three" babies—the stores and her two small children. She can often be found in the stores "chatting it up" with customers, and occasionally you might find her four-year-old quietly snacking on bread and balsamic dip at the counter. She loves to hear from her customers about all the great ways they use the products. Send her your favorite recipe to penny@ oliotastingroom.com.

Since opening, Olio Tasting Room has expanded its product lines to include pastas, sauces, teas, sea salts, tapenades, specialty condiments, and more. "We aim to source locally when possible, to know our producers, and to buy foods with ingredients we can pronounce. Olio products have graced the kitchens of many happy clients near and far, as well as exciting spots such as the Italian embassy, Salamander Resort and Spa, local wineries, gourmet shops, restaurants, and even a few wedding tables."

Calfkiller Brewing Company – Don and Dave Sergio, Owners

It all began in 2001 with two brothers who dreamed of having some sort of business together. Coincidentally, they were also beginning an aggressive home brewing hobby—expanding their palettes and those of their families. Growing up in a family construction company, the brothers converted a horse shed in Don's backyard into a home brewery using 100 percent recycled materials. They then began brewing Calfkiller beer in 2004.

The brothers loved their beer and enjoyed serving it at family functions, friends' weddings, and other festivals and contests. They became known for making great beers and decided to pursue a side business producing Calfkiller beer on a larger scale. From 2006 to 2010, the brothers fought legal battles, raised families, worked full-time construction jobs, and honed their Calfkiller beer-making craft. They collected old dairy and brewing vessels and constructed a building at night and on weekends, again using recycled materials.

Today, they continue brewing Calfkiller beers on the brewing system they pieced together. The duo are always adding equipment when possible, continuously dreaming of the future, but never losing sight of the beer that is being brewed today.

UniSource Mortgage Services, Inc. – Bill Fletcher, President

UniSource Mortgage Services is a privately owned mortgage brokerage that was founded by Jim Fletcher in 1996 (opened for business in January 1997). The goal of establishing the company as a dynamic brokerage was a family affair from the start. Jim's youngest son and daughter-in-law, Jonathan and Sharon Fletcher, were among the company's very first employees as loan originator and loan processor, respectively. Jim's oldest son, Bill, joined the company in 1998.

The company initially served clients in South Carolina and Georgia, but as the company grew, so did its territory as it expanded to include five other states (Virginia, North Carolina, Florida, Mississippi, and Tennessee). Following the 2008–2010 recession, the company reduced its footprint to South Carolina and Tennessee. The company's headquarters are located in Bluffton, South Carolina, and Bill Fletcher currently serves as the company's president and chief operation officer while Jim, a former certified public accountant, serves as the company's chief financial officer.

APPENDIX II

YOUR COMPANY BUSINESS PLAN

One owner told me, "I'll put my business plan together on Friday." A good business plan requires time, extensive research, and careful consideration of numerous business issues. The following outline serves as a guide for development of your business plan. Some items may not apply to you, and there may be unique factors in your business that aren't addressed in this outline. This outline was derived from an interactive business planning software program, *Business Plan Pro*. There is also a companion program, *Marketing Plan Pro*, which goes into more depth to develop your marketing plan.

1 – Executive Summary

1.1 Summary
1.2 Objectives
1.3 Vision
1.4 Fundamental Purpose
1.5 Fundamental Values
1.6 Fundamental Operating Principles
1.7 Success Determinants
1.8 Value Proposition

2 – Overview

2.1 Corporate Structure
2.2 Ownership
2.3 Financing
2.4 Location
2.5 Facilities

3 – Product/Service

3.1 Market Case for ____________________

3.2 Product/Service Offerings
3.3 Sourcing: Manufacturing/Purchasing
3.4 Technology
3.5 Product/Service Cost
3.6 Future Products

4 – Sales & Marketing

4.1 Market Trends
4.2 Industry Trends
4.3 Market Growth
4.4 Market Size
4.5 Market Segments
4.5 Target Market/Customers
4.6 Target Market Strategy
4.7 Value Proposition
4.8 Branding
4.9 Competition
- 4.9.1 Alternative Products
- 4.9.2 Competing Companies
- 4.9.3 Competitive Advantage

4.10 Marketing Strategy Options
4.11 Selling Price Range
4.12 Potential Distribution Outlets
4.13 Advertising
4.14 Public Relations
4.15 Website
4.16 Sales Channels
4.17 Strategic Alliances
4.18 SWOT Analysis
4.19 Sales Strategy
- 4.19.1 Employees/Outside Sales Reps
- 4.19.2 Sales Programs
- 4.19.3 Territories
- 4.19.4 Lead Generation Plan
  - 4.19.4.1 Generation
  - 4.19.4.2 Conversion
  - 4.19.4.3 Qualification
  - 4.19.4.4 Follow Up
  - 4.19.4.5 Tracking

6.7 Professional/Advisory Support

7 – Risk Assessment/Mitigation

7.1 Hazard Risk
7.2 Financial Risk
7.3 Operating Risk
7.4 Strategic Risk

8 – Financial Analysis

8.1 Summary
8.2 Financing
8.2.1 Investors
8.2.2 Borrowing
8.3 Startup Costs
8.4 Summary P&L
8.5 Detail P&L
8.6 P&L Assumptions

9 – Exit Plan

9.1 Key Performance Indicators
9.2 Exit Strategies

10 – Management Profiles

11 – Investors/Legal

11.1 Investors
11.2 Payout
11.3 Legal Documents

ABOUT THE AUTHOR

H. Roy Austin, CPA, CMA, MBA, founded Rockwell Business Solutions in 2007 to provide coaching and training services for small businesses. His passion is "getting underneath the numbers" and developing information systems to help management understand what drives financial performance. His prior positions were as chief financial officer for D. J. Powers Company, Inc., a third-party logistics provider; controller for Savannah Manufacturing, an aseptic drink manufacturer; and various accounting, sales forecasting, and market research assignments over twenty-nine years with Eastman Chemical Company in Kingsport, Tennessee.

Mr. Austin earned a BA in economics from Bethany College and an MBA in marketing from Michigan State. He is founder and chair emeritus of Savannah CFO/Controller's Council, which has grown to over 425 financial executives since its inception in 2004. He Chaired the Council for ten years. He is also an ambassador for the Bluffton Chamber of Commerce and is a Gold Club member of Business Network International, where he served as mentor coordinator and education coordinator in his chapter. He has been a member of the Institute of Management Accountants since 1984, and in 2004 he received the Financial Executive of the Year award for the Florida Council region. Formerly, he served as chair of the Volunteer Advisory Board for the Tennessee Department of Corrections, as well as chair of the board for the John R. Hay House, a halfway house for convicted felons. In 1998, Hay House named its new building in his honor.

Roy served nineteen months in Vietnam as a First Lieutenant and was awarded three Bronze Stars and two Army Commendation medals.

His website is www.rockwellbusinesssolutions.com.